The Lion
&
The Unicorn

By the same author and published by Collins

The Story of England
MAKERS OF THE REALM B.C.-1272
THE AGE OF CHIVALRY 1272-1381

KING CHARLES II 1630-1685

RESTORATION ENGLAND

Samuel Pepys
THE MAN IN THE MAKING 1633-1669
THE YEARS OF PERIL 1670-1683
THE SAVIOUR OF THE NAVY 1683-1689

The Napoleonic Wars
THE YEARS OF ENDURANCE 1793-1802
YEARS OF VICTORY 1802-1812
THE AGE OF ELEGANCE 1812-1822

ENGLISH SAGA 1840-1940

The Alanbrooke Diaries
THE TURN OF THE TIDE 1939-1943
TRIUMPH IN THE WEST 1943-1946

THE FIRE AND THE ROSE

English Social History
THE MEDIEVAL FOUNDATION
PROTESTANT ISLAND

JIMMY

The Lion
&
The Unicorn

A HISTORIAN'S TESTAMENT

Arthur Bryant

COLLINS
14 St James's Place, London

First Impression   December 1969
Second Impression December 1969

SBN 00 211471 2

Printed in Great Britain
Collins Clear-Type Press
London and Glasgow

IN MEMORY OF BOB PITMAN
1924-1969
*who was both Great Heart and
Valiant for Truth*

England

No lovelier hills than thine have laid
    My tired thoughts to rest:
No peace of lovelier valleys made
    Like peace within my breast.

Thine are the woods whereto my soul,
    Out of the noontide beam,
Flees for a refuge green and cool
    And tranquil as a dream.

Thy breaking seas like trumpets peal;
    Thy clouds—how oft have I
Watched their bright towers of silence steal
    Into infinity!

My heart within me faints to roam
    In thought even far from thee:
Thine be the grave whereto I come,
    And thine my darkness be.

WALTER DE LA MARE

Contents

PRELUDE

Lion and Unicorn

I   The Tower of Memory

1 *Ere We Be Young Again*   page 19
2 *Her Secret None Can Utter*   32
3 *On Discovering the Past Was Real*   36
4 *Blue Remembered Hills*   48
5 *Sterner Days*   63
6 *Brave New World*   108
7 *Back to Dear Old Blighty*   123

II   Avons of the Heart

8   *The Country Habit*   153
9   *Creatures Great and Small*   172
10 *Forty Years On*   191

III   True to Ourselves

11 *Sinks the Fire*   219
12 *Who is for Liberty*   247
13 *To Thee My Country*   292

EPILOGUE

The Faith Within Us   322

Lion and Unicorn

When the organisers of the 1951 Exhibition of Britain labelled the Pavilion devoted to the intangibles of our national heritage, "The Lion and the Unicorn", they hit on a large and happy truth. The Lion himself was mainly conspicuous by his absence: King Harry before Harfleur, the disciplined ranks on the *Birkenhead*'s deck and the *Victory*'s cockpit at Trafalgar, St. Boniface going out unarmed through the forests of Central Europe to convert the pagan Germans, and Livingstone a thousand years later emulating his feat in darkest Africa, Florence Nightingale in the Scutari wards and Howard in the felons' stinking jails: such are the children of the Lion, and, as such, had little place in this glittering plastic show of the first decade of peace. Yet even then the Lion was conducting himself in his usual way in Korea; nor, so soon after Alamein and D-Day, was he likely to be forgotten by even the most unthinking visitor.

On the other hand, the Unicorn was well and happily to the fore, and, represented in particular by the White Knight, fully equipped at all points of his lovable eccentricity and absurdity. Incidentally, what might have been the finest Unicorn exhibit of all was provided by a she-mouse who established herself and her family in the Pavilion lion's mouth which, being fashioned of straw, provided her with both a home and a larder. Unfortunately, this unplanned item was accidentally discovered by the Authorities a few days before the opening and hastily removed. Had it been allowed to remain, whatever the effects on the lion's mouth, it might well have proved the greatest attraction of the Exhibition, at any rate to British visitors. That enterprising mouse and her offspring had done exactly what was needed to delight the British public. In making herself a home with such psychological discrimination, she had placed herself where she would arouse in them, not the Lion, but the Unicorn. Like the wren who made her nest on the roof of a perambulating railway carriage on one of our quieter branch lines and struck the headlines in every newspaper, she knew the way to Britannia's heart. She was unfortunate—and the Authorities, I think, foolish—and was given, I suppose, to the Exhibition cat. Had she lived, the bulk of the nation's then exiguous cheese ration would probably have been laid at her feet.

The British public is like that. It has a lion's heart and a unicorn's mind. It is a mind which, though prosaic in its approach to nine out of ten of life's concerns, is eccentric and nonsensical in the other tenth to the point of near lunacy. Perhaps this strain arises from the mixture of blood: from the Celtic contending with the Saxon; I do not know. All one can be sure of is that it is there and has been there for a long time. That delightful poet, John Skelton, possessed it as long ago as the fifteenth century. So did his anonymous contemporary who wrote a poem enshrined in *The Oxford Book of English Verse*, round a dialogue between a farmer and his wife about an old cloak.

Throughout our history runs a long succession of eccentrics who carried this trait in our character to an abnormal length: country gentlemen among whom, in a more spacious age, it was almost an occupational disease; explorers, dons, schoolmasters, clergymen; even kings and princes of the blood. Nothing, it will be remembered, so endeared George III to his subjects as his characteristic enquiry as to how the apple got into the dumpling; it almost compensated them for the loss of the American colonies. In the most humdrum, ordinary English men of business and affairs there is frequently a strain of the same escapist lunacy: the kind that makes them spend all their holidays playing golf and even longer talking about it, or causes them to collect postage-stamps or coloured match-boxes. It is a trait of which dogs and cats are great beneficiaries; one wealthy and highly respected nineteenth century nobleman filled his house—a vast Hertfordshire palace—with these fortunate creatures, let them sit at table and took them for drives, dressed in smocks and hats and lolling on the carriage cushions. In a less expansive age, in which the economic opportunities for eccentricity are fewer, the same phenomenon can be observed in the form of dogs riding in sidecars or in the baskets of bicycles.

This capacity for absorption in the inessential has obviously been a source of strength to the English. It may have made them occasionally neglectful of more important matters, but it has preserved a margin of reserve in their souls which in crisis has stood them in good stead. Drake, finishing his game of bowls, was merely exercising the Unicorn in him while resting the Lion against the hour when it would be needed. Indeed, the exclusion of the Lion in favour of the Unicorn by the promoters of the South Bank Exhibition was probably instinctive wisdom. As a people we had recently had to put on the Lion too much and might well have to do so again in the future, and an interval of relaxation with our unicorns, private and collective, was all for the good. Lord Baldwin, when Prime Minister, used to spend his spare time reading detective stories; Winston Churchill prepared for his supreme hour of blood, sweat and tears by spending a great many pleasant hours sketching and laying bricks. Even Neville Chamberlain, most prosaic of Ministers, was never happier or nearer the heart of his countrymen than when watching birds in the garden of No. 10 Downing Street—a hobby he shared with Lord Alanbrooke, the man who, perhaps more than any other save Churchill, bore upon a single pair of shoulders the burden of directing Britain's war effort between 1941 and 1945. And what Englishman does not regard Dr. Johnson as a more compelling moralist because he collected orange-peel, fed his pet cat, Hodge, on oysters, and deliberately placed his feet in the middle of every paving stone encountered on his walks abroad? It is what makes him so lovable and therefore, to us, so great. A man who does that sort of thing, we reckon, will be able to stand firm in all Hell's despite.

Indeed, the success of Britain in war has not been wholly due to the Lion. Its eccentric and curious companion and rival, the Unicorn, has taken its place in battle too. It was there, for instance, in the London blitzes, soaring fantastically out of the irrepressible Cockney heart amid crashing masonry and the ruin of human homes and hopes—a perennial source of laughter and whimsical absurdity so valiant that, encountering it, one never knew whether to laugh or cry. And as long as it takes its wonted, honoured place on the quartering of Britain's arms, we shall remain what we have long been, a joke to everyone, a source of sustenance to a large number of little animals who might otherwise fare ill in a harsh world, and a force so resilient in adversity that it has never yet been ultimately defeated and, by the grace of God, never will be.

* * *

These reflections on our national characteristics first appeared in 1951 in an article in the *Illustrated London News*. For thirty-three years, succeeding G. K. Chesterton, who had contributed to it for almost as long, I have been writing that journal's weekly page, "Our Note Book"—the oldest continuous column in British journalism. The Fates have certainly given me plenty to write about—the greatest global war in history, a major social revolution, the disintegration of the British Empire and its transformation into the Commonwealth, and more economic crises than one can count. Produced in the interstices of historical work and often written in swaying trains and cars, and, sometimes, during the war in aeroplanes or on upturned boxes on airfields or the platforms of crowded railway stations, these contributions—a contemporary, if rambling, commentary on our times—reflect the personal and political philosophy of an onlooker, holding no office or public responsibility except of a purely voluntary kind, and speaking only for himself.

One day it may seem worth publishing such a week-by-week commentary on a period of historical importance—one in which Britain, after saving herself with the help of her global empire from the consequences of past folly, rallied the forces of human freedom to destroy an immensely formidable aggressor, and then, in the hour of victory, like a weary and disillusioned Titan, divested herself of the power ever to do so again. We are too near the events, even of a quarter of a century ago, to see them in historical perspective. But since my articles have covered a wide range of subject, and as many readers have asked me to reproduce them in a more permanent form, I have chosen some seventy or eighty out of the seventeen hundred I have written, and, adding a few longer pieces, like the "Summer of Dunkirk", have quarried from them the material to make a book which is partly reminiscent, partly a commentary on our times and partly a confession of faith. Mirroring the instinctive dichotomy in our national make-up, I have called it "The Lion and the Unicorn". Its early chapters recall memories of my youth and of events, places and impressions which have shaped my outlook and beliefs: its later ones set out those beliefs and my view of the problems, political and economic, which concern our future as a people, including the faith out of which our civilisation grew and without which it must, as I believe, perish. Where necessary I have grouped together several articles, written at different times, to provide a fuller and balanced treatment of a particular subject. Others are printed much as they appeared, with a footnote to indicate the date of publication, though, wherever possible without impairing the sense of the original article, I have cut out redundancies and repetitions.

I cannot pretend that my views are fashionable or in tune with contemporary ideology. If anyone wonders why my column in the *Illustrated London News* has any readers, I can only suggest the answer Charles II gave when, asked to explain how a particularly stupid clergyman, whom he had made a bishop, had converted his flock from dissent to orthodoxy: "I suppose his sort of nonsense suits their sort of nonsense!"

PART I

The Tower of Memory

CHAPTER I

Ere We Be Young Again

The eternal dawn, beyond a doubt,
Shall break o'er hill and plain,
And put all stars and candles out
'Ere we be young again.
R. L. STEVENSON

If I had a time machine, I should start by setting it to carry me back to the opening years of this century. For I should first like to revisit the country where I was born and the city where I grew up. That country was called England and the city London.

Much that I should find in that faraway metropolis still stands; the Victorian houses where the Forsytes lived, with their tall classical windows and iron area-railings; the plane trees in the squares—or at least some of them; the Houses of Parliament, St. Paul's dome and the Abbey, the Law Courts, the iron railway bridge over the river at Charing Cross, and the embanked river. Though London was then a far smaller place, not half its present size, the outline of its streets was much as today. Except for Kingsway, which had still to be built, the street map of central London has altered little since the beginning of the century, and no Londoner, suddenly thrown back seventy years in time, would have much difficulty finding his way about it. Yet for all this he would be translated to a city so different to ours that, despite its many familiar buildings, he would feel himself in another world. Its inhabitants, traffic, sights, sounds and smells would be as unfamiliar as those of some city of the Orient or of the American or Siberian prairies.

For his overwhelming impression as he looked out on the streets would be that he was in a land of horses. Instead of petrol fumes and the roar of internal combustion and changing gears—to which the young today are so accustomed that they take them for granted and scarcely notice them—he would immediately be made aware of the smell of horse-dung and hot leather, the sound of clopping hooves, the jingle of harness and bells and the thunder of iron wheels on wooden paving blocks. In the more crowded thoroughfares—Piccadilly or the Strand—the volume of sound would be nearly as great as today, though far more varied and less monotonous, with a strong undercurrent of street cries—for the art of advertisement was still almost as much vocal as visual— and of barrel-organs and brass bands, to both of which the Londoners of my youth were much addicted.

But it would be far easier to escape from the noise. In the quieter residential streets and squares there would, compared with today, be remarkably little traffic. Only the rich had carriages; the dust-cart, the tradesman's van, an occasional hansom or four-wheeler, and men wheeling barrows or a Punch and Judy show, usually with a ruffed terrier in attendance, these would be the chief occu-pants of the roadway. It was still a pedestrian's London; even the toffs walked. I can see them doing so on a Sunday morning, in their glossy top hats, long, wasp-waisted, square-cut frock-coats, spats and shiny, pointed boots, accompanied by their feather-hatted, boa-ed and highly-upholstered ladies, as they made their way from St. Peter's, Eaton Square, through the dusty Belgravia streets to Hyde Park Corner or Albert Gate for the great after-church parade near the Achilles Statue. There were wonderful carriages and horses, gleaming and prancing, with ethereal creatures sitting in them, and liveried, cockaded footmen riding on high. Yet these were only part of the show; shoe-leather was the most important of all the ingredients that made up Edwardian London. Indeed, the most essential sartorial distinction of a gentle-man was that his footwear was neat, clean and well-made. Pro-vided he was sound in this respect, he could still pass muster in that snobbish but highly individualistic world though the rest of his attire was shabby. He could even get away with turned-up trousers.

It was a world in which it was easy to distinguish the classes into which society was divided, for every class had its own garb. Yet it was also one which, though divided by class and class distinction, was unified by a common religious and moral belief and code. The prayers my nurse—a farm labourer's daughter—

taught me to recite morning and night by the bedside, the grace said before meals, the hymn sung in every church and chapel in the land were common to aristocrat, bourgeois, artisan and peasant and helped to keep England a single nation. For this reason it was in some ways a less divided community than ours. The unity of conviction with which, despite Party divisions and animosities—never stronger than in the decade before 1914—it entered the war against imperial Germany after the latter's invasion of Belgium, was proof of it. There was a wide divergence in the way men lived, socially and economically, but little in what they regarded as right or wrong, even if, as in all ages and societies, they often failed to practise what they preached.

I suspect it is the lack of this unity of conviction, as much as the ubiquity of the internal combustion engine, the aeroplane and the shadow of the nuclear bomb, that makes London seem such a restless place today and Britain so unsure of herself. Certainly the background of life, even for a boy born into the professional classes who had to make his way in the world with no hope of inherited wealth, was by modern standards extraordinarily secure. One had to fend for oneself, work hard and live a sober, godly and righteous life, but, provided one had the character and stamina to do these things, one could look forward to a life full of hopeful possibilities and satisfaction.

It is to see the reflection of that certainty in the eyes of men and women that I should like to revisit the London of my youth. I know there was much squalor and tragedy in it: the drab dirt of the slums, the destitution and drunkenness of those who had failed in the hard, strenuous race of life, the pathetic beggars and crossing-sweepers and ragged children, the sight of whose poverty wrenched at one's heart as one walked the thriving, confident streets of the world's greatest metropolis. Yet, on the whole, it was a London with conviction, faith and, with what comes from these things, vitality and energy. I should like to see and hear again its familiar sights and sounds: its horse-buses and jingling cabs and carriages, its tinkling hurdy-gurdies, the gleaming, varnished shop-fronts and striped awnings in the Bond Street sunshine, the fine brown of horse-dung eddying on the dusty summer pavements, the parade of men and women and horses at Hyde Park Corner on June afternoons, and the quiet of the royal parks of Kensington and the Pimlico squares before the first motors invaded them and the long Victorian peace, which lasted from Waterloo to Mons, came to an end.

* * *

II

Though Norfolk-born, and by love and adoption a man of Dorset, most of my earliest impressions were formed in London. My world was a narrow one, bordered by Kensington Gardens on the west, Trafalgar Square and the Strand on the east, the shops of Oxford Street and Lord's cricket ground on the north. Only occasionally did I penetrate south of the river, to Battersea Park or the Oval, or, during walks at weekends, when my father was free to take me to Wimbledon Common, Bushey Park or Hampton Court, travelling there through the smoke-grimed tunnels of the still unelectrified Metropolitan District Railway or later—for he loved to experiment—by one of the first motor-buses, Union Jack or Vanguard, which nearly always at some point on their journey broke down. Mine was both a sheltered and an austere life; I might almost have been in a monastery, though a monastery whose obedientiaries wore petticoats. My father was an official in the Secretariat of King Edward VII, whom for twenty years before his accession he had served at Marlborough House and Sandringham. He was a man of great method and integrity, whose word was his bond and whose life was governed by unchanging, inexorable rules based on work. Except on holiday his routine never varied—breakfast, after a cold bath and exercises, at eight and never a minute later; a short walk in St. James's or the Green Park with my nurse, my brother's pram and me before crossing the Palace courtyard to his office, a small upright figure dressed in the regulation top hat and frock coat of his calling; a frugal vegetarian lunch when he returned from the Palace for an hour; then home again to five o'clock tea. After that—except sometimes on summer evenings when he took me to Lord's or the Oval—he worked at dispatch-boxes in his library until it was time to dress for dinner, a meal invariably begun at 7.30 p.m. sharp. By ten or, at latest, ten-thirty he was in bed.

My mother, who was nearly twenty years younger, delicate, a poet and dreamer, and had come from a much easier and less regulated home, adapted herself to this life with admirable philosophy and to the comparative poverty which was our lot. I say comparative because, though my parents' income at this time of their lives was sternly inelastic and used with a frugality whose necessity impressed itself deeply on my mind even in the nursery, our modest household included a resident cook, two maids and a nurse, as well as a part-time laundress who came in every week for two days of strenuous boiling and mangling in a spacious steam-filled laundry which existed in an annexe at one end of the official residence in which we lived.

My own part in this life of routine was at first remote. I lived alone with my nurse, and, after his birth, with my brother at the top of the house where we had a floor to ourselves shut off by a wicket-gate from the grown-up goings-on below. My nursery looked out on one side to a busy street down which a stream of hansom cabs trotted more or less continuously. Here from my monastery window I could watch the workaday world whose doings filled me with envy and a wild longing to be part of it. Almost immediately opposite was a fashionable fish-shop beside whose well-filled slabs a succession of ladies, all boas, furs and gigantic feathered hats, bargained genteelly with fishmongers in blue and white aprons. A door or two away was a coach-builder's establishment out of which, on Levée days, there were trundled the most wonderful-looking state carriages and coaches, ornate with coronets and gilding, and which, harnessed in the street, were driven off by multi-cloaked and bewigged coachmen to collect from Mayfair or Belgravia mansion the stately beings who owned or hired them.

From the other nursery window, which opened across a little garden yard on to the back of the Royal Mews, one could occasionally see, but more often hear, the doings of a different kind of society; the equestrian community which ministered to the king's horses. Sometimes, beyond the faces glimpsed in the windows, one would hear the sound of angry shouting, revealing the existence of undisciplined passions unknown in the rarefied air of the nursery flat or of my mother's drawing-room below. There once a week, on her At Home day, I used to descend to carry on halting and reluctant conversation with her visitors, or sometimes, when she was alone and I was allowed a brief escape from the nursery, to pretend to help her with the accounts of the St. Peter's, Eaton Square, choir school, to feeding which—for she was an enthusiastic disciple of our popular vicar, who once, during the children's service, rebuked me from the pulpit for crawling up the aisle to retrieve a clockwork mouse—she devoted much of her time and the talent for frugal and wholesome housekeeping which she had so improbably, in the light of her temperament, acquired from my father.

Beneath the latter's impenetrable armour of devotion to work and routine and my mother's conscientious subjection to the slavery of domestic and ecclesiastical economy—I can see her now, with a faraway look, meticulously adding up, or trying to add up halfpennies—were deep reserves of tenderness and tolerance which became increasingly apparent with age. But the society they created for their children was no permissive one; its keynote for them, as for themselves, was duty, not inclination. And what in retrospect I recall most vividly from that vanished life—in which, year in, year out, until I went to school, nothing seemed to happen but the repetition of the familiar and gentle enforcement of a discipline as inescapable as the sequence of day and night—were the impressions of two very different worlds that lay outside it and from which I was both shut out and protected.

One was a world of glittering wealth and display which I used to watch with envious amazement and longing on summer afternoons as there poured in and out of Hyde Park a procession of brightly gleaming horses and carriages whose riders and passengers were arrayed like Solomon in all his glory and possessed, or seemed to possess, the earth and the fullness of it. The other, encircling the familiar streets and parks where I walked with my nurse, was a vast ocean of poverty and drab, yet strident, squalor, the recollection of every glimpse of which haunted my childish dreams. One saw it in the crossing-sweepers shivering in the winter rain, in the sodden processions of sandwich-men shuffling listlessly by with their huge advertisement boards; in the raucous-voiced touts, with gaunt, haggard faces, who ran beside the cab on one's return from a country holiday in the hope of a few coppers for unloading the heavy, iron-bound trunks on the roof. Particularly, I recall, a ride one day on the top of a horse-bus all the way to Victoria Park and back through the grimy dinginess and sour stench of the East End. It was supposed to be a treat, but for me it proved an interminable nightmare over which I brooded for long afterwards.

*   *   *

III

Almost my first memory is of waking on Christmas morning in a firelit London nursery and feeling a sense of awe and mysterious expectation. The whole room was full of the spirit of love and of an intense, yet secure, excitement. Everything was in shadow yet touched by a living, flickering warmth. I remember lying there listening to the friendly clock, looking at the fender rail and the gently burning flames, and then noticing an unfamiliar and intriguing shape at the bed's foot. I must have been told not to touch it until I was called in the morning, and I lay still and possessed my soul in patience. Perhaps I was too happy—for the recollection is of great happiness—to do anything else. On later Christmas mornings I used to crawl down the bed and cautiously investigate the stocking's contours, peering into its recesses, and even, tremulously, fingering the articles at the top: a projecting end of a box of lead soldiers, an Ally Sloper or bear, a bag of sweets, a tin trumpet. Once I disarranged the top of a stocking so much that one of these precious objects fell with a clatter in the darkness to the floor, and I momentarily stained my Christmas morning with a sense of guilt, almost of sacrilege. Yet when the longed-for moment came and the curtains were drawn and went up, as it were, on the crowded delights and excitements of this great day, nothing of my wicked impatience and disobedience was noticed, or, at any rate, nothing was said. It was a day in which scolding was almost unknown; all the more awful, therefore, if it should, by ill-chance and one's terrible, incorrigible frailty, befall.

One of the treats of those Christmas mornings was that my brother, four years my junior, was allowed to join me in bed with his stocking as soon as we were called, so that we could go through our treasures together. Later—a carefully rehearsed surprise—we crept downstairs to break out, with a startling spasm of joy, into carols at our parents' door. It must have been a somewhat weasel-like sound, for neither of us knew much about singing and my brother at that time was incapable of rendering a note in tune. Afterwards we joined the grown-up part of the family at breakfast, greeting them in an ecstasy of jumping about and excitement. I imagine that during the meal we wriggled more than we spoke, for our souls were on tip-toe with expectation. For this reason I can recollect little about the meal except that the sideboard was adorned for the occasion with such delicacies of a now vanished age as Christmas-pie, into the making of which all the beasts of venery and the air appeared to have entered. I do not recall that we ate any of it, yet its presence was a kind of guarantee of recurring good cheer and abundance, like the red-berried holly and coloured paper streamers with which on Christmas Eve we had, with much falling off chairs and ladders, bedecked every picture in the house. The conflict here between my own flamboyant and my brother's very austere taste was apparent, the pictures decorated by me being almost forced to the floor by the weight and pressure of greenery, while those left to him were starkly and centrally crowned with a single stick of holly pointing upwards.

Ours was not a rich home, except in love, but at Christmas the sense of good things was almost overpowering. My parents would have gone to the stake, I feel, to ensure that it was so for us. After breakfast we went into my father's study, where, in neat piles, the presents awaited which in theory we all gave to one another, but which, in practice, constituted a kind of heaped tribute for my brother and me. As we untied each ribboned parcel, we hurried round our little family circle in gratitude, showing our treasures and our ecstatic delight in them to one another; in my case and my brother's with complete sincerity and every reason; in my parents' case with a good deal of praiseworthy but convincing dissimulation.

Even on Christmas day there were sights in the prosperous West End streets to tear a pitiful heart. I remember well, on our way to church, the aged crossing-sweepers at the corners awaiting their Christmas-boxes of silver coins, and whose wintry vigil and shabby clothes afforded a terrible contrast to the scenes of domestic warmth, comfort and bliss from which we had just come, and to which we were soon, with such glowing anticipation, to return. The thought of them used to haunt me at intervals during the day, strengthened as it was by my early reading of a harrowing book, a great favourite of mine, about the East End of London, called "Froggy's Little Brother", and whose hero, I like to think, is now magically transformed into one of the elder and ennobled statesman of our triumphant Labour Party. There was one crossing-sweeper in particular who used to stand at the corner of Grosvenor Place in distressingly ragged attire. Looking back, I suspect this may have been partly dictated by his profession which, on such a beat, must have been fairly lucrative. I always had a secret hope, as later we returned from our devotions with the sound of "Hark the Herald Angels" resounding in our ears, that we should invite him to accompany us home to partake of our luncheon. As this meal was invariably both cold and frugal—for we had our Christmas dinner at night and were never allowed to spoil it by premature guzzling, however longingly we might look at the mincepies and pineapple on the sideboard—the poor man would probably have been less grateful for this splendid act of Christian charity than my brother and I imagined. Once on a Christmas afternoon—when, in anticipation of the impending feast, we were always taken by my father for a long walk in some suburban park or pleasance—we encountered on the banks of the Thames near Putney a man who had rescued a poor woman who had been attempting to commit suicide:

> One more unfortunate
> Weary of breath,
> Rashly importunate
> Gone to her death.

I can still see that cold riverside scene; my father telling me to stand still and hurrying down to the rescuer to offer help, our hasty walk to the police station, the injunction not to upset my mother by telling her when we got home. Somehow the horror of it brought home to me, better even than the sermons and the carols of the children's service in St. Peter's Church, what Christmas was really about.

I am grateful to that early background of faith and those who created it for me. When on Christmas Eve the streets begin to clear of traffic and quiet descends on London, I can almost hear the silence of that firelit room of more than half a century ago, the jingling and clop-clop of a distant hansom, the ticking of the big wooden clock on the mantelpiece with its brass face faintly reflecting the embers in the grate below, the sound of my nurse's breathing on the other side of the room, and, for me, a sense of listening and waiting for something that I certainly could not have explained then and still less can explain now, but which Christian children for countless generations before had awaited and experienced and the poet-parson of Wiltshire Bemerton, George Herbert, put into words:

> *Church-bells beyond the stars heard, the soul's blood,*
> *The land of spices, something understood.*

*   *   *

IV

It was a hillside of beeches in a western coombe that taught me to love England. The air smelt wooingly there; 800 ft. above sea-level it was free from the lazy, enervating languors of our south-western shires, yet, for all its vigorous breezes and clear, starry winter nights, balmy with the tenderness which is the West's peculiar benison. One came on it down a winding drive whose white-trunked beeches were like the pillars and tracery of some great Gothic cathedral; then, suddenly, the trees opened out on to a clear green space of lawn riding above a steep, sloping park. Before one, stretched at ease on the hillside under its high crown of beeches, lay an old, grey, plain stone house, with a slated roof and a Regency verandah, as unassuming as the vista beyond was breath-taking. Below were the trees of the park, two lakes with rushes and willows on their northern banks, and, beyond, rising like a wall closing in the valley to the south, a high forest of beech and oak stretching in unbroken glory for nearly two miles. Above the encircling woods, armadas of rooks constantly wheeled and swooped about their business, making morning and evening musical with their anthems. Only to the east was there any break in the encircling horizon of trees, far enough from the eye to give a sense of space, yet near enough to induce an indescribable feeling of security, guarded as one was by those beloved woodlands, the unbroken peace of the green shires beyond, and the fleets of England that rode, invisible but invincible, still unchallenged arbiters of the world's seas. For where the valley opened out to meet the rising sun the skyline of trees ended and a horizon of chalk downs took its place, noble and bare, four miles distant. Peace, gentleness, beauty were the guardian spirits attendant on the place; spirits evoked out of the long English centuries by the courage, labour and piety of the men and women from whom we derive our blood.

This was my boyhood's second home: the day-dream of many an exiled hour in city streets, school and camp. Here all the journeys of imagination ended. I used to lie awake at the beginning of a new term at school, conquering in fancy the stubborn miles and interminable weeks that separated me from my heart's desire, speeding in fancy between the dusty hedgerows of a still unspoilt England towards the spired cathedral town in the West and the cool avenues and winding lanes of ancient cultivated valleys eaten out of the chalk through centuries by sparkling trout-streams, each more sacred to me than the one before, because nearer the place I sought. I saw in dream the grey Norman church on the hillside, the high hazel hedges between which slow horses dragged enormous loads of hay or mangels in bright-coloured, curved wagons of antique design, the little Gothic-windowed lodge with its brightly-painted white gate at the entrance to the beechwoods, the drive whose every bend and tree and bush were symbols of boyish adventure, romance or dream, the sudden gasp of excitement as the woods began to drop away into space and that ever-new, never-changing vista of enchantment came into sight. "God gives all men all earth to love," wrote Kipling,

But since man's heart is small
Ordains for each one spot shall prove
Beloved over all.

For me, it was that little corner of earth where Wiltshire joins
Dorset and the infant Nadder rises. Just as Ely is the gateway to
the Fens, by which all who approach them from the south must
pass, so is Salisbury for the traveller from Waterloo to the south-
west of England. It is the key to the kingdom of up-and-down,
where the landscape starts to up-end, where fields and parks are
no longer spread before one at eye-level but fall and rise in green
walls so that sometimes, as one looks out from lawn or window,
some great tree, with cattle sheltering under its shade, is either
far below or high above one. Everything is rounded, and the sky,
except on the high downs which can occasionally be glimpsed
through tiny openings of wooded valleys, instead of being remote
and far away as in Cambridgeshire and the Midlands, is only just
above the tree tops. More often than not it is full of clouds.
Indeed, in my old home these frequently descended and encompassed one in a gentle dripping mist, resting for the first time on
terra firma after their long Atlantic journey. For the hills above
the Blackmoor Vale are the first real landfall for the great aerial
water-bags which, entering England from the West Bay between
Devonshire and Portland, float across her, dispensing her
aqueous climate. It is only here that the solid land squares up
to meet them and there is an end, for them, of ocean. Stand on
Melbury Down and look south-westwards, and the gentle Dorset
plain below, with its grey stone churches and villages, is green
like the sea, hidden thirty miles away by only the low, tempest-
blown hills above Kingston Russell and Burton Bradstock.

It is here, when I was a boy, that I used to repair on foot or pony
for long solitary communings, dreaming of deeds that I was never
to perform or scribbling absurd verses—long consigned to the
flames—on the back of torn envelopes, inspired by the unconscious
grace of some long-legged maiden shyly admired at tennis-party
or in the churchyard after morning service, or by romantic
dreams of a happiness as elusive and illusory as the military glory
which I then imagined to be the supreme prize of life. As I gazed
down from that commanding height I would people the vale

with the figures of its long history—Cavaliers and Roundheads,
their breastplates caught in gleams of sunlight between passing
rain-clouds, or parties of boar-crested Saxons winding through
Celtic coombe and forest ever deeper into the reddening west to
do battle with Arthur's knights, or, centuries later, marching to
the summons of the greatest of Wessex's sons, Alfred the King,
to grapple with the Danish invaders on the downs above Edding-
ton.

There are some heights in Wessex, shaped as if by a kindly hand
For thinking, dreaming, dying on, and at crises when I stand,
Say on Ingpen Beacon eastward or on Wylls-Neck westwardly,
I seem where I was before my birth and after death may be.[1]

Those dreams of an Edwardian boyhood seem strangely far
away from the motor-ridden England of today. There are times
when one wonders whether the world of sixty years ago was an
illusion or whether the world of today is, for they seem so in-
compatible with one another that they cannot both be reality.
Yet, in the broad perspective of time, both are. The contours of
Wessex hill and plain and the clouds from which the great Dorset
and Wiltshire trees draw their life-giving moisture will still be
there when the age of Joseph Chamberlain and the age of Harold
Wilson are equally memories of a remote and seemingly unreal
past.

---

[1] T. Hardy, *Collected Poems*, p. 300. Macmillan.

CHAPTER 2

Her Secret None Can Utter[1]

Know you her secret none can utter?
—Hers of the book, the tripled Crown?
Still on the spire the pigeons flutter;
Still by the gateway haunts the gown.
ARTHUR QUILLER-COUCH

To revisit Oxford is always an adventure in time. I have known it so long, and it has changed for me so much and so little. I knew it first as an Edwardian city, still quiet with the leisure and scent of horse-drawn traffic and, except to the north, so near the fields and unsullied water-meadows as to be a country town. In the two Hinkseys, by Matthew Arnold's earlier and more exacting measure, nothing was the same; yet, once past Folly Bridge, the reservoir and railway, a lad could ramble into a still unravished pastoral landscape of gently rounded fields, heavy elms and hedge-rows full of dog-roses. Rural Oxfordshire began a mile below Summertown; North Marston was still as cradled in bucolic antiquity as Wood Eaton and Ambrosden. There were no petrol fumes in the High, no industrial Cowley, no concrete-fronted twentieth century shops. The towered, domed city still lingered on—a relic of the age of cobbles and horse-dung. And there, oblivious of impending death on the Somme or a sur-taxed old age at the scullery-sink, were " the young barbarians all at play"— the *jeunesse dorée* of a rich, carefree age, in their tweeds, flannels and boaters, gods to my childish eyes, the apparent inheritors of a, for them, goodly earth of rod, dog and gun, Gaiety chorus and cigar-scented Piccadilly promenade.

That was my first Oxford, and I can still hear its quiet bells across the stately water-meadows. My second was a camp, not a campus: a place of bugle calls, drab uniforms and morning parades. Here, in a high, streaky-bacon, Betjemanic, goblin-

[1] *Illustrated London News* 21 April 1951; 11 June 1949.

market villa in the Banbury Road I studied, with patriotically tempered boredom and distaste, the nobbly internals of Lewis and Vickers guns. I lived in a sixteenth century college, rowed in leisure hours in an eight on the Isis past emblazoned, if rather shabby, wartime collegiate barges, and enjoyed for a few strenuous weeks, in uniform, some of the delights of an undergraduate's life.

Yet the supreme and, as I was to learn, most essential delight was wholly lacking: liberty. I was to discover her later in the same place, magically transformed, when, sudden victory on tired arms descending, I and my fortunate comrades were released into a still austere but infinitely welcome January England: free of every military restraint and obligation, heirs of victory and unassailable, eternal peace, young uncrowned lords of the Turl and High and of an Oxford which, it seemed, had been waiting and growing for us for six centuries. It was all ours: the grey quadrangles, the flowered gardens, the towers and domes; the learned men at their lectures and orisons; the gay lunches and suppers—when we could afford them—of salmon mayonnaise, ices and steaming chocolate sauce; the willow-shaded afternoons in Cherwell punt and canoe; the gala, parasolled visits in Eights Week and Commem of lightly-chaperoned, cousinly young ladies who opened, for romantic and unreckoning hearts, vistas of eternal, breath-taking happiness; the endless talk, wit and glow of friendship while St. Mary's deep-tolled bell proclaimed to unheeding ears the midnight hours:

> They say that in the unchanging place
> Where all we loved is ever dear,
> We meet our morning face to face
> And find at last our twentieth year.

That Oxford lasted for me less than two years. Foolishly, or perhaps, wisely, I felt the spur of the lost war-years and impatiently wanted to storm the workaday world. I soon found myself in it, and the Oxford of the young released captains who had so gaily thrown their Sam Brownes over the moon became only a precious memory. Then, a few years later, I returned to the magical city, trundling in an aged motor-car every few weeks out of the elmy, clayey North Buckinghamshire plain along a still winding

Bicester highroad, and past the rising suburban horrors of an already doomed Kidlington, on my way to Extension lecture or shopping expedition. I was now Benedict, the married man, making my little niche in profession and home, a supernumerary of one of Oxford's neighbour agricultural shires, a man with his foot more in the soil than the college, his mind more set on teaching than on learning. Yet all the while, during the fifteen years of peace when North Buckinghamshire was my home, Oxford remained an essential part of my background—sometimes prosaic and associated with crowded business, sometimes romantic and idyllic, always, when one had time to let one's mind and heart assimilate what one's eye saw, indescribably lovely, despite the growing industrial encroachments on the peace and dignity of its historic streets and the green, willowy beauty of its surrounding countryside. Once the two currents mingled when I produced a pageant in front of the lake in the park of Worcester College with a caste composed of men and women drawn from almost every Oxfordshire village, looking in their mediaeval dresses against the grey stone of Oxford's narrow streets incredibly like their prototypes and ancestors of five centuries before. One experience, a new one, was added in those years to my Oxford associations: the quiet delight of working long, peaceful hours in Duke Humphrey's beautiful library, looking down, whenever my glance strayed from the seventeenth-century manuscripts before me, on the garden of Exeter College and, sometimes, on sunlit summer afternoons, on the dons of that blessed institution having tea in a green shade, Chaucerian Mr. Coghill, I like to think, among them. I was so happy up there among the oaken shelves, with my dusty, sere-coloured letters linking me to the flesh-and-blood of the English past, that I did not even want to come down, on the hottest, thirstiest afternoon, and join them.

Those were days of peace. Then, for the second time in my life, I became familiar with Oxford in wartime, lecturing to audiences of soldiers and airmen gathered together in colleges where, a quarter of a century earlier, I had been one of them; forcing my way, in the course of hurried visits, through drab streets out of which all beauty and dignity had apparently been drained and filled with shabby, grey-faced, shambling evacuees. There were times when it seemed that Oxford could never again become what she had been, and must remain for ever an unhappy, congested suburb of a vast, amorphous, industrial Cowley. But her power of survival was greater than I had supposed, and I have lived to see her once more, as Matthew Arnold saw her, still "steeped in sentiment, . . . spreading her gardens to the moonlight and whispering from her towers the last enchantments of the Middle Age."

For her inner secret heart remains as beautiful as ever. One can pass out of the petrol-scented, piston-banging barbarism of the twentieth century High into the green serenity and quietude of College garden and quadrangle, flanked by buildings rich with the patina of centuries. To sit on some hallowed lawn in the long, quiet dusk of May, to dine off ancient mahogany and silver in Hawksmoor's cool and temperate English baroque, to stand amid whispering ghosts on the long, cold floor of a noble library, with the darkening twilight flooding through the great traceried windows, to see the dome of the Camera glowing rose-like against the blue of night or the eagle-topped glory of a Wren façade floodlit for a College play; to walk under the ancient city wall with a friend in darkness, while the flowers of the limes give out their first fugitive scent, to lie listening to those magical bells which hour by hour have made music for half a thousand years, to rise from one's bed and gaze on the enchanted scene—moonlit garden, tower, dome, spire, pinnacle and lichened wall—and see the ghost of an English Creseid, as Chaucer pictured her, tiptoeing down the mediaeval stone steps to the waiting lawn and the dark, blossoming trees below; such are the enchantments this magical city of learning still offers to successive generations of her sons. For it is Matthew Arnold's Oxford that has the last word. "Apparitions of a day, what is our puny warfare against the Philistines, compared with the warfare which this queen of romance has been waging against them for centuries, and will wage after we are gone?"

CHAPTER 3

On Discovering The Past Was Real

> The zummer air o' this green hill
> 'V a-heaved in bosoms now all still,
> An' all their hopes an' all their tears
> Be unknown things ov' other years.
>
> WILLIAM BARNES

At school I had loved history in a desultory sort of way, but never seriously enough to impress either myself or, with one exception[1], my schoolmasters. My chief acquaintance with the past was a meticulous knowledge of the details of Napoleon's campaigns, learnt with the aid of a set of halma men and the diagrams of battlefields in Alison's *History of Europe*, that stupendous work in twenty volumes which proved, as Disraeli put it, that Providence was on the side of the Tories. Then came the First World War with its ceaseless transfers and coming and goings, little conducive to the study of history, and thereafter the post-war Modern History School at Oxford, which, in that hour of release and youthful pleasure, was almost less so. After that, being at that stage of my life an idealist with an unorthodox itch to practise what I preached, I taught such text-book history as I possessed to bright-eyed little boys in an L.C.C. school, till the authorities with delicious illogicality brought these labours to an end by making me, at the age of twenty-four, Principal of an Art and Technical College.[2]

But during the next two years of administering classes in drawing from the life, art metal-work, motor engineering, bookkeeping, printing, plumbing, mothercraft and home-dressmaking, the generosity of an ancient Cheshire house to whom I had become

---

[1] George Townsend Warner, father of Sylvia Townsend Warner the novelist, and Senior History Master at Harrow until his death in 1916. G. M. Trevelyan was one of his first pupils and I one of his last.

[2] Now the Cambridge Technical College.

akin put into my hands the stuff of which history is made. Put into my hands is a misnomer, for it would have required a giant's hands to have clasped at once all the Shakerley papers. One grey December day in 1923, a concealed door in the wall of the Somerford library, decorously camouflaged by an eighteenth century hand with the names of books that were never written—Bishop Allworthy's *Sermons*, Lear's *View of the Stage*, Dr. Maggott on *The Hereafter*—was opened for me and I found myself standing in a vast stone cell, with shelves all round me loaded with almost all that remained of the life record of countless Cheshire men and women.

I did not, of course, know this at the time. All I saw were bundles and bundles of documents, tied in dirty grey parcels, and on tables round the walls an indescribable litter of parchments and papers. There were also some great seals of England lying about on chairs as though they were waiting to be thrown away as too old to keep. And the whole floor was powdered fine with the dust of broken seals.

Such was my first introduction to the Shakerley MSS. As casually I began to turn a few of the papers over, something of their meaning came dimly to me. Here was the actual past, of which I had read unimaginatively in books. I could touch it and peer into it and savour its musty, faint but vivid perfume. Curiosity gripped me.

After my first discovery I asked to be made free of the muniment room. Every day during that Christmas holiday I turned the great silver key, pushed back the heavy door and then closed it after me and sat down in that cold storage chamber of the past. The living life of the house without, the misty trees in the park and the sodden landscape of wintry Cheshire beyond receded: I could only hear the whispering voices of men and women who, after the silence of centuries, had found a listener and were trying to speak. And gradually I learnt to attune my unaccustomed ears.

At first I did little more than follow an idle curiosity, picking up such letters as lay on the surface and tasting rapidly wherever the unfamiliar handwriting admitted of such easy reading. For the most part the papers had been untouched; successive generations of family solicitors had occasionally entered to search for some ponderous conveyance or will, but had never attempted to penetrate farther. Once an eighteenth century antiquarian had busied himself for a short while among the papers, and some traces of his intrusion—a letter or two to the Shakerley who then owned Somerford and an occasional scrawl of indication on the back of some document or parcel—betokened his limited interest. Since that time a herald or a local antiquarian had on rare occasion made his entry to pursue momentarily some particular search, heraldic or genealogical, leaving behind him an untidy trail of rummaged papers. And the last of Somerford's chatelaines, a woman of character and intelligence, had spent some curious hours, as many as ill-health and a crowded life of many activities admitted, pursuing some long-forgotten theme of family history. But systematic search there had never been; the early Historical Manuscripts Commissioners had not set foot in Somerford— probably they had been roughly repelled by the spoilt, ill-tempered aristocrat who, surviving from the heyday of the Regency into the decorous order of Victorian England, had closed the doors of Somerford to all but dancing girls and his own toadies. The great bulk of the Shakerley papers lay as they had lain for centuries.

What began as a relaxation from the monotony of a winter holiday in a lonely country house soon became a regular hobby. When I returned to my professional labours in southern England, I took a few of the bundles with me and fell into the pleasant habit of occupying my evenings by copying the more interesting parts of the letters they contained into a large exercise book which I bought for the purpose. When Easter again released me, I hurried north to renew my acquaintance with the muniment room, silent and unvisited during my three months' absence— that tiny pin-point of time in its long generations of oblivion. The letters I had copied during my absence had aroused my curiosity to pursue a dozen different trails, and my blood was whetted for the chase. I began to undo bundle after bundle to discover what each contained, and whether they could assist my searches.

Many of the bundles, I soon found, revealed only legal documents, long disused, the titles to land in Cheshire and Lancashire villages of homely names, some of which, however, during the nineteenth century had grown into household words of semi-humorous, wholly industrial connotation, but which, at the time referred to in these documents, had been merely rustic and local. Many of these deeds were of almost terrifying antiquity—tiny slips of parchment, beautifully written in Latin in hands reminiscent of the more individual examples of modern script and in far finer preservation than their eighteenth and nineteenth century successors. There seemed at first something uncanny in turning over and fingering conveyances of land in places like Stockport, Wigan and Macclesfield, made in days when King Henry II sat on the throne of England and whose minute pendant seals bore the devices of long-vanished monasteries and of semifabulous beings like the seven palatine Earls of Chester.

Others, taking up as much cubic space as a hundred of their forerunners, when unfolded presented thick sheet after sheet of closely writ parchment of apparently prodigious importance, but, when examined, proved to be only some cumbersome eighteenth century will or marriage settlement. For the lawyers, who in days of universal illiteracy had secured their craft monopoly by the simple device of being able to read and write, had learnt to preserve it, as the nation became literate, by ingeniously constructing a wordy jargon which no man but themselves could understand and which they ever expanded as the march of human reason toiled vainly after them. All this, which others learn from books or teachers, I came to discover for myself.

But what I sought and learnt to treasure were not the deeds. The jewels which lay thick to my delving hands were the letters, still folded as their long-dead recipients had left them, the very sand from the stand-dishes of their first writers glittering in their folds, so that often my fingers and wrists were stained with a minute dust. Sometimes I found them in hundreds, tied into parcels by some impatient solicitor or agent and marked omnisciently, "Of no importance." I learnt to value these indexes of the barren precision of the legal mind, for they pointed to me my richest veins of gold. At other times I would come unexpectedly on letters buried deep in bundles of conveyances, whose context seemed to have no connection with theirs. I learnt to seek for them in all places; pressed between the pages of account or house-keeping books, trodden underfoot beneath the dust of the broken seals on the stone floor, thrust into corners of cupboards or patching the mouldered lids of deed-boxes. Then I would unfold them and with excitement pursue their contents.

Those were the days of the first chase; I pursued wildly and scarcely knew what I pursued. My quarry, I came to learn, needed staider hunting. A casually opened letter would give a glimpse of some—to me—thrilling intimacy; a Jacobean elopement, the scapes of an Elizabethan undergraduate, a harassed Governor of Chester receiving royal orders from James II to admit a priest to say mass in defiance of law in Chester Castle. One jumped wildly to conclusions, but soon found oneself checked and the scent lost. For a time I was content to follow some other trail, where so many presented themselves, but the check was always repeated. Curiosity, and something quietly insistent inside me, in time prompted to a more laborious pursuit. Patience, method, above all, industry, these plainly were the disiderata for the discovery of what I was seeking.

They came to my aid. The work was so absorbing that it grew on me imperceptibly. It was not till the last hour struck in the history of Somerford, and the great house, dismantled, opened its doors to a barbaric invasion of antique dealers and auctioneers before its final agony at the hands of the estate breaker—product characteristic of our petulant, uncreative age—that I was able to survey the full scope of the work before me. Then the papers, in vast wooden boxes and trunks, were moved to their new home in Buckinghamshire, where humbler but even older doors opened to receive them. And here, in a room whose walls had shadowed Elizabethans, the vast array of the Shakerley MSS. was spread day after day on the unswept floor, despite the protests and entreaties of womankind—"worse enemies to papers," as one of Pepys's correspondents described them, "than rats and mice." Yet, now that I recall it, it was one of that destructive sex, my wife, who knelt beside me on the floor night after night as together we turned over countless papers, ever sorting and arranging till all lay in the neat folders prepared for them.

Every year from 1560 to 1850 was given its own folder—the deeds, which strayed back into the misty antiquity of the twelfth century, were arranged separately according to their nature or topographical context. Every letter, spread out, took its exact chronological place in the year-file to which it belonged. Nearly all the letters were folded as they had first been sent, the old practice till the coming of envelopes in the early nineteenth century being elaborately to fold the single or double sheet on which the letter had been written, seal it across the open fold and address it on the back: many of the missives so made were little bigger than a book of stamps. Only the extreme quality of the old hand-made paper on which they were written had preserved them against cracking along the folds and so falling to pieces. It was noticeable that the nineteenth century letters were mostly in far inferior condition to those of the seventeenth century, while the paper on which an English gentleman of 1850 corresponded with his friends was of infinitely superior quality to that used today.

Dating was not always an easy matter. Many of the letters were undated and had to be fitted into their proper place by their context. This was rather like doing a jigsaw puzzle with half the pieces missing, for, of course, much material that might have guided one had long ago perished, while the correspondence as a whole tended, like that of nearly all country house collections, to be rather one-sided, the outgoing letters reposing, if at all, in the muniment rooms of their recipients' descendants. Here the calendars of the Historical Manuscripts Commissioners and of the various learned societies who have published works on family papers proved helpful; the indexes perused would often reveal a Shakerley, a Buckworth or a Vernon whose letter fitted neatly into some vacant niche in the Shakerley collection. More often there was nothing to guide us, and we had to keep a number of spare folders roughly dated into which we cast doubtful letters according to such broad characteristics as style and handwriting, there to wait until I became sufficiently familiar with the tiny intimate allusions they contained to date them with greater certainty.

Yet, though there was much delving in the dark and at first

a good deal of the usual mis-dating consequent upon the confusing habit of our forebears of dating their Lenten letters sometimes according to the old style and sometimes the new—it is
surprising how often even the learned editors of the early Historical Manuscripts Commission Reports fell into this fault through
not paying sufficient attention to the minutiæ of the context—
there were other factors, familiar to all who work on records,
which lightened one's labours. The old practice of addressing
letters on the back of the paper on which they were written
almost invariably enabled one to identify the recipient as well as
the sender, a thing that would have been almost impossible under
the modern usage of separate envelopes, which are usually consigned after opening to the waste-paper basket.

Another great boon was the pre-nineteenth century custom of
attaching surnames to uncles, aunts and cousins. Uncle Shakerley
of Gwersylt is a far more recognisable character to the historian
than Uncle George. Against this must be set off the minor incon-
venience of finding a man's "in-laws" described by the same style
impartially as the closer kinship of father, mother and brother.
And, until one became used to it, it was often confusing to find
intimate friends and lovers concluding their letters: "Your
humble and obedient servant," while tax-gatherers and other
officials almost invariably ended their unpalatable communications with "Your loving friend."

After about 1670 elementary postmarks, at first of date alone—
though of the day and month only and not, unfortunately, the
year—and later sometimes of the place of posting, often proved
useful. Nor was the occasional help to be obtained from the
armorial devices on the beautiful red seals to be despised.

When at last the letters were all sorted and the year-files placed
in a vast oak spice-chest with innumerable drawers—made by a
Welsh carpenter for the writer of many hundreds of them in the
early eighteenth century—the education of an historian had
begun. A chance curiosity had grown into a holiday task, and a
holiday task now became the regular routine of every evening
and leisure day. Each night, when I came home and the lamps were
lit, I unlocked the spice-chest, pulled out the particular folder on
which I was working and transcribed or calendared, as the inter-

est or reverse of the particular document dictated, letter and bill. Sometimes months would elapse before I could dispose of some particularly bulky folder, containing many hundreds of letters.

At first I transcribed by hand with a tall feather pen which seemed appropriate to my subject. But as I became wiser I learnt to prefer a typewriter, which by enabling me to take carbons saved much wearisome cross referencing and gave me files of transcripts arranged under subject as well as date. The sweet, regular labour of it taught me what school or university—though they laid the foundations of it—had never taught, a craft; to do one thing thoroughly without evasion or omission. It is a lesson learnt by most men who practise a handicraft in their own way, but seldom provided by the rather "slap-dash" and desultory general reading of modern literary education. Yet it is well worth attaining, for though it may not increase a man's moral stature, it tends to give him a sense of balance and values, makes him love quality and shun shoddy, and teaches him to judge men and things.

This is a digression, yet I owe too much to the Shakerley MSS. not to record that debt. The play's the thing. And the play, if there was much labour in it, was none the less all delight. The interest of slowly unfolding the course of one human life after another, with all its desires and aspirations, its joys and pathetic failures, was such that only a very dull man could have failed to be absorbed. And here were real lives that had once meant as much to their possessors as mine to me. One got a queer, almost godlike, sense of being able to see the future of these long-dead beings as well as the past, of being able to feel and yet to be unswayed by feeling. And with it a sense, too, of humility, for even as one now beheld these, so might one also be seen and judged hereafter. Something of the quality—emotion recollected in tranquillity which Wordsworth held to be the essential of poetry—was present in those silent hours of the night, looking over the shoulders of those far writers and tracing in equally transient shadow on the wall of one's own age the words they wrote.

The variety in the human interests revealed by the papers was almost endless. In various ways, at least a dozen correspondences of different Cheshire, Lancashire and North Welsh families had found their way into the general body of the Shakerley MSS. and each started some new pursuit. One, which gave me intense excitement at the time but led to no capture, was a collection of letters and documents belonging to that Fitton of Gawsworth who was the father of Mary Fitton, the elusive being whom some have claimed as the Dark Lady of the Sonnets. Suppose, I hazarded, one came across some allusion to this suspected, lost relationship; suppose even—but that was hoping too much! Yet sometimes I wonder whether in some unexpected collection of papers somewhere in the Midlands, a bundle of letters may not one day be unearthed bearing Shakespeare's signature. There were so many unsuspected things lying among these Shakerley papers, of whose existence no one had before been aware, that nothing of the kind would surprise me.

Many were the delightful vistas down which one gazed as one pursued one's task. I recall one such, glimpsed at the moment when I had just moved the MSS. to their new home. My neighbour and landlord, Sir Harry Verney, sent me as a welcoming gift a copy of the first and best of all printed country house collections, the *Verney Memoirs*, whose originals were, and still are, housed in Claydon House, a mile or so away. I read them with delight and was particularly enchanted with the character of that prince of seventeenth century letter-writers, Tom Verney, the "importunate beggar," for whom, as an American wrote with truth, "nature had not broken the mould in which Falstaff was run." Stimulated and enthused, I opened one of the boxes of Shakerley MSS. that had just arrived from Cheshire, and took a handful of letters out at random. To my amazement almost the first I opened was a neat missive signed Tom Verney and addressed to that warm-hearted, irascible cavalier, old Sir Geoffrey Shakerley, the Governor of Chester Castle. It proved to be just such a letter as I had learnt to expect from honest Tom, urging in superlative and almost irresistible eloquence the prospects of some primitive mining venture on which he was engaged on Sir Geoffrey's Welsh lands. Nor did it fail to conclude with a request for a loan of £3. Thirty years had elapsed since Tom Verney had written the last of the begging letters quoted in the "Verney Memoirs," but here he was still at his old game and with gusto undiminished for all his three score years and ten. I hurried down to Claydon House to verify the hand-writing by Tom's letters there: the identity was unmistakable.

The personalities whom I learnt to know and grew to love, as I copied their letters by my fireside, gradually became more real to me than many of my own contemporaries. They lived for me and still live, just as Elizabeth Bennet and Mr. Micawber and Colonel Newcome and all that glorious company live for lovers of books, only with the enhanced vitality of having actually been alive. The two Yorkshire sisters, for instance, one of whom, in 1628, married a Cheshire squire and the other a Lothbury merchant of the house of Lowther—"I hop to God I have got an onast religas man", wrote the latter on her wedding day—who used to end their letters to each other with touching formality:

I leave you to God and rest
Your true loveing sister till death.

Yes; and after death; the sweet piety of the home on the Yorkshire moors which bore that love still shines through the faded ink and has power to touch the reader after more than three hundred years. "Sweet sister, I have sent you a little suegar lofe: I pray you accept of it, tho' it be but small. I left behind my lute," she added, "it is in a canvis bag upon the bed in the best chamber."

I remember one letter that gave me particular pleasure. It was from a small boy at school to his guardian, and written in the year 1700:

"Honored Sir,

I received your cloaths you sent me: they are a little to long but that is no fault and a little thing makes the goold buttons being worne before to unravel and Maddam Thellwall thinks they are too good to spoil and advises me to keepe them till Christmas againe, and to wear the cloaths with silver olive buttons, and sais a frise would have been much better for every day, for all the boys that are Gentlemens sons wear them, for it is so cold, and are very cheaper.

I was not well but have taken fisik. One day I was taken in the Scoole with the griping of the guts, which Mr. Prise thinks

to be the wormes. No more at present but my seruis to your
Lady from him who is

Your humble servant

ROGER BRADSHAIGH."

Dearest, I think, of all the dead men and women I grew to care
for was Peter Shakerley. The old man still beetles at me from
under his great Hanoverian wig in the gold frame above the table
where I write; the house he built in his old age was where I found
the Shakerley papers, and though it is now perished and the tall
trees he planted all felled, his careful, far-seeing spirit still broods
over the wasted parklands of Somerford, and in the little panelled
chapel which alone survives of the ordered paradise he created in
what was formerly a wilderness and has now, by man's greed
and folly, been made a wilderness again. Yet Peter was not always
old. Once in his youth he stampeded, to his father's fury, through
the slow formalities of a marriage settlement; "we had much
ado," wrote his delighted father-in-law, who had gained greatly
by his impetuosity, "to keep him from kissing his bride before
matrimony was all read." The tender and beautiful woman he
took to himself so gallantly that day gave him sixteen years of
happiness, but no children, and more than twice that time of
loneliness after her early death.

Yes; it is easy to love Peter Shakerley—the bold sloping writing
so full of strength and character, the terse, manly style—"so,"
he wrote to his erring undergraduate ward, "I shall judge of
your devotions in the future by the balance remaining in your
hands at the end of each quarter"—the splendid virility that could
cause him at the age of seventy to issue a challenge to two
relations, thirty years younger than himself, "to undertake me
either at shooting, angling or walking" during a stormy March
holiday upon the Derbyshire moors. And, most of all, one loves
him for his work, treasured up in that great legacy of papers he
collected and left behind—the record of a life spent in the service
of his country and his neighbours, ten years a soldier and Governor
of Chester, twenty-five years a member of Parliament, corres-
ponding voluminously with his constituents on every aspect of
the trade and rising industry of the third commercial city of

England, faithful executor and trustee of half a dozen of the great estates of Cheshire and Lancashire, two at least of which he saved from destruction and ruin.

No man can live for ever; neither can his work. To read the lives of the ancient dead over their own shoulders is to con that mournful lesson; they lived, desired, and strove.

> *And all their hopes and all their tears*
> *Be unknown things of other years.*

Yet, as I read, I found that even that had in it some sense of quiet satisfaction and companionship; the gulf of loneliness which divides man from man is bridged in that enchanted moment; one knows the nature of one's lot on this dream-visited planet, and accepts it with all its implications:

> *I know my life's a pain and but a span;*
> *I know my sense is mock'd in everything;*
> *And, to conclude, I know myself a Man—*
> *Which is a proud and yet a wretched thing.*

CHAPTER 4

Blue Remembered Hills

"Into my heart an air that kills
From yon far country blows:
What are those blue remembered hills?
What spires, what farms are those?"

A. E. HOUSMAN

*In the years before the Second World War—"the long weekend"—
I lived in rural North Buckinghamshire, lectured on winter evenings for
the Oxford University Extension Delegacy and wrote my first historical
books on the English seventeenth century, including 'Charles II', 'Restoration England', the three volumes of 'Pepys', and 'Postman's Horn'. I also
produced pageants at Cambridge, Oxford and in the Fens, and in 1933
the Greenwich Naval Night Pageant—the Navy's counterpart to the
Aldershot Tattoo. As Educational Adviser and a Governor of the Bonar
College, Ashridge, and as a contributor to the Illustrated London News,
and* Observer, *I had, too, some minor connection with politics and
public affairs, holding views which, like those of many Englishmen in
that confused time, seem in retrospect almost contradictory. For I was a
passionate advocate of the then highly unpopular cause of rearmament—
in which I was right—and of the hardly less unpopular cause of appeasement—in which I was wrong, not because it was wrong to try to avert
the tragedy of a second German war, with the apparent waste of all the
lives lost in the first, but because no appeasement of a rearmed and
revengeful Germany was possible so long as Britain herself was in-
adequately armed.*

A Buckinghamshire Home · Hunter's Moon · The Bells · Doomed Treasures · The Last Easter of Peace

I

A Buckinghamshire Home[1]

At Harrow School we used to sing a song to the effect that, in the view of all right-minded boys, there was no month like October. The reason for this preference—and it was always expressed with immense noise and gusto—was that it brought the cold weather down, "when the wind and the rain continue." Few of those singing it forty years ago would be hardy enough to endorse such sentiments today, for we have reached an age when we could do with much less wind and rain and a great deal more sun. But Edward Bowen knew his boys, and so did John Farmer, the composer, and a splendid song they made of it, with its thundering chorus of

> *October! October!*
> *March to the dull and the sober,*
> *The suns of May for the schoolgirls' play,*
> *But give to the boys October!*

Personally I plump for September. Keats had the same preference; what could be lovelier than an English walled garden, full of flowers, fruit and drowsy insects, on a sunny autumn morning? The sun seems to shine more consistently in early September than in any month of the English year. Yet it is for one memory in particular that I love it. It was on an early September day in 1925 that I bade a sad farewell to a great house in the north country which a few months later was to suffer under the hands of the housebreaker. All day I drove southwards, through the rich Midland countryside, past noble parks and trees—still untouched by the fate which a generation ahead was lying in wait for them too—until towards evening of a calm, lovely day I reached the little North Buckinghamshire village where I was

[1] *Illustrated London News*, 5 September 1953.

to live for the next twenty years. The ancient moated house on its outskirts which was to be my home was still in the hands of the builders and decorators. I can even now recall the faces of the local worthies who were the unchanging members and employees of the firm that carried out the work and who, during the next three intensely exciting, yet peaceful weeks, were to become my allies and friends.

Until the house was ready for occupation I had arranged to stay in the village post-office half-a-mile away—"a cottage well-thatched with straw", kept by some of the kindest people I have ever met. Thence every morning my wife and I set out along a grassy, nut-grown, elm-bordered lane which took us, without crossing or touching a road, to the old white house, with its tall Elizabethan chimneys and beautiful red-brick seventeenth-century wall, on which all our immediate worldly hopes and interests had become centred. Beside us walked a great, thick-ruffed, deep-chested dog, of Gladstonian dignity, wolf-like appearance and almost unbelievable gentleness, who from the first moment adopted his future home as though he had always lived there and already knew that beneath the grass of its quiet lawn, sheltered from wind and sound by high yew hedges, he was to find after seven happy years his eternal resting-place. Then, until we returned for our evening meal down the elm-lined lane, each calm September day passed in a whirl of activity as we supervised and helped—or hindered—builder and gardener, un-packed boxes of books, papers, china and glass, arranged the furniture and hung the pictures as each room was made ready for habitation. I can still see the glittering white of the newly-distem-pered walls and the beautiful brown oak of the beams stripped of their many coats, the shining elm staircase, the vast fireplace we undug in one room and the carved Jacobean stone overmantel of another, the ancient walnut and mahogany furniture we had brought with us which fitted into their places in their new home as though they had been made for it, and the seventeenth and eighteenth century ladies and gentlemen in their gilt frames who seemed to accept, so surprisingly and naturally, their new and humbler home as if it was part of the eternal order of things. They looked down as though they were happy, and as though the serenity of that enchanting, welcoming little house had won their hearts, as it had ours.

Outside were the gentle, rolling fields and guardian elms of the North Buckinghamshire plain, imperceptibly turning from green to gold at the warning of the first night frosts after those warm, sun-kissed, misty days. There was no sound of anything but birds and human voices, of the cattle in the fields, and the distant noises of the quiet village street. All the houses in it were either of rosy seventeenth-century brick, with high-pitched roofs, or of white-washed walls with half-timbering and thatch, and all stood almost hidden from one another and the world in groves and clusters of elms. There were no aeroplanes, no sounds of wireless, no lights but the soft glow of oil-lamps, round which we sat at night reading in a profound country quiet. The restless modern world existed, but it was still far away, though we were only fifty miles from London. I have never known so peaceful a place, or so gently happy a one, and that September for me was like a kind of honeymoon between man and earth, dweller and home. I became naturalised, as it were, into the quiet land I had chosen and which was to be my background for so long. There was no sense of strangeness, none of unfamiliarity; it was as though I had been born there, and even the beloved Wiltshire haunts of my boyhood did not seem more home than this. Perhaps it held such magic for me because this unassuming countryside drew its atmosphere from an incredibly ancient woodland past; once part of the forest of Bernwood, it constituted a watershed between the Norfolk pinewoods, where I was born, and the south-western beechwoods where I was bred. I cannot explain it, but can only record the fact of my sudden and glad enslavement, and the love and gratitude I still feel for that friendly land of elms, sloping meadows, oaks and leafy hamlets,[1] and for the benediction of the kindly autumn month in which I was made free of it.

* * *

---

[1] Now threatened, with the whole of the Vale of Aylesbury, by the proposal to site the third London Airport at Wing and Cublington.

II

Hunter's Moon[1]

Summer leaves the Buckinghamshire plain more reluctantly than
other lands. Weeks, even months, before she finally goes she gives
her first signs of departure; a cold breeze slips warningly down
from the north in late July, chilly fogs rise out of the warm
August fields, and all through the sun-drenched days of early
September the swallows flit, restless and afraid, outside their
familiar habitations. But still, though the call of the sun hurrying
southward is urgent, summer cannot altogether bring herself to
be gone. She lingers and lingers. October still has days full of
the illusion of June, and even December displays in chilled
gardens her damp and faded roses. Like the sea-going sailors of
earlier days, shedding wives and sweethearts all down the River
to the Downs, summer sings her swan-song, "Loth to Depart."

Yet in one's own life the change from summer afternoons to
winter evenings comes quickly enough. One Saturday one is still
hopefully pounding away at tennis in the failing light, and the
next sitting snug before the fire, listening to the wireless and
wondering how many weeks it is to Christmas. And once faced,
the change from summer routine to winter is not unpleasant.
There is something invigorating about the earliest cold crisp
days: for the first time since we got back from the holidays we
find ourselves feeling our old vigorous selves and ready for anything. The period of melancholy regret is over: the flowers are
vanished, the leaves down and there is nothing further to mourn.
We have touched bottom at last, and it is not so bad as we thought.
In fact, it is almost enjoyable. Resigned, a sensible man squares his
shoulders, puts on his overcoat and even welcomes the brisk walk
home from the station in the early dark.

This annual revolution affects men's lives in different ways.
For most it alters the hours of leisure more than hours of labour.
The coal miner no longer ascends from the pit into the light of
day, the Whitehall typist cannot eat her sandwiches beside the

[1] *I.L.N.* 17 October 1936.

lake, and there is no more gardening in the long evening twilight for the suburban breadwinner. In office and factory, however, the old round remains much the same. Yet there are plenty of exceptions. Sailors and farm labourers, lorry drivers and policemen find their employment in winter very different to what it was in summer. And there are a few whose occupation changes completely. What happens to professional cricketers and the men who collect the pennies from the occupants of deck-chairs in the London parks?

One can best speak of one's own experience. For years I was in the habit of spending winter evenings lecturing for an ancient university in small Buckinghamshire and Oxfordshire country towns and villages. It cannot be a common form of vocation, for human patience and powers of endurance could not permit of many lecturers. But more than most it is a seasonal one, for who would listen to a lecture when he might be sitting in the sun or enjoying himself out of doors? As Dr. Johnson said of fox-hunting, attendance at lectures proves the paucity of human pleasures, at least as afforded by the English countryside between October and April.

So it came about that for the writer for a whole decade the coming of winter spelt a new life, or rather an old life revived after a summer's lapse. The leisurely hours of study between tea and dinner had to cease; instead, the stroke of five became an alarum to depart. It was now my lot to rise from the fire, collect great-coat and lecture-notes, and grope my way to the garage. An hour or more's driving through the chill hostility of a winter's night would bring me to hall or institute, where the frugality of the illumination and the uncompromising hardness of the chairs only heightened the impression of earnest endeavour which the audience politely contrived to convey.

It sounds, I dare say, a comfortless picture. Yet strangely those evenings of sober discourse—a parliament of half-hesitant, deeply thoughtful countrymen round a stove—were as stimulating as any in my remembrance. And the homeward journeys afterwards are as pleasant to recall. For solitude, the ranging silver beam of headlight on hedgerow and sleeping meadow, and the hazards of wintry weather made them partake of some peculiar and inexpressible romance. Now, far to south or north, the light of a distant town would make an arc of dim fire in the sky, now the moon would rise cold and vibrant to ride visible clouds, now wisps of white fog enfold road and bonnet and transform the guiding beam into an impenetrable wall of emptiness. Six times in nine years a fox ran swiftly across the car's course, and twice an owl slept unscathed in the midst of a lane, and the wheels passed on either side of it. Such hours of moving isolation afforded time for thought and meditation seldom allowed by the conditions of modern life. There are compensations in the hurry-scurry of an age of transport, and the solitude of the wheel by night may give the peace and inward content which in former times men sought for in the wilderness. Nor did the sight of familiar gate-post and topiary ever seem sweeter than they did in those nights to the homecoming traveller.

These things must seem trivial to record in a world of marvels made manifest by headlines. In reality they are the essence of life and more significant than all the chronicles of all the kings. That summer has gone and winter come in her place touches deeper chords in each of us than anything we read in the newspapers. For the wars and revolutions of the moment are quickly forgotten and their place soon taken by new, but harvest home and the hunter's moon will endure as long as the sons of men.

*　　*　　*

III

The Bells[1]

Last year I spent my New Year's Eve with some old friends who entertained me lavishly with all the most up-to-date delights of the season. I dined in company with strangers in an expensive restaurant; was taken to the theatre; was ensconced in a great limousine for half an hour in a New Year's traffic block in Piccadilly Circus while a howling mob—nearly all presumably strangers to one another—made whoopee around, and was lavishly supped in a splendid house, where all thought of encircling winter

[1] *I.L.N.* 31 October 1938.

was banished by the luxuriously heated air, and the New Year was toasted in in brimming cups of vintage champagne. It could not have been better done, and we kept it up, if I remember rightly, till after two. Yet, somehow, for all the kindness and hospitality, I felt a little wistful, and out of it. I wanted to be somewhere else.

This year I shall be there, watching where I have seen so many new years succeed the old. The house will be quite dark, for in the village where I live we keep early hours. But I shall be standing at the window of a little seventeenth century room looking out where countless men and women have looked out on previous New Year nights. It may be one of those ordinary, still, black nights common to the English midlands at this time of the year, with not a light in the sky and no sound but the rustling and snuffing of the cattle beyond the garden wall. It may be raining, with a soft wind from the south or south-west, with soaked primulas drinking in the border below. Or it may be a traditional December night with frost on the ground and a thousand stars sparkling through the crisp air, and the house lying like an old white ghost in wintry glory. But whatever the weather there will be an air of waiting: of a certain familiar and hallowed suspense. And the silence will make it all the more intense, recalling the age-long significance of a great traditional human occasion better than all the rejoicings and loud good wishes of strangers.

For there is this essential difference between New Year's Eve in the city and in the country. In the former it is a pagan festival, in the latter part of a Christian feast. Rioting gaily in London restaurants and cabarets is at the farthest possible remove from the simple manger birth under the arch of the heavens which is still the dominating fact of the Christian New Year. For the latter falls within the Christmas feast, whereas New Year's Eve in the metropolis is merely the recognition of a recurrent landmark in the secular calendar. The old year is out and the new year, which we hope will be rather more prosperous, is in. There is little more to it than that, and we join hands with strangers and sing "Auld Lang Syne", conscious, at least for the moment, that, being mortals, we are all in the same boat and might as well put a friendly convivial face on it.

But in the stillness of the country night we hear sounds which the din of the city drowns. All the bygone centuries of Christian belief and worship and the dead men and women from whom we sprang are plucking at the chords of our consciousness. We are still under the spell of that other mystical and symbolical night of a week earlier. The words of an old carol ring in the mind: "It came upon the midnight clear." Here we are watching a spectacle as solemn and eternal as men's eyes can behold. The grandest show the city proffers has nothing to equal this. We are beholding and experiencing a miracle; one no less because every man and every age has been able to take part in it. Not only is all living mankind symbolically linked by the occasion as by the cheering crowds and the toasts in city streets and taverns, but the whole human race, past, present and future, is for the moment made one. All the generations that have ever been or are to be are waiting there in the dark night, wondering and listening.

Presently the bells will begin to ring from every grey church tower within earshot. Across the wet, green fields the sound will come, rising and falling with the undulations of the wind. And beyond the bells heard will be other bells, not audible to the terrestrial ear, but pealing for all that out of the night with a sweet joyous clarity from the shires which lie beyond sight and hearing. For men listening to the farthest bell within range of my straining ears will hear other bells that I cannot, and these, again, will link one to more distant audiences.

The circle of consciousness grows and grows by giant leaps till it includes the whole earth. As clearly as the loved invisible meadows and hedges that encircle the dark garden, I shall see in vision the North Buckinghamshire landscape sloping away to an encircling horizon of rejoicing bells, and simultaneously imagine other scenes known and loved in the past—stone villages in folds of the Cotswolds, high white Wiltshire walls where pollards wind fantastically across water-meadows, Celtic sanctuaries amid the stark, wind-swept slopes of Cornwall. Here, also, the bells will be clanging as though the spirits of men were gone mad with sudden jubilation: some great discovery having been made, some new America of the soul. For in those midnight minutes the whole of Christendom, that great catholic union of the living and the dead, is at one with itself, realising with rejoicing the significance of its existence and recognising amid all the disappointments and shocks of the terrestrial hurly-burly that man is heir to a great estate.

* * *

IV

Doomed Treasures

Sitting by a blazing fire on an October evening,[1] in a room lit by lamps and candles, I could not help counting my treasures and wondering how many of them may never be enjoyed by such as I again. To have walked across the misty fields of autumn and come out of the raw afternoon with tingling veins and a memory of sad elms and crimson and gold gleaming down the sentenced hedges, to feel the embracing warmth of the house even before one reaches the line of its latticed, lighted windows, to raise the latch and enter into one's own home—not a concrete and steel box in a skyscraper, but a solid, ancient house that had seen successive generations of children and won the love of its owners for centuries—is to enjoy great wealth. It is a wealth of a kind which was common enough a generation or two back, but today is becoming increasingly rare. Probably not one in ten of our new urban population, town dwellers now for at least four generations, would recognise it. Its continuance is threatened by every kind of modern development: by joint-stock capitalism, by the regimentation of goods and minds, by Communist theory and Socialist practice, by the confused thinking and defeated living of those who are filing in slow procession into the shadow of the servile State which our wise men have for so long been building for us. It is a form of life which must be accounted passing away; I doubt whether our children's children will see its like. It will be remembered only by antiquarians, who will have it from books and reconstruct it in lectures and learned theses—a pale, intellectualised ghost of what was once vital, but from which the glow of life will have faded. Those who hear or read of it will be as

[1] *I.L.N.* 30 Oct 1937. Written two years before the second World War.

little able to recapture it as we are to comprehend the emotion of those who built the Pyramids or walked among the hanging gardens of Babylon.

It is curious to reflect how many of the simple things which have given pleasure and content to generations of men and women living in this island will never give that particular pleasure and content again. For all our myriad wonders and achievements of scientific discovery and invention, ours is an age more conspicuous for destruction than creation. The soul of things—built up by centuries of repeated usage, hallowed by heredity and instinctive feeling—is dying. The deep thrill of recognition for the sight, scent and sound of things that our fathers loved is no longer part of the human birthright; we seem set on a slippery slope that leads through ceaseless change for its own sake to lassitude, decay of the spirit and ultimate anarchy and barbarism.

That is the way all civilisations die. The moment that the ordinary everyday phenomena of life cease to have any other significance than purely utilitarian purpose, the man who so perceives them has passed the zenith of life. So it is with civilisations. They rise with the capacity of their citizens for taking joy and finding significance and understanding in the daily framework of their lives, for enriching that framework by accumulated, loving and joyous labour, for giving it reverence and protective care. They die when their citizens cease to find joy in and care for these familiar essentials of living. The old customs and festivals cease to be honoured, and along the horizon of the fading past the old lights go out. When men turn their backs on their institutions and cease to hold them in account, the communions of which they are social and political members are destined for the dark. The unity has gone out of them: men and women become mere economic units, each set on the fulfilment of his or her own selfish interests. There is nothing any more to keep the body politic together.

Such musings may be those of a pessimist, happily doomed to be falsified by the future. It may be that, in the interstices of our busy modern life of change and new invention, all kinds of binding habits and common associations are growing up that will cause unborn generations to find joy in the social framework of their existence. The fierce clang of changing gears at night, the roar of the internal combustion engine, the loud nasal inaudibilities of the platform loud-speaker announcing in tinned cockaigne the destination of trains, may become to our children's children sounds that inspire and comfort as much as the tunefulness of Bow Bells did their London forebears. They may already do so to our own children.[1]

Right or wrong, optimist or pessimist, let me recount a few of my treasures: they were those of millions of English men and women before me. The sound of horse hooves on the road in the early morning; the smell of autumnal fires and the haze that hangs just now like a halo round faded sunflowers and dahlias and thatched barns; the sight of hounds and pink coats against the russet hedges; a tea-table of gleaming silver and the curtains drawn against the damp night; an old brown folio beside an open fire, with the soft flicker of lamp or candle-light on ancient furniture; the slow, measured march of time noted in the peaceful serenity of a grandfather clock.

> *Now stir the fire, and close the shutters fast,*
> *Let fall the curtains, wheel the sofa round,*
> *And, while the bubbling and loud-hissing urn*
> *Throws up a steamy column, and the cups*
> *That cheer but not inebriate, wait on each,*
> *So let us welcome peaceful evening in.*

The new men of the towns, with their chromium-plated flats, chairs and cupboards of steel, their central heating and clanging lifts and buttoned porters, know and care nothing for these old friends and comforters of civilised men. Nor is it reasonable to expect that they should respect our love for them. We must needs steel ourselves against their passing. An old home full of hallowed associations and treasured belongings is up for sale: the auctioneer Progress awaits to give them a quick dismissal, and soon the dealers' men will come to carry them away. It is not unfitting to salute them before they go.

* * *

[1] By now, more than thirty years later, they probably do.

V

The Last Easter of Peace[1]

At the time of writing a cold wind is blowing out of the east. It gives England a bleak, strained appearance alien to her. There is no colour to be seen from my window save in the ugly outlines of some raw red-brick houses, their untoned garishness emphasised by some kindred quality in the harsh uncompromising wind. At such moments one might almost fancy England to be part of the Muscovy plain, as perhaps once it was in some far grim ice age.

Yet soon all will change. The cold harshness will be succeeded, in the manner of things English, by a soft day and a wind from the south. The earth, after its long parching, will suck vapour out of the clouds, mist will lie in the valleys, and shafts of sunlight give promise of the coming hues of the vivid grass, and the trees, ready to burst into life, will wear a mysterious tinge of dull copper-red over their wintry greys and blacks. It will still be cold, but all bitterness will have gone from the atmosphere. In the town the pavements will glisten and the dust of March be laid by showers of rain, and the early flowers in the parks no longer mock the passer-by behind his turned-up over-coat. Perhaps by Easter the sun will be shining.

Unfortunately today there is not only a wind blowing out of the east. There is a threat as well. It is the threat of steel—of steel instruments of war and steel men, made grim by a harsh history, casting angry and covetous looks at our peace and security. It will take more than a south wind to melt that threat or a sunny day to warm that icy chill between nation and nation. With our divided councils—the price we pay for our freedom in peace time —we have lost many opportunities in the past of easier remedies than those that now lie before us. Now nothing can absolve us from the penalty of old follies but our own sacrifices.

Not once or twice in our rough island-story,
The path of duty was the way to glory.

[1] *I.L.N.* 8 April 1939.

Nor shall we fail to make them. For all the talk of the doubters, our people are ready. If we are threatened, we shall meet iron by iron—by iron of our own making and tempered by the wind of our freedom. If anyone imagines that he can make the English give way to threats, he is a poor hand at reading our history. He will have to destroy us first. The national character has no more changed now than it had—as foolish prophets supposed—in 1914. We love pleasure and love to be at peace. But we know how to lay pleasure aside, and, if need be, peace also. It may be that by doing so we shall still win peace at the eleventh hour, and so save not ourselves alone, but the world, from its self-destruction and folly. We owe it to the world to try to do so, for we must bear our share of having contributed to that folly in the past. Our demagogues have cost us a good deal. But, if it comes to the point, there is no likelihood of our refusing to pay the price, and to the last penny.

That is the expression of what may well seem a grim mood, though it is one that almost every Englishman shares, be his love of peace never so great. One recalls the words that Scott wrote in 1807, mourning the loss of Nelson, Pitt and Fox and our allies' defeat at Austerlitz and anticipating a long period of national struggle and suffering:

> *To mute and to material things*
> *New life revolving summer brings;*
> *The genial call dead Nature hears,*
> *And in her glory reappears.*
> *But, oh, my Country's wintry state*
> *What second spring shall renovate?*

To many at the time they must have seemed words of despair. Yet, as events showed, there was no need for despair, nor was there any in the poet's mind. Sadness he knew, and the sense of coming danger, but his faith in his country was unshaken, and he knew that, if winter came, spring must follow.

That is the message of Easter to those in the shadow. The great Christian feast, and the coming of spring with which it coincides, are reminders that nothing human endures for ever, and that if our earthly joys and treasures cannot last, neither can our afflictions and sorrows. Everything is relative: victory has no meaning save as the corollary of defeat, peace save as that of conflict, joy save as that of grief. One cannot have one without the other. So, however dark the political clouds may seem this Eastertide, we can share in the gladness of the festival and be happy in the return of spring—that return which men have welcomed in all the troubled years of our planet's history and will continue to do so as long as it endures. We pray that the storms which threaten us may pass, but if they do not, we are reminded how we can face and overcome them.

Twenty-four Easters ago, at the end of the first winter in the trenches, a young English officer, outsoaring the dark shadow world around him of mud and frostbite and bursting shells, wrote of his gladness at the first sight of returning spring:

> *The naked earth is warm with spring,*
> *And with green grass and bursting trees*
> *Leans to the sun's gazeglorying*
> *And quivers in the sunny breeze.*[1]

Nor did that reviving warmth, so strangely in contrast to his grim surroundings, cause him any pang of regret—only joy. He had had everything in the past which life could offer, and was ready to give, as a few weeks later he did, his life into the hands that had created him, secure in the knowledge that spring and beauty were immortal, and that he himself was part of their immortality.

> *The fighting man shall from the sun*
> *Take warmth, and life from the glowing earth;*
> *Speed with the light-foot winds to run,*
> *And with the trees to newer birth;*
> *And find, when fighting shall be done,*
> *Great rest and fullness after dearth.*[1]

---

[1] Julian Grenfell, 'Into Battle,' *The Muse in Arms*, Murray.

CHAPTER 5

Sterner Days

"Do not let us speak of darker days; let us
speak rather of sterner days. These are not
dark days; these are the greatest days our
country has ever lived."

WINSTON CHURCHILL
Speech at Harrow School, 29 October 1941

To Find us in the Way · The Ship · The Summer of Dunkirk ·
London Pride · Childhood from the Blitz ·
Hitler's Fateful Choice · The Knocking on the Door ·
The Cathedral · The Turn of the Tide ·
Maintaining the Initiative · D-Day ·
A War-Time Journey · The Final Act

I

To Find us in the Way[1]

The changes wrought by time are very curious. Twenty-one years
ago we were still in the orbit of the Great War. A general or an
admiral was regarded as a species of god, remote, omnipotent
and exceedingly to be feared. Even a man with quite a modest
red tab or a small quantity of gold braid was a person held
universally in awe. A man's importance could be reckoned by
counting the bands on his sleeve or the stars on his shoulder.
Service to the State, and naval and military service at that, was
the criterion by which everyone was judged. A good war record,
it was held, would remain an essential passport to a man's success
to his dying day. A bad one would ruin him.

[1] *Illustrated London News* 1 April 1939.

How different has the reality been. Within years, almost it seemed a few months, the whole scene had changed. Generals and admirals had shrunk in public esteem into slightly ridiculous, loud-voiced old gentlemen who, after a life of useless activity, had retired to Cheltenham or Bournemouth to bore a contempt-uous younger generation with antiquated *clichés* and outworn prejudices. Colonel Blimp became the laughing stock of a more adult and civilised age. The old values counted no more. Physical courage, discipline and devotion to duty were at a discount: war heroes—V.C.s, sergeant-majors and the like—sold at two a penny. The best man was he who most professed contempt for the soldierly virtues. I seem to remember that one of the most popular plays in the first decade of broadcasting was one in which the heroes were the citizens of an attacked State who showed their utter scorn for the whole silly business of soldiering by ignoring the invasion of a warlike neighbour. The latter's troops were com-pletely nonplussed by this pacific and non-resisting behaviour, and finally returned in shame to their own country after first laying down their arms. Imagine the B.B.C. today solemnly advocating a similar conduct towards acts of Nazi aggression. Yet, curiously enough—though no one, so far as I know, has commented on the fact—this was precisely the procedure adopted by the un-fortunate Czechs when Hitler marched into their country. Un-consciously, no doubt, they were merely pursuing the technique advocated so strenuously for more than a decade by most of the younger publicists in this country.

There was nothing new in this English post-war reaction to things military. The cry of Farewell to Arms and Good-bye to All That has been heard in England many times before. Who wanted to listen to Uncle Toby's antiquated stories of the trenches in Flanders? What was the use of talking about singeing the King of Spain's beard at the pacific court of James I? Ten years after Waterloo, such had been the strength of the national drive towards economy and disarmament, the Duke of Wellington complained there were not enough troops left in England to bury a Field-Marshal! It is a fallacy to suppose that we are a people so stolid and impassive that we never change our course or veer with the emotional gales of the hour. Our moods of impulse are not, perhaps, easily aroused, but when once we fall into them we are apt to take them, for the time being, very seriously. And our strong habit of national unity in times of emotion tends to make such moods more powerful than they would otherwise be.

Though it is hard to credit it today, when our whole existence as a people once more depends on sea-power, the fashion of decrying our own arms has even been applied to the Navy, "whereon under the good providence of God, the wealth, safety and strength of the Kingdom chiefly depends." It is only a year or two since the present writer was taken to task, on the complaint of some of those who are today most strenuous in their demands for armed resistance to force, for having selected Nelson as a suitable subject for an educational lecture to a class of working-men. It was felt that the example of the great seaman's life of single-hearted devotion to his country's service would somehow corrupt these humble, but earnest students and accustom their still virgin minds to the forbidden delights of militarism. Nelson as a subject was taboo: he was no longer proper. Yet every member of my audience, who, in spite of the views of their betters, were sympathetic enough to my theme, and every one of the well-meaning, but misguided, progressives who objected to the use of Nelson's name, were dependent for almost every mouthful they ate on that sea-power which Nelson had established beyond challenge on the day of his death a century and a quarter before. The freedom of the seas was then, as now, a vital necessity of our being. But they had forgotten it.

They have remembered it now. Only a day or two ago I listened to one of those whom the B.B.C. employ to enlighten us on foreign affairs telling the nation to be grateful for sea-power—a blessed and comforting thing, he called it. Blessed and comforting it certainly is when one's enemies are in the gate—like the sight of the guardship lying off Dover when one returns to England after a long sojourn abroad.

> *I travelled among unknown men*
> *In lands beyond the sea,*
> *Nor, England! did I know till then*
> *What love I bore to thee.*

The innumerable pacifists of a decade ago were not, it seems, pacifists really. They were merely playing at being pacifists, because there were no enemies. And now, when a pirate sail has appeared on the horizon, they have come swarming over the gunwale to the familiar protection of His Majesty's Navy like children running to their nurse's apron when surprised at play by the ugly face of a passing tramp. It is a return to the unchanging realities of our national history.

Long before Nelson put the crown on a century of naval achievement by his final victory off the Spanish coast, even before Drake had made his first voyage to the West and grasped the potential value of sea-power as a means of making England's influence felt in every corner of the world, an English ambassador epitomised the essentials of our blue-water policy in a letter to the Secretary of State: "Bend your force, credit and device to maintain and increase your Navy," he wrote, "by all the means you can possible, for, in this time, considering all circumstances, it is the Flower of England's Garland. Animate and cherish as many as you can to serve by sea. Let them neither want good deeds, nor good words. It is your best, and best cheap, defence." Since that time, at first spasmodically, and later—ever since Pepys's great spell of service at the Admiralty—with unbroken method and purpose, the service of the King's ships has been directed to the command of the oceans.

Far beyond the coasts of this little island the effects of that consistent resolution have been felt. They are still felt today. "Wherever there was water to float a ship," Napoleon said to the captain of the *Bellerophon*, as she bore him at last to captivity, "I was sure to find you in the way."

* * *

II

The Ship[1]

Yesterday crossing an ancient harbour I saw a great ship. She lay along the quayside, with innumerable gangways climbing steeply up her tall sides and with white-capped men in blue and khaki swarming across them on urgent, ordered errands. She was making ready for sea, and wisps of smoke were curling from her funnels and her great guns were swung seawards. There was something gaunt about her, and her superstructure towered above the water, for she was an old ship. She had fought for England a quarter of a century before, when those guns had swept the misty horizon and hurled their offspring of flaming death across the seas at Jutland. Now once more her hour had come, which was England's. As the ferry-boat chugged and fussed its way through the waters of Portsmouth Harbour, I could not help reflecting on the mystery of this great fighting-ship and the significance of Britain's sea-power. On her and a dozen like her depended in the last resort the lives and well-being of every inhabitant of the crowded island she was sailing to defend and of many millions of others in every part of the world. It was through that power, exercised by the ordered labour and skill of countless Britons, that this country's word had been heard in the past and her slow wrath feared. It was a power so great that it had needed to put forth its full strength but once in a century to keep the world's peace.

Between 1914 and 1918 the mere existence of that force hundreds of miles away from the struggling armies and the smoking cities that fed the battlefield had been sufficient to decide the fate of mankind. The terrible purpose of England beset by foes was expressed in its final form in remote silence; among the islands of the north the Fleet was in being. The only half-hearted attempt to challenge it ended in the thunder of Jutland. Yet when the smoke of that confused cannonade lifted, the silent seas remained as before—Britain's forbidden waterway. The peoples of Central Europe suffered privation till their armies broke and fled, and

[1] *I.L.N.* 16 September 1939. Written on the day before war broke out.

their ships, manned by hungry, mutinous men, tailed in mournful submission to surrender at Scapa Flow. And the contrary of all this was also true, that without this power we in this overcrowded island would have starved.

It is to force that the German leader has appealed. It is a state to which he has constantly resorted in the course of his extraordinary career. Until now his appeal has been successful. It has succeeded because those to whom it was applied were weaker than himself. Now, despite every reasonable warning, he has employed it against the pledged ally of a maritime Power which, for all its reluctance to resort to force, is accustomed, when compelled to exercise it, to do so with relentless and unyielding pressure. His is an act of tragic and criminal significance. It unlooses a flood of evil which no man can dam and whose ultimate effect no one can calculate. It inflicts upon mankind suffering which no human being has any right to impose upon his fellow-creatures. The lust for power is a terrible thing. And in the last resort it can only be restrained by force. That is what the fleet of England is for.

This question of the use and effect of force poses for good men a terrible dilemma. There are some who solve it by abjuring force under all circumstances: their lot is hard, but at least simple. There are others—the great majority—who do not question its necessity but loyally obey their orders, sacrificing themselves on the altar of a proud obedience to their country's call. And there are others who see that lawless force must be resisted, but fear lest the force they create to redress an outraged balance may itself become, in its ultimate triumph, lawless and oppressive. For the exercise of all force, as the painful experience of the past quarter of a century has shown, produces calamitous results. It is this that constitutes the wickedness of the act that has now once again unloosed it. Though force may coerce the body, it also has the effect of embittering the mind. He who uses it, though in defence of the right, may, in the hour of victory, shut his heart to pity, and in doing so render himself or his children liable to the terrible penalties which the gods sooner or later inflict on the arrogant. The pages of history reiterate this truth with mournful monotony.

Perhaps the British have come nearer to solving the problem

than any other people. Alone among the recorded rulers of mankind, they have shown in their chequered history the ability to use force and, having used it, to refrain from oppressing their adversary. Like others, they have sometimes failed, but, having made mistakes, they have learnt from them. That is why we believe that victory, when it comes, must not be ours alone but that of all mankind.

* * *

III

The Summer of Dunkirk[1]

The days between May 29 and June 3, 1940, proved a turning point in history. They marked the first check in Germany's triumphant march towards world dominion.

In one sense Dunkirk, like Corunna, was a tactical British victory, and, as such, has tended to obscure the events that preceded it. In another it was the greatest military disaster in our history. An army of more than a quarter of a million men, a force far larger than any commanded by Wellington or Marlborough, with practically the country's entire available field equipment, was surrounded and penned in a narrowing corridor to the sea with no apparent choice but surrender or death.

The fault was not primarily that of the army but of its allies, who had been defeated on either flank. But in a larger sense the great disaster of May 1940 was as much the responsibility of Britain as of any other nation. It marked the apparent collapse of all the values which an easy-going parliamentary democracy had stood for in the years between the wars. It marked equally the apparent triumph and material vindication of Hitler's barbaric revolution and of the cruel and ancient tyrannies he had enthroned. Right based on mere good intentions, it was proved, could not stand in the field against evil based on might. At that moment the miracle occurred. It did not reverse the verdict of the

---

[1] Written to commemorate the third anniversary of Dunkirk, this appeared on June 3 and 4 1943 in the *Daily Sketch* and was subsequently published privately by Kemsley Newspapers in aid of the Daily Sketch War Relief Fund.

"Battle of the Bulge", but redeemed it. It was like a rainbow at the climax of some terrible storm. In the midst of it, long columns of men, tormented, utterly weary and in deadly peril, were seen going down unperturbed to the water's edge.

Their only means of escape were a single port blasted by enemy bombs and shells, and a line of exposed beaches with shelving shores from which evacuation would have been impossible in anything but a dead calm. They stood there in long patient queues, as though waiting for the last bus home, or sheltered in impromptu holes excavated in the sand, while overhead dive-bombers roared and screamed, and fantastic air battles were fought out in the midst of immense pillars of drifting smoke and fountains of water.

After the traditional fashion of their race in the hour of crisis, the waiting men showed no sign of panic or despair; nor, it would seem, of any visible emotion at all. They merely waited with a kind of dogged faith, and presently their faith was justified. Guarded by lean, crowded destroyers, hundreds of little boats came out of England and bore them away. By some strange magic of courage and improvisation, these hundreds of thousands of men were taken on board and borne out of the reach of the dragon's fiery breath and closing jaws. For five days and nights the miracle continued, until no one remained on the beaches at all save the dead. The living came back out of the delirium of modern war to the quiet and ordinariness of England; to neat railway carriages and smiling policemen, and girls holding up cups of tea; and there they lived to fight another day.

For a few days England breathed again, and the free world with her. Then the terrible surge of German victory was renewed. The newspapers were filled with pictures of tanks, motorised guns and trucks, packed with proud, fanatic-looking young Germans, glowing with health and vigour and passing in seemingly endless procession through the streets of cowed French and Belgian towns; of great black bombers and troop-carriers with hooked crosses swarming overhead in droves, of the horror and devastation wrought wherever they swooped; and of pitiful staring refugees flying through the rubble before the terror that nothing could stay. There were photographs of Hitler smiling in triumph in the midst of his staff, of General Giraud being borne away to captivity among clicking, staring Nazis; of grim-jawed parachutists, ready to drop out of the clouds as they had done in Holland, and shoot down all who dared resist. For those who were not Germans the world was being taught there was only one virtue—instant and unconditional surrender; for those who delayed, only one fate—certain and imminent destruction.

Under that knowledge France, for two generations the military Colossus of Europe, crumpled, broke and yielded, while every road to the south-west was blocked with fugitives, and the Panzer surge swept unresisted into the Rhone valley. The men of Bordeaux, after Premier Reynaud's last, vain, despairing appeal to an unarmed America, made their abject surrender. In the eyes of the overwhelming majority of mankind, there seemed nothing else for them to do.

The world prepared itself for the inevitable. The last Americans hurried home across the Atlantic; the anxious Russians pretended not to be interested and talked of the end of an unnecessary capitalist, imperialist war; and those within the European prison house who were not already slaves queued up to kiss the conqueror's chains. From Bordeaux and Budapest, from Bucharest and Sofia, from Madrid and Helsinki, in top-boots and medals, in Homburgs and summer suitings, the respectable of a fallen Christendom made the pilgrimage to Berchtesgaden. There, amid the clicking priesthood of the jackboot and the hip-revolver, they made their obeisance and paid the first instalment of Danegeld. And looking over their shoulders they waited for the proud, rich, helpless island State, which had led Europe into the illusion of government by debate and agreed rules, to follow their example. The cheats and thugs had won. The time had come for the mugs to pay up.

But the voice which came out of England at that moment was neither repentant nor submissive. It was not the voice of the hypocrite saying acceptable things before sacrifice, nor of the humbug temporising to save his face. It was the voice of a man angry, defiant and utterly resolved; or rather of forty-seven millions looking in a single direction, and that direction seawards, and intoning in their hearts the words which one of them spoke for all. "We shall defend our island whatever the cost may be. We shall fight on the beaches; we shall fight on the landing-grounds; we shall fight in the fields and in the streets; we shall fight in the hills; and we shall never surrender."

It sounded to the world the wildest extravagance. For outside the British Empire, and the White House in Washington, there was scarcely anybody to whom such words at such an hour made sense. The *Herrenvolk*, who were too busy counting their gains and herding their prisoners into pens to listen, announced them to be the drivel of a "broken down drunkard in the pay of impotent moneylenders", and contemptuously offered the English peace in a global concentration camp.

Churchill and the doomed islanders did not hear. With the minimum of fuss and chatter and the maximum of speed, they were girding on their armour. They were no longer interested either in Hitler's beguilements or threats. They had long ceased to believe in the former, and they had now ceased to notice the latter. They knew that he could and would do his worst; but they were not thinking about what he could do, but about what they could do. With all the terrible concentration of their race, they were resuming a craft which they thought they had abandoned for ever. In the words of their leader, they meant to make war, and persevere in making war, until the other side had had enough.

The miracle of Dunkirk was twofold. It not only restored a British army: it revived the nation's soul. It made the islanders realise themselves, to know, under God, of what they were capable, and resolve to do it. Their arms, save at sea, were negligible. Their military equipment had mostly been fashioned for the troglodyte campaigns of 1917, and the bulk of it had been lost at Dunkirk, their vital trade routes were outflanked from Biscay to the North Cape, their shores were threatened with invasion and their cities with destruction. But since there was now no one but themselves to save the truths and decencies in which they believed, and they could not conceive of a world without them, there was no longer any question in their minds as to what they had to do. Doubts, divisions and sloth, blindness and fear, fell away from them at that hour like the mists of morning at the rising sun. Britain was herself again.

This was the real miracle of Dunkirk. The genius of the Navy, the dogged patience of the men on the beaches and the calm of the summer seas had wrought the conceivable out of the inconceivable. Yet from it had sprung something still more wonderful than the evacuation under the Luftwaffe's nose of 300,000 men in yachts and paddle steamers. The England of the Peace Pledge Union and the dole queue had been changed in a flash of summer lightning into the England of Nelson and Alfred:

> *Greed and fraud, unabashed, unawed,*
> *May strive to sting thee at heel in vain,*
> *Craft and fear and mistrust may leer*
> *And mourn and murmur and plead and plain:*
> *Thou are Thou, and thy sunbright brow*
> *Is hers that blasted the strength of Spain.*

No one who lived in England through that wonderful summer of 1940 is ever likely to forget it. The light that beat down on her meadows, shining with emerald loveliness, was scarcely of this world. The streets of her cities, soon to be torn and shattered, were bathed in a calm serene sunshine; and in forge and factory, field and mine, her people worked with a fierce, unresting, yet quiet intensity, as they had never worked before. In every village men dragged out primæval carts that might have barred the way of Napoleon's Grand Army, and, wreathing them in farmyard wire, placed them across the roads. Signposts were taken down, trenches and gun emplacements dug in fields, and in city and country millions of citizens strove to make themselves soldiers. Factory hands and retired ambassadors, greybeards and boys in their teens, middle-aged men holding themselves taut, after twenty years of easy living, in memory of their former prowess in war, paraded side by side in working clothes with armlets lettered "L.D.V." Many of them wore medals; they had little else. Many made arms during the daytime which they learnt to use in anticipation at night. By doing the utmost that they could, they reckoned with the sober patience of their kind, they would "whiles do mair".

For—and this was part of the miracle of Dunkirk—the British people were already thinking, not of averting defeat, but of earning victory. Like Pitt when Napoleon's Grand Army was waiting to cross the Channel, they were concentrating not on saving themselves, but on delivering Europe. In doing so they were instinctively following the historic path of their salvation. For a small island, moored off the coast of a Continent, cannot indefinitely survive when the whole of the latter is mobilised against her. Before a cowed Europe can be consolidated by her foes, Britain must take the offensive or perish. Never in her history had victory seemed more remote or improbable than in 1940. Yet at the very hour when, in the midst of unparalleled disasters, he offered his countrymen "blood, toil, tears and sweat," Churchill defined her goal. "You ask," he said, "what is our aim? I can answer in one word: Victory—victory at all costs, victory in spite of all terror, victory however hard and long the road may be; for without victory there is no survival."

Already, with empty arsenals and housewives mobilising their pots and pans to make enough fighter planes to save London from the fate of Warsaw, Britain was planning the four-engine bomber programme to wipe out the cities of the Ruhr. With invasion hourly expected, she was sending out her only armoured division on the long sea passage round the Cape of Good Hope to guard the Nile Valley and lay the foundations of future offensives. Her own preservation was seen only as a means to the greater end of saving mankind.

Meanwhile, the angry Germans, slowly and incredulously realising that the British would not make peace, prepared with Teuton thoroughness to smash them to pulp. The men of Bordeaux, who had good reason to know the might and ruthless power of Germany, supposed that the island State which had withstood Napoleon would have its "neck wrung in a few weeks like a chicken". The swastika rose over the Channel Islands; Mussolini's legions, outnumbering Wavell's Middle East Forces by ten to one, marched into Egypt; the Japanese sharpened their swords at the gates of Hong Kong; and the victorious, greycoated hordes danced and revelled in the streets of a dazed and ravished Paris preparatory to a final triumph amid the burning villages of the Weald and the smouldering debris of London. All the while the long procession of barges floated down the rivers and canals of Europe towards the Channel ports, the endless columns of grey and steel moved to their appointed places, and the great black laden aeroplanes gathered in their thousands on the airfields of Northern France, Belgium, Holland and Norway. And as the world watched, the world suddenly realised, with a thrill of wonder and awe, that England was going to fight.

Scarcely anyone imagined she could survive such a contest. Even in America, where so many generous hearts bled for her, where the Nazis were generally hated and where British agents, aided by every device open to a far-sighted President, were desperately buying up machine and tommy-guns, the general belief was that Britain and Europe were alike finished. Yet all over the world backs bowed to slavery stiffened instinctively at the sight of the British mongoose poised to spring, with every hair taut and bristling as it faced the giant Teuton cobra.

That was the rallying-hour of freedom, and from every country brave men who had fled to England—Poles and Czechs, Frenchmen and Norwegians, Dutchmen and Belgians and Jews—stood side by side with the islanders and their faithful kinsfolk from overseas, unshaken, unseduced, unterrified. For though Europe had relapsed into barbaric darkness, a light had been lit that summer that could not be put out; or rather an ancient flame long secretly tended had been revived.

Already on the Kentish aerodromes, as the sirens began their low wail over the London streets, the few who were to save the many were preparing for battle, and the Spitfires were warming up. Already in the cities tens of thousands of men and women, dedicated to death, calmly awaited the hour when hell would descend out of the skies to blast their homes and pulp and tear their bodies. The Battle for Britain and of the world's deliverance had begun. The love of the British people for their native land— long derided by intellectuals as a barbarous and antiquated superstition—their faith in their enduring destiny and their stubborn refusal to admit the possibility of defeat had given mankind another chance.

"Hitler knows," their leader told them, "he will have to break us in this island or lose the war. If we can stand up to him, all Europe may be free, and the life of the world may move forward into broad sunlit uplands. But if we fail, then the whole world, including the United States, including all that we have known and cared for, will sink into the abyss of a new Dark Age, made more sinister, and perhaps more protracted, by the lights of perverted science. Let us therefore brace ourselves to our duties, and so bear ourselves that, if the British Empire and its Commonwealth last for a thousand years, men will still say, 'This was their finest hour'."

*   *   *

IV

London Pride[1]

The lady who bundled into my already overcrowded taxi, asking cheerily, though a little anxiously, if I still had room for a little one, was obviously a person of knowledge and character. She settled her ample self down with infectious assurance, patted the younger woman by her side—a complete stranger to her—and called her "dearie", and addressed herself to me, the original charterer of this communal vehicle, as to her destination, which was a large, popular emporium in the middle of London. She apparently kept a small store in the outer suburbs and was on her way to secure that personal satisfaction on some matter of business which correspondence by post could not give. She seemed confident that she would receive it, and I have little doubt she did. I felt I was taking some part in the great business of buying and selling by speeding her on her interrupted way, the more so as the interruption had been caused by that general disturber of business, Herr Hitler. Some aspiring German in the dark, knowing not what he did, had dropped a bomb between her and her destination. It was my privilege—expelled like her from a stranded train in a blitzed and taxiless wilderness—to undo the damage this unconscionable aviator had done.

Our new friend—for she was that almost before she had opened her mouth—expressed herself with some force, but also with great good humour, on the contemptible activities of the enemy. What had to be, she said, had to be. Of course, they did a lot of

---

[1] *I.L.N.* 2 November 1940.

damage, those bombs: made a nasty mess where they fell, and cruel hard on some poor people it was. For herself, she did not care—and here, watching her Chaucerian mouth wagging, I trembled, though needlessly, for the modesty of the typist at her side, at whom she gave a quick, motherly glance—well, anything for them. One could always get on somehow: now up, now down —life was like that. What she always did when things went wrong was to make herself a cup of tea: even if the gas was off, one could always do that with a few sticks, and there one was, better in a moment. She gazed out of the window at that passing London which was her joy and kingdom, and had she been the dome of St. Paul's she could not have looked more proud and seemly to my English eyes. I could not help wishing that Hitler could encounter this jolly atom of English earth and spirit; remembering the far days when he also was poor and humble, he might have recognised his match in resolution.

There was a pause: a gentleman going to a Government office began fussing about the best stopping-place for the last stage of his journey. Suddenly this stout wife of London spoke again, banishing all lesser thought and speculations. "My!" she said, "what an armistice it's going to be this time! The last'll be nothing to it!" And at this her smile was like five hundred beeves at pasture. Looking at her, I could all but hear those triumphing sirens blowing down the sombre years before that far day of triumph, and see the lights blazing across the rejoicing London sky. "Yes, the last was a good 'un," she added, "mere slip of a girl I was then. Not one of us where I worked was sober, not for twenty-four hours we weren't. Our boss, he stood us all champagne: bit of a lad he was, and liked the girls, mark you: not that we minded. We didn't mind anything! Not 'alf." After this enigmatic reference to the past, she slipped for a moment into the pleasures of reminiscence. "Nothing," she added, "can ever take that away! I shall remember it till I die."

Something in this good woman's courage, her love of life, her invincible cheeriness made me feel that in asking her to share my taxi I had unwittingly entertained angels. I asked her whether she found her retired suburban life quiet. "Yes," she said, "it's quiet; but then"—with great cheerfulness—"I'm growing old.

One feels different when one's old." Perhaps one does, I reflected, but it doesn't seem to make any difference; the flag stays flying just the same. For here, as though it had been the rainbow, was the sign from Heaven that horror and waste and destruction could never break the spirit of my country or her great-hearted, battered, indomitable capital. Sometimes in the peaceful past I used to fear for London, fancying her degenerate, and seeing only the "great Wen" of Cobbett's indignant yeoman phrase. She seemed to have grown so vast and straggling, to have been vulgarised and deprived of all indigenous character. Yet now I was shamed and proved utterly wrong; my poor imagination had never pictured the greatness of my own city or comprehended it.

London pride! I remember seeing a play of that name during the last war, with Gerald du Maurier taking the part of a coster. As the taxi rattled through the interminable drab streets, with their broken, boarded windows and patches of pathetic match-wood marking the attempts of the Third Reich to break the spirit of London, the thought of the Cockney poor—of a great people who had lost everything but its cheerfulness and courage—filled my mind. I recalled other expressions of that indomitable spirit— of Hampstead Heath on Bank Holidays and Hackney Marshes where they exploded the great bomb from St. Paul's—of costers in all their pride of pearls and feathers, with frolicsome young people singing and dancing, and old parties with bottles of stout and jests for every passer-by, of something that was older and stronger and more communal than all the *volk* pride and strident unity of the Reich. And I knew that a people who had lived through the long shades of the industrial revolution, and endured the rigours of the nineteenth-century labour system and the slum and the shadow of the workhouse and still retained its spirit and gaiety and love of life, was a harder nut to crack than anything conceived of by Hitler's iron philosophy.

*   *   *

V

Childhood from the Blitz[1]

To see the familiar landscape of one's own city slowly vanishing in bursts of flame and rubble is to experience a curious sensation. It is like growing old: there is age and evening about it. Not that the landscape of London is really changing very quickly under its repeated nocturnal bombardments. I doubt whether the main change effected by a winter of bombing has been much greater than that normally carried out in pursuit of private profit in an average London year between the wars. The *Luftwaffe*'s work did less to change the face of, say, Berkeley or St. James's Square in 1940 than the building contractor in the years immediately before. Yet to a Londoner who can remember two-score years of intimate daily London life, the perpetual process of erosion and destruction is no light thing. One after another the landmarks of one's youth are destroyed or changed: the old, familiar accompaniments of one's human pilgrimage cast away. One is reminded forcibly of mortality, of the transience of life. And, like growing old, it is not wholly an unpleasant experience. For one begins to realise how true it is that the existence that matters to one goes on irrespective of material surroundings. One closes one's eyes, as in the hour of sleep, and still lives.

Amid these battered terraces and squares my own childhood was passed. Within that blackened church—in whose crypt the body of its rector, faithful to his charge and flock to his last hour, lay only the other night, murdered by the architects of the New Order—I first learned to worship. Under its gilded Byzantine roof I sat beside my mother and spelt out in letters of gold, clearly writ on black marble, the Ten Commandments: "Thou shalt not make to thyself any graven image"; "Thou shalt not covet"; "Thou shalt do no murder". Near at hand was another text to which my childish eyes often strayed, a memorial plaque in the wall which related the exploits of an English admiral who fought at Trafalgar as one of Nelson's young captains, and who, twenty years later, commanded a British fleet in the battle that established

[1] *I.L.N.* 3 May 1941.

Greek independence. It added to the mysterious thrill his memorial gave me that the dead admiral's grandson was generally sitting a few pews away from me, with his son, a school-fellow of mine, by his side. It made the past seem the more real—a thriving and continuing existence of which I was part, as were also the pastoral Hebrews and their flocks, whose passionate record of national and religious struggle the lessons, read from the great brass eagle Sunday by Sunday, enfolded.

Today's spasm of angry destruction brings back those early days. As the familiar walls crumble and the windows are shattered, the strangers who have barred the doors against one's own youth depart. The intervening years are obliterated: one is back again in the city of one's beginnings. It was a place of mystery and expectation, offering so much more to the quick imagination of childhood than the paltry humdrum compromise of the smart-Alec London of yesterday now vanishing in smoke and fire. In the dusty hush after the bombardment we are returning to the vanished city of promise from which we set out. Our travels have proved but blind; we are back after our vain circle; here we may begin again. This is our stronghold.

In this hour of revived memory the fireman standing by the blackened wall is less real to me than that same wall as I saw it, decked with window-boxes, on a summer evening at the start of the century. The brown dust of a London still drawn by horses eddied with the breeze over the broad, hot pavement; across the way, in the square, the chestnuts were in bloom. I was coming home from the Park, walking beside my nurse and my brother's pram. I felt a faint sense of frustration: I had been feasting my eyes for an hour on a scene of what was to me indescribable beauty, and now I was returning through the empty streets to go supperless to bed while the sun was still shining. In those days the Park after tea became the prelude to a wonderful pageant of which I repeatedly saw the beginning but whose climax I could never share. Every evening in that glamorous May I had walked beside my nurse to the great stone screen before Hyde Park, waited tight-wedged in the decorous, scented throng of glossy-hatted men and frilled, flowery women who pressed in and out of the foot gates, and taken my minute uncomprehending turn

in that now amazing and long-departed procession of humans and
horses and tinkling harness that seems as remote from the London
of 1941 as the chariots of Boadicea's army. I never saw myself as
part of that spectacle, but always as a spectator. For instinctively
I knew that I was watching only the overture and that before the
curtain rose I should be hurried back to bed. All the hot afternoon
I knew that London Society slumbered, behind shuttered blinds,
only to wake to expectancy as Big Ben and its attendant towers
and spires chimed four. Then, like me, it drank a cup of tea and
set out for an hour in the sunshine, to see and be seen against a
background of leaves and flowers in its varnished, crested
carriages. After that the real life of the evening began: bright
lights, blazing stars and jewels, tables gleaming with silver and
laden with wonderful foods and wines; the stirring of the great,
draped curtains between the gilded pillars of the proscenium;
music, dancing, warm, happy life. Perhaps I was a strange child
to have envied this, seeing only its flowery prelude in the late
afternoon sun. Or do children today, seeing the shadow-life of
the film, glow with the same unattainable desires?

> And life is colour and warmth and light,
> And a striving evermore for these.

Perhaps it was for this reason that the happiest memories of
the London of my early childhood are of winter rather than
summer. If there was life there from which I was excluded, I
knew nothing of it. What a joy it was to climb, well muffled, to
the top of a horse bus and sit tense above the steaming horses on a
bright October day, watching the Hampstead trees nod mysteriously over the vast distance of Baker Street, or come down
Piccadilly at lighting-up time a little before Christmas, when the
shop-fronts were hung with enormous hams and turkeys and
the windows were full of gargantuan pies and iced cakes, and,
with my hand reluctantly clutching the attendant grown-up, to
sense the coming magic of the top of St. James's Street and the
descent down that splendid thoroughfare to the friendly Tudor
palace at its foot. The sentries, in their red coats and bearskins,
reminded me of my own soldiers gleaming before the nursery
fire at their still unfinished game, and, as I passed them and

rounded the corner into the Mall, the sea wind out of the west gave me a relish for my tea. The thought of the black toasting-fork waiting on its nail by the fire speeded my feet, capering a little ahead of my protesting escort; the last hundred yards to the threshold of my father's house, I remember, I always ran and then waited breathless until the latch-key arrived. No bomb can deprive me of these things, which were already taken from me by jailer Time when Hitler was painting houses in imperial Vienna. But as the bomb dust clears away I find that I can sense them a little more clearly.

*   *   *

VI

Hitler's Fateful Choice[1]

When I was a boy with a passion for military history, I found myself perpetually thinking of the familiar landscape of my school and holiday haunts as the terrain of a battlefield. This loved ridge was held in force by the French or Austrians; across that broad valley the cuirassiers of the Guard were charging; between the gleaming trunks of a beech wood the dark green tunics of Craufurd's Riflemen were skirmishing in the forefront of Moore's or Wellington's army. To the outward eye I was a rather untidy, impracticable, dreamy lad mooning across a field: to myself I was St. Cyr or Augureau executing a difficult operation in the face of the enemy. I advanced in open, but unbroken, order towards the crest of the downs amid an imaginary hail of bullets, fought every inch of my way across the Wiltshire meadows to church, and galloped with the Heavy Brigade, a small, breathless forward in a black and yellow shirt, over the clayey football fields of Harrow towards the touch-line and the Russian guns. There was scarcely a hedgerow within a mile of any roof under which I slept that I had not taken in flank, or a spinney which I had not, after pro-longed and intricate manoeuvres, surrounded!

[1] *I.L.N.* 14 and 21 June 1941. All my wartime articles had to be written a fortnight before they appeared. These two were written immediately before Hitler invaded Russia, the second of them appearing on the day before the German blow fell.

Later, when I was learning to fly, I looked at country with a different eye. I was perpetually seeking large, flat fields for forced landings—in those days one of the most frequent of aeronautical operations. As I drove through the countryside or gazed out of the train window, I swept away likely-looking parks and meadows with my mind's eye and levelled golf courses, recreating in their place ugly and commodious aerodromes. In the same way I remember that my father, an enthusiastic golfer, used to consider country largely in the light of potential golf courses. So fishermen eye running water in one way and sanitary engineers in another: each human mind sees the whole of God's creation as the background of a gigantic ride for its own peculiar hobby-horse.

Historians are not immune from this curious trait. They see contemporary events not so much as the uncertain pulsating stuff of an all-absorbing present, but as the raw material of history. They are always judging or trying to judge contemporaneous acts not as they appear to those who initiate them, but as they will one day appear to posterity. This, as they know from their explorations into the past, is seldom what the opinion of the hour supposes. They therefore tend to diverge from, and often to quarrel with, the popular contemporary view. They are frequently wrong in their surmises, for the first essential of the historian's trade—the bricks of accurate and ascertained fact—are seldom available to them. But they cannot help making them, for their craft has become second nature. Like the tailor in Shakespeare's *Henry IV* they are ready to prick as many holes in an enemy's battle as in a woman's petticoat.

Engaged, in the interstices of wartime work, in chronicling the British people's struggle against the French Revolution and Napoleon, I find myself automatically trying to judge the news of the present war—so like that earlier one in its issues and essential character—as our descendants may judge it. What we see, not knowing the future, as a long period of rather purposeless waiting, they, from their wider knowledge, may see as a vital preliminary to the climax, while some event, which to us seems all important, they may regard in retrospect as irrelevant. And it is possible that the next few weeks may see an intensification of the war more rapid and decisive than we can visualise from our newspapers and broadcasts. For with the Greek expedition and the Cretan and Abyssinian episodes out of the way, we and Germany are back to essentials. We are on the defensive, and have no option for the moment but to remain on it. But our enemy also has no choice—or, rather, no real choice. For, with neutral America already arming against her, she cannot remain indefinitely on the defensive without courting ultimate and certain doom. A long war for Germany, as so many Teutons can recall, is a war of suffocation. They cannot afford to wait for such a doom. They must strike now to break out of the ever-strengthening ring about them, or see their last opportunity, week by week, month by month, dwindling into a forlorn hope and, finally, into an impossibility. For that bogey of encirclement, with which their greedy leaders in their happier days attempted, with such fatal success, to excite them, has become today a very real one. For all her glittering victories, the Third Reich is encircled by steel. And the instrument of that encirclement is the sea-power of the British Empire and its still passive but very real and potent supporter, the United States of America. Germany must break that ring or go down as surely in the end as she did in 1918.

The question which the next few weeks may well decide is whether she can break it. That she has mighty forces with which to do so, and that this country will have to exert every ounce of courage, brawn and brain to keep the ring intact, there is no denying. There would appear to be four ways in which Germany can end her encirclement. The first and most obvious is by a direct invasion of this island. That it may be attempted is undeniable, for we are dealing with a gang of very desperate and bold men. But to undertake an invasion of Britain without preliminary command of the sea is, as Napoleon observed, a forlorn and desperate expedient. Today, as we know to our cost and our pride, command of the sea comprises command of the air above the sea. Without the latter, for all the valour of our people and resolution of our leadership, we could not hold out for a month. But so long as our fighters can exact the same toll on the German striking force as they did last September, any attempt to invade Britain can only end in one way.

An easier and equally decisive option for Germany is to break the ring by an under-surface and overseas blockade of our supply and trade routes. Past neglect of the Navy and of our agriculture have made us terrifyingly vulnerable in the vital point of our stomach: here, as some have long warned us, was the weakest joint in the armour of our peacetime democracy. But there are signs that the resource and courage of our naval and merchant seamen are turning the swaying fortunes of the Battle of the Atlantic in our favour, and the destruction of the *Bismark*, albeit hardly and tragically paid for, has helped greatly. For if Germany cannot turn the tables on our blockade in the Atlantic and dare not resort to the desperate expedient of a sea and airborne invasion without command of either sea or air, it means she must break out elsewhere. She must break out eastwards into Asia and southwards into Africa: that is, unless she enlarges the scope of widening destruction by involving Russia or Spain and thereby opening still more perilous issues for herself. And here, in Syria, Palestine and Egypt, she has to face our armies, not on her own chosen and favoured ground, as in Flanders, France and Greece, but on ground where the numerical odds against us are discounted by geography and our command of the sea. Every week in which that, for Germany, unavoidable assault is delayed is a week in our favour, and every league of desert and sea which lengthens the spearhead of Germany's outward drive from her continental base one in her disfavour.

* * *

For the Nazi cannot sit back and wait for us to attack. He must take and sustain the offensive even if the offensive is the losing card. So far, with one exception, he has attacked on ground which gave him an overwhelming advantage. He had it in Czechoslovakia, in Poland, in Norway, in Holland, Belgium and France, in Greece. He even had it in Crete, though here his advantage was more doubtful and may have been contributed to by some neglect of our earlier chances. The exception was the Battle of Britain last summer, when in the skies above our southern counties he found himself operating far from his own and close to our air bases. He then discovered the difference between leaping on a herd of goats in the open plain and attacking a lion in his den. . . .

Yet attack he must. In a year he has conquered and virtually enslaved all Europe save for the Iberian peninsula and the Russian marches. But Europe is not enough for him. So narrow a *lebensraum* cannot content him; like a rat which has eaten some burning, urgent poison, he must seek water, expand or die. He must resume the attack, not now against continental neighbours with beckoning plains and crowded cities conveniently adjacent to his own airfields and Panzer bases, but against the tough, outer-world empire which, like Napoleon, he sees as his ultimate enemy. For that empire encircles his European dominion in a far more real way than ever Frenchman, Czech and Pole encircled the Teuton homeland. It encloses it with the "army of unalterable law": law that has been outraged and must be avenged and enforced. There, for all his seeming strength and omnipotence, lies the German's dilemma. He must break out or, as the ingrowing pressure of Britain, Canada, Australia, New Zealand, South Africa and India and their mighty American arsenal reaches its inevitable climax, one day go under. And his road to untrammelled power lies across the historic fighting-grounds of Englishmen: sea and desert. Can he cross them?

We do not underrate—we should be foolish to do so—his will and power. The speed, tenacity and originality of his attack on Crete show what the Nazi is ready to dare and do in his attempt to smash through the lines encircling him. The struggle is about to enter on a more intense period. The enemy must either invade this island, master our command of the seas, or break out of Europe into Asia and Africa. The Battle of the Atlantic now waging is the answer to the second, while to achieve either the first or the last Hitler's men must fight under the same disadvantage that ours fought under in Norway, Belgium, France and Greece: that is, without the protection of their own fighter aircraft and subject to the attack of ours. For the range of aircraft is governed by geography, and in the next stage of his advance geography will no longer be the German's friend, but his enemy. We shall be fighting him at last on equal terms.

And if he shirks the issue? The question is: can he afford to?

If he could win the Battle of the Atlantic, as he so confidently boasts in his broadcasts, he would have no need to take that fatal lunge across sea and desert. But to win the Battle of the Atlantic he has first to beat the Royal Navy, and no one has ever succeeded in doing that. Everything points to an early blow against our encircling lines across and beyond the Mediterranean. It is true that to achieve his end Hitler may attempt to encircle our position or take it in the rear, either by striking through Russia or through Spain or by calling in the Japanese against our communications in the Pacific and Indian Oceans. That he may strike either at, or with the possible connivance of the Kremlin, through Russia into Iran is obvious. Strategically this is now the only "easy" road left to him. But such desperate steps cannot be taken without evoking human and racial imponderables which may well benefit us far more than the enemy. Hitler knows this, and his hour of decision is at hand. It is his fate to strike, and ours to resist and strike back[1].

*　　*　　*

VII

The Knocking on the Door[2]

The opening days of December 1941 were among the most dramatic in modern history. They recall the moment in Shakespeare's *Macbeth* when the knocking on the door began. It was Fate speaking: reality's hour. All over the world the same sound was heard—at the same moment. In Russia, Hitler's legions were discovering the reality of the Russian winter and the Russian character. In North Africa, Germans and Italians were discovering the reality of sea-power and its effect on land operations. In the Pacific, Americans were discovering the meaning of aggression and of the might of prepared force against unprepared. And in the China Sea we, too, were discovering or, rather, rediscovering, the peril of using battleships close to an enemy coast without overwhelming air protection; and the difficulty of opposing a

---

[1] On the day after this article appeared, he struck—at Russia.
[2] *I.L.N.* 27 December 1941.

strong naval Power at the far side of the world. All these things men knew before by hearsay; by what their fathers and school-books had told them, by what their seers had prophesied, even by what they themselves had affirmed or denied. But they only knew them as men know that which they have not experienced. Now they have become apprehended realities, like the bombs which fell on London a year ago.

The entry of Japan and America into the struggle, coupled with the earlier German attack on Russia, makes this now a world war. As in 1917, all mankind is in the fight. Strategically, it is a war fought in concentric rings. Its centre is some Siberian village, far from the scenes and sound of battle. On that invisible pivot the whole world turns. Around it and the vast, unexploited lands of Central Asia is grouped the greatest mass of humanity resident on earth: the teeming populations of Russia, China and India. They constitute over a thousand millions, or more than four times the total population of the aggressor Powers. But, save in Russia, they are only partially armed, and even in Russia are dependent to a large extent on the supplies which their allies in Britain and America can send them. And around them, broken only in places by the tentacles of British sea-power, are the hundred per cent mobilised forces of Germany, Italy and Japan. These form the greater part of the circumference of an inner armed ring round Asia and European Russia. It stretches from Manchuria to the Burma Road, is broken for several thousand largely inaccessible miles of coastline, desert and mountain between India and the Turkish frontier, and continues again along the bloodstained battlefront from the Black Sea to the Arctic.

If this were the whole picture, the Slav and Asiatic myriads, hemmed in by the fully mechanised Axis partners, would be doomed. Even the heroic resistance of Russia and China could not save them from ultimate defeat by numerically inferior, but infinitely better armed, forces. They would be condemned to become hewers of wood and drawers of water to the Teuton and Japanese overlords, and the riches of the Asian hinterland would fall to the aggressors. But, happily, this is not the whole picture. The Axis is not the ultimate circumference. Beyond the military ring of Germany, Italy and Japan is another ring, formed by the sea-power of the United States and the British Commonwealth of Nations. Numerically a little less than the joint population of the three Axis Powers, and still not so well armed, they can ultimately throw into the battle a fighting force and an industrial potential greater than anything the Axis can boast. These mighty resources are still only partially developed, especially in the United States. But that they will now be developed to the full there can be no doubt.

There are various possibilities. The Axis can try to do one of two things. It can fight a delaying action against the British Empire and the U.S.A.—the outer ring—while devoting its offensive power to smashing the growing resistance of Russia, India and China before the help of the former can arm that immense reserve of man-power and render possible a gigantic outward offensive movement aimed at Japan through China and Manchuria, and at Germany from her vulnerable eastern frontier. Or it can try to hold Russia and China in a passive ring while employing its offensive force to knock out Britain or the U.S.A., or both. But this would only be possible if the Axis gained virtual command of the sea and air in the Atlantic and Pacific. Equally, the ability of the U.S.A. and the British Commonwealth to reinforce and strengthen beleaguered Russia and China, and to keep open the few channels through which they can at present contact them—Murmansk, Persia, the Burma Road and Alaska air-route—is dependent on sea and air power. What has happened so far, in the first phase of this wider war, has been that, after dealing a stunning and treacherous blow at American striking sea and air power—sufficient, it was hoped by Tokyo, to keep the U.S.A. inactive for many weeks or months—Japan is now concentrating on closing one of the principal gateways through which outer help can come to the Asiatic mainland. The attack on Malaya and the Burma Road is a vital part of offensive Japanese strategy. The assault on the Philippines is part of the delaying action against the U.S.A.

It seems fairly clear from the events of the past few days that the Japanese hope by their delaying action at Pearl Harbour to be able to expel the Americans from the Philippines and their other west Pacific bases, while simultaneously capturing Singapore and closing the Burma Road. In this way the door through which China can be helped would be slammed, and the relieving attack of the United States suspended across many thousand miles of ocean. The rich islands of the south-west Pacific could then be seized one by one, to provide the supplies for the next stage of war, and to deny them to the Democracies.

Whether this programme, so successfully opened, will be completed remains to be seen. There is no denying that the sinking of the *Prince of Wales* and *Repulse*, the damage done to the American battleships at Pearl Harbour and the surrender of Thailand have carried the Japanese a long way down the road they have set themselves. There is, however, many a slip between the cup and the lip—particularly, history suggests, in wars against the Anglo-Saxon. One thing is certain, and it is this. That the heroic Russian resistance to the might of Germany has already delayed, and possibly halted for ever, Hitler's eastward drive which the Japanese offensive in south-east Asia was to have seconded. Instead of being in Moscow, the Teuton hordes, at the time of writing, are sullenly drawing in their frozen horns. The Nazi plan for totalitarian world domination postulated a vast continental military and economic bloc stretching from Brest to the Pacific, and possibly from the North Cape to Table Mountain. Hitler could then advance to the next stage: the destruction of an isolated Britain and America. Japan has begun her share of the sinister work with customary efficiency. Yet, looking at the latest news from Moscow, one begins to ask: Has Germany?

*   *   *

VIII

The Cathedral[1]

The train into the West was crowded with the usual wartime company: soldiers, laden with gigantic packs and exchanging familiar observations of a grim, semi-humorous kind, a few cheery sailors, a sprinkling of muffled civilians going rather doggedly about their business in the cheerless grey of February.

[1] *I.L.N.* 7 March 1942. Written after the fall of Singapore.

There was nothing much in the news or the immediate prospect ahead, or in the wintry landscape seen from the carriage windows, to cheer the heart. Dogged endurance was the best hope life could afford for most of us for a long time to come. Even the thought of exhilaration would have seemed a kind of weakness: our business, we all knew in our uncommunicative English way, was to grit the teeth and win through. Yet as we steamed into the outskirts of the cathedral city, every eye automatically turned to the window, peering over the suburban roofs and penthouses at the strip of leaden sky beyond, as though in search of something. And then, as the old houses in the heart of the city glided by, we saw it; strong, tapering, exquisitely right in proportion and significance. And at that momentary vision there was a kind of inaudible sigh: our eyes dropped back to our papers or began calculating the allocation of our luggage as we rose to unload the racks. We withdrew each into our own grim spiritual dug-out, ready for the next arduous or harsh experience. Yet in every heart there burnt a little flame of hope. We had taken inspiration from our gallant past. For we had seen it: the spire!

Hundreds of years ago men had built it: tough, gnarled men in strange garments, remote from us as some other planet, yet our own forebears. Some part of our blood, some facet of our daily vision, came to us from them. They were the far-off forefathers of our own fathers: without them we could not have been. And in their ignorance of most of the diffused knowledge we take for granted today, and lacking nearly all the comforts and conveniences which those of us outside the Western Desert would feel lost without, they built the Cathedral and crowned it with its spire. Judged by material standards—by human thought, effort and labour—it must have been at least a hundred times, perhaps a thousand times, as difficult for them to do so as it would be for us. Yet the fact remains that they could and did build it, and we, were we to essay the task, would almost certainly fail. We are their masters in material and accomplishment, but they were our masters in spiritual comprehension. We could tell them more about this world than they even dimly guessed, yet they could teach us more about life itself. For their souls were at one with their existence, and ours are not. For all the harsh discomfort and squalor of their lives, theirs was a vitality and physical and spiritual awareness that still speak to us across time from the buildings they raised to commemorate their faith. That glorious spire, which in a dark hour gave me and my fellow travellers a breath of inner vitality, was their handiwork.

* * *

IX

The Turn of the Tide[1]

Early this year, when the tide of defeat was running heavily against us and criticism of Mr. Churchill was rife, I made a prophecy—it was an easy one for an English historian—that the time would come, and perhaps at no very distant date, when the tide would flow as strongly in the other direction and when wives would ask their husbands in the morning what new victory we had won. And I ventured to suggest that it was for such a time that the Prime Minister was planning, and that the defeats and disappointments of the moment were a necessary and probationary prelude to that epoch of triumph. The other day a reader wrote to remind me of my prediction and to point out that such a day had come. Wives *were* asking their husbands in the morning what new victory the United Nations had won.

Not that, with so many obvious rocks ahead, and with our enemies squatting squalidly over such vast and once free tracts of land, we can claim the present favouring tide as an epoch of triumph. It is little likely, as yet, to be the beginning of the end: it is far more probably, as Mr. Churchill has said, the end of the beginning. Yet whatever it is, and whatever new set-backs and disappointments are waiting for us round the corner—and they may be grave and many—there is no denying that it is very cheering. At the time of writing, it is just three weeks since we read in our morning papers that the twelve-days' slogging match at Alamein had resulted in a British victory. We had had so many disappointments in that quarter, had had our hopes suspended

[1] *I.L.N.* 5 December 1942. Written after Alamein, the British American landings in North Africa and the Russian counter-offensive at Stalingrad.

and dashed so often, that one had received the earlier accounts of the battle without much tincture of optimism—a luxury one had long laid aside. The fillip to one's spirits, at the news that our troops and their brilliant commander had at last won the reward they so richly merited, was instantaneous. I had occasion, on the following night, to give a monthly Ministry of Information War Commentary in a little Midland industrial town. The audience, so sober ordinarily, so patient and enduring in adversity earlier in the year, seemed charged with electricity. They apparently even found their lecturer so, for they subsequently commented on the marked improvement in his usual pedestrian style: a circumstance which, unless attributable to a head-on collision in the black-out with a lamp-post while walking to the meeting, could only be explained by the exaltation caused by unwonted victory. One felt as though one had suddenly grown younger: the cramp of weary mind and body seemed to loosen. It was in such a mood that ten days later we rang our church bells for the first time since we had tautened our nerves against invasion in the high, perilous summer of 1940. I hope some echo of their ringing could be heard by the brave victors in the Libyan desert.

It takes more than one swallow to make a summer. Yet since then we have had a whole flight of swallows. Hard on the news of Alamein came the startling transformation of the scene in North West Africa. The American and British forces landed in Morocco and Algiers, the civil population received them with open arms, and even Darlan, after a brief and apparently symbolic resistance, unexpectedly threw in his lot with the rising cause of the United Nations. Since then, other good news has followed: the swift check of the Germans in the Caucasus, the suspense of the third naval battle of Guadalcanal broken by an American victory, the pounding of Italian arsenals and ports by the R.A.F., successes against the submarines in the Atlantic, the American and Australian advance in New Guinea, the repudiation of the Axis by the authorities of Dakar and French West-Africa, and now the spectacular Russian break-through behind the German armies at Stalingrad. By the time these lines appear, of course, the unwonted ups of war may have been succeeded by some of the

more familiar downs, or the tide of victory may have temporarily
ceased to flow in our favour. It may, on the other hand, have
flowed still further in the right direction. Yet, whatever befalls,
we have had three weeks of continuing good news. And that,
after three years of mainly bad, is much. It is a portent of things
to come. . . .

All that at present is certain is that at long last we have passed
from the defensive to the offensive. The enemy, at least for the
time being, has lost the initiative, and we have gained it. The four-
fold Axis offensive of 1942—which was to achieve decisive results
before the effects of belated American armament could be felt—
has failed on every front. The Russian armies are still undefeated
in the field; the Japanese Navy, held by the Americans and
Australians on its vulnerable eastern flank, has been unable to
drive westwards across the Indian Ocean towards its European
partners, the sea-lanes have been maintained against the sub-
marine packs, and Rommel has failed to reach the Nile Valley.
Now the Russians are attacking strongly before Stalingrad and
in the Caucasus, the United Nations have taken the offensive in
North Africa, and the Australians and Americans are nibbling
at the Japanese outposts in the South Pacific. Four great obstacles
lie in our way, and it is easy to see that trouble may be looked for
from all or any of them: the German power of recoil in Russia,
the use by the Axis of interior lines in North Africa, the potential strength of a highly militarised and mobilised Japan, and
the shark-like ubiquity of the U-boats. The last is perhaps still
the greatest danger to the United Nations; the second that on
which the eyes of this country are most naturally and immediately
fixed.

For the Axis bridge across the Central Mediterranean still
remains; it has, indeed, been shortened and strengthened by the
German and Italian entry into Tunis—the inevitable price for
our own gains further west. Until that bridgehead has been
captured, whether from east or west, the Mediterranean cannot
be reopened to our convoys. The virtual increase of two million
tons of shipping which that achievement would guarantee has
still to be won. The Axis supply lines through Southern Italy
and across the Sicilian Channel are short: the supply lines of our

converging armies from Egypt and the Atlantic long. If Germany can build up a sufficient army in Tunisia and Tripoli, her commander will have the geographical option of striking either at Eisenhower or Montgomery. The issue will depend largely on air power, and in the crucial triangle between Sicily, Tunisia and Sardinia we may be about to witness an air combat almost as decisive for victory as the Battle of Britain.

* * *

x

Maintaining the Initiative[1]

Tunisia has been won and the Mediterranean reopened. The question which all the world is asking, including, of course, Hitler—who in earlier and, for him, happier days used to provoke such questions in others—is: What next? We shall all, including Hitler, know in good time. Yet certain truths stand out as old as the history of war. An enemy possessing the advantage of interior lines is being faced at last with a superior force of men and arms assembled against him on the perimeter of a wide circumference. Until those men and arms can be brought to bear against him simultaneously he still enjoys a chance to recover the initiative by throwing his main weight against such of his adversaries as are already in contact with him—in other words, the Russians— while facing the remainder with a comparatively small holding force. The fact that to engage at all that remainder must force a landing on fortified beaches against a continental Power controlling everything that runs on wheels inside that continent summarises the difficulty of the attackers' position. The defenders, in other words, do not need overwhelming strength to hold the first surge of an attacking force coming from the sea, because, even if the initial landing or landings are successful, a considerable period must elapse before the attackers can build up on the enemy shore a sufficient reserve of war material, ammunition, fuel and transport to enable them to stage a major offensive.

The delays and disappointments of the first five months in

[1] *I.L.N.* 29 May 1943.

Tunisia afforded an illustration of this: the more valuable because it has almost certainly indicated ways in which this inherent handicap can be overcome, or at least reduced. Yet the fact remains: that, as regards operations on an enemy-held continent, a bird in the hand is at first worth two in the bush. Other things being equal, one soldier already there, fully supported and supplied for immediate battle, is likely to be for some time the equal or superior of two landed on the beaches with their heavy armour, artillery and transport and the wherewithal to maintain them still to be landed. In the early stages of any landing, so long as the enemy possesses a reasonable sufficiency of troops and material and retains his fighting morale, we might well, but for the growing might of our air-power, have to start with the immediate odds heavily against us. We have, in short, to reverse Dunkirk. With air-power, it can be done, but no one can suppose that, so long as the Germans possess reserves and fighting spirit, it is going to be easy.

Yet here the general principles of war, above all of England's past wars, guide and encourage. That profound student of military history and mechanised battle, General Fuller, reminded me a little while ago that history affords no example of a world war being won by the side with the advantage of interior lines. It has always been the side attacking from the circumference which has proved the final victor—in other words, the side with sea-power and untrammelled sea communications. I am not suggesting that we yet possess such untrammelled freedom, but I am convinced that, thanks to our new offensive against the U-boat and our growing air superiority, we are going to gain it before long. When that hour comes we shall be able to attack wherever and whenever we like on a wide circumference. And the wider that circumference, other things being equal, the better. The further the enemy has to fight from his own central bases the easier for us and the more costly for him. Obviously a blow close to his heart is the best offensive weapon of all, but only—and this is an important point—if and when it can be pressed home. If it cannot be, such a blow is likely to be less damaging to the enemy than an attack on some outlying limb, since it can be parried with comparative ease and at moderate cost.

It is the wasting campaign at the remote circumference which most speedily and surely drains the strength of a military giant still too strongly entrenched to be destroyed at close quarters: the Spanish ulcer, as it were, that wore down Napoleon. The losses sustained by Germany in Russia, both in men and equipment, have always been heaviest at the point furthest from Germany; at Tula and Kalinin in the winter of 1941-42, and at Stalingrad and in the Caucasus last winter. It is infinitely more difficult and costly for the *Wehrmacht* to wage war on the Volga than it is, shall we say, in the Pas-de-Calais or in Holland—heavy though the price be in suffering and destruction that Russia has had to pay to bury so many Fritzes and Hanses on her steppes. To slay the evil dragon who desolates Europe at the earliest possible moment is our duty: but a thing does not become immediately— as opposed to ultimately—possible merely because one wants it. Until we can actually kill our prey, the best way to hasten his death is to bleed him, and to bleed him where the wound cannot easily be staunched. That is what we have been doing in North Africa and what our allies did last winter in the remote lands between Don and Volga.

In such a process, Britain, by virtue of her sea-power, possesses a peculiar advantage. We can make the enemy fight in positions where our command of the sea facilitates our own problems of supply, transport and manoeuvre, and complicates his. The classic example in the wars against Napoleon was the Iberian Peninsula; in our own war it has been, up to date, North Africa. The German was forced to give battle in Tunisia because its conquest would afford us lateral command of the Mediterranean and a bridgehead against Sicily, Sardinia and the Italian main- land. Yet by giving battle there, he suffered a far heavier ratio of loss than he would have done on his own continent. For every German killed or captured by British gunfire in North Africa, it may well prove no exaggeration to say that at least another was killed or captured either by direct loss at sea or by the handicaps imposed by imperfect communications. The final collapse, we have been told by correspondents, was partly the result of a breakdown in transport, principally through lack of petrol. We all know whom we have to thank for that: "bell bottom-trousers and suit of Navy blue"! Also, one should add, his brother in Air Force blue. Though we cannot always expect to fight the enemy on as favourable a terrain as North Africa, with salt water between him and his bases, there are plenty of outlying positions in Europe, particularly Southern Europe, which the foe is forced to defend for fear of worse to come, and which, being either islands or peninsulas, offer us—once the initial landing has been secured—a growing advantage by virtue of our sea- and air-power. The fact that there are so many of these, and that the enemy, not knowing where we will strike, is forced to man them all, is an additional advantage. For to man the circumference compels him to draw on his central reserves—the instrument by which he can alone reap and retain the benefit of interior lines. The more extended the circumference, the greater disability this becomes.

There is one other principle—a ruling one. Not only for the sake of our allies but for the sake of ourselves and of the whole world, we must renew our battering and bleeding of the enemy at the earliest possible moment and at whatever point or points we judge most likely to achieve the maximum results. For if we did not, the enemy could make hay while the sun shone, and, using his interior lines, recover the initiative. This is something which those who have so boldly, and—in the upshot—successfully, directed our fortunes till now, are unlikely again to allow him. The foe, we can be sure, will be hit and hit soon, and repeatedly, cost what it may.

* * *

XI

D Day[1]

Everything comes to him who waits and, under God's providence, works hard enough for it. It has come to Mr. Churchill, and to Generals Alexander and Montgomery, in this month of June 1944, and to all those who from Dunkirk and Tobruk and other places

[1] *I.L.N.* 24 June 1944.

of vicissitude, have returned to keep a promise made in a dark hour to their own souls. To take Rome one day and land on the coast of an enslaved France on the next, almost four years to the day after we were so violently flung out of Europe by an aggressor, is a not unsatisfactory achievement for the champions of a once-forlorn cause. And Britons can congratulate themselves that they have had at least a fair share in the achievement. Four years ago— even three—they were the only people still on their feet who had any share in it at all.

There is so much to be said about this miraculous invasion— still at the time of writing only at the beginning of its second week—that it is hard to know where to begin. First, it has come almost at the precise moment and place that anyone using his reason—which few, however, do—would have expected it to come. Secondly, that the Germans apparently did not expect it at that moment and place. But by far the most impressive thing about the whole affair has been the magnitude of the venture. How right General Montgomery was, in his Order of the Day before embarkation, to use Montrose's words:

> *He either fears his fate too much,*
> *Or his deserts are small,*
> *That dares not put it to the touch*
> *To gain or lose it all.*

That is what Churchill, President Roosevelt and their naval, military and air advisers did. They staked the free world's victory on mounting the greatest act of amphibian warfare in history.

The first thing to rejoice at is that we have made our lodgement; the second that, so far, there has been no holocaust. The third is that our shipping losses have proved, comparatively speaking, extraordinarily light. The three fears which have haunted every thinking mind since the great adventure was first mooted have been: should we, in the face of an enemy dug in and possessing every unit of transport on the continent, be able to make good our landing and hold it against the fury of his immediate counter-attacks? Would the damage inflicted on our shipping by enemy mine, shell, torpedo, rocket and bomb be greater than our Navy and Merchant Marine—the central pillar of our entire war structure—could sustain? Would the losses on the beaches be so vast as to cripple us, like those of the Somme and Passchendaele, for a generation to come and ensure that, while we won the War, we should again lose the Peace? The Germans doubtless comforted themselves by answering these questions in a way very different to our own hopes, and even a year ago they would almost certainly have been right. Their dive-bombers, submarines, E-boats, mines, submerged stakes, wire entanglements, concrete defences, batteries, fire-throwers, rockets and tanks would have had free play on the bodies of our soldiers and the hulls of our ships.

By meticulous planning over many months, even years, and by intensive, sustained and multiple work to implement that planning on a scale unequalled in the history of co-operative military endeavour, all the enemy's obstacles and weapons have been overcome or mastered. There has been no booby-trap so small, no adverse chance so unlikely that has not been brooded over in advance and the antidote patiently sought and exactly worked out. For every one of a million tasks the men have been appointed and trained. There was no other way in which an invasion against such apparently overwhelming odds could have been launched and sustained without disaster.

Immense difficulties and dangers still remain. But the success of the first week has already deprived the enemy of his initial advantage. He is now confronted with a baffling dilemma. His tactical reserves have failed to throw us back into the sea at any point or even to impede our build-up on the captured beaches. To secure a decisive result before it is too late—and every day sees his chances dwindling—he must throw in his strategic reserves. Yet he knows that our amphibian strength may be used at any moment and at any point of a wide circumference. His failure to molest our sea and air transport has left us the means, not only to sustain our original landing, but to strike again and again. If he throws in his strategic reserve against forces which are strong enough to hold them, those other impending blows may well prove fatal. Yet if he does not do so, the blow already struck may gather such strength as to prove fatal, too. And all the while he is forced to keep vast armies in being, not only on the Russian front and in the south, but manning every mile of coastline upon which we might elect to descend.

Here lies the peculiar strategic advantage of amphibian power— power, that is, where the twin advantages of complete command of the sea and of the air, which today goes with it, and of military striking power go hand in hand. The defeat of the U-boat and Luftwaffe, and the creation, arming and training of the vast armies of the United States and British Empire have given us this advantage. Today the foe has had to deploy his armies along thousands of miles of coastline. He cannot safely withdraw a single division from that extended, exposed, static position. Yet we can keep in reserve our entire military force not already landed, ready to use in decisive strength at the right place and moment. It is a tremendous advantage, and one for which there is no parallel in military history.

For if ever a war has proved the importance of command of the sea it has been this. Far from blunting an age-long truth, the new factor of the air weapon has sharpened and accentuated it. In the four years since 1940 we have seen the exercise of both the two great uses of sea-power in global war: first, the ring of water stretched and kept round an otherwise uncontainable land victor; then the mounting of overwhelming military force from behind that ring and its delivery across waters over which absolute air and sea supremacy has been obtained. The men, dead and living, who fought the U-boat through four weary years on water and in the air have contributed as much to the invasion as General Montgomery and his troops. So have the men who, night after night, have used the new weapon of strategic air striking-power to dislocate the enemy's communications and slow down his war production. The battles of the Ruhr and Berlin, like the cruises of the *Audacity* and the anti U-boat escort vessels, were the indispensable preludes to the Battle of Caen.

*   *   *

XII

A War-Time Journey[1]

The other day I had occasion to travel several hundred miles by rail on a Saturday, returning on the Monday, to lecture at an Army school in a remote Welsh village. Having often to move about the country on such business, and knowing from experience what was likely to happen, I had taken the precaution of applying for a place to enable me to get through the work which I am compelled to take with me on such journeys. The authorities did their best, but the most they could achieve when the train appeared was to get me on it at all: at that moment I should have been considerably relieved had they failed! Looking at its crowded corridors, the wonder was that it did not burst open and disgorge its passengers in one convulsive explosion. As it was, large numbers fell out in every direction when the doors were opened, only to scramble back before newcomers from the packed platform could take their places.

By some miracle of military persistence, my escort succeeded in winkling me into a luggage-van already filled by more human beings than even the frugal French contrived to pack into their freight cars during the First World War. Here, for the next five hours, till I was due to change trains, I stood or reclined in a variety of highly restricted but varying positions—varying because at every station it became necessary for harassed porters and postmen to uproot the trespassing passengers from their knobby niches on the luggage and mail-bags in order to carry out their almost impossible duties. At one station the police intervened to eject everyone from the van who was not travelling on official business, but at the next stop it immediately refilled, not only with newcomers, but with several of its old inmates who had somehow managed to retain a foothold elsewhere.

There was a small number of soldiers travelling at my end of the van on special passes. At the sight of the massed holiday-makers on each platform—most of the original passengers seemed to be hard-tried Londoners removing their wives and

[1] *I.L.N.* 22 July 1944.

families to country quiet after three weeks of what Uncle Nat Gubbins calls "Hitler's flaming daggers"—these martial travellers, weighed down by their packs and belongings, waxed very caustic, in terms traditionally dear to the British soldier, at the selfishness of those who were defying the Government's appeal to spend their holidays at home, and who were presumably spending good wages in pursuit of private pleasure at a time when their fellow-country-men were dying on a soldier's pittance to free the world. But the British soldier is a strange person, and neither logic nor bitterness have much part in his make-up. Those who at one moment he reviled as profiteers and traitors he greeted in the next as old friends and fellow-sufferers. Within a few minutes of the renewed scramble for places at every station, the newcomers at our end of the van had become part of what was almost a family circle. Smiles and anecdotes were exchanged; everyone helped everyone else to find such comfort as our cramped quarters admitted, and, as the next station revealed its crowded, waiting platform, all became united in a single bond of fiery unity against the new-comers until they, too, had entered the charmed circle and became our brothers. An American soldier—a dark-jowled, ebon-haired private of plainly Latin extraction—particularly distinguished himself by the contrast between the ferocity of his threats and the warmth of his welcome. Repeatedly announcing in a nasal and expurgative snarl his low view of British wartime railway travel and British holiday-makers, he proceeded, the moment the van doors had finally closed again on the struggling, elbowing mass of Midland humanity, to make room for all the children within earshot and to entice them and their goggling mothers into an ecstatic sing-song among the mail-bags. It was not at all conducive to work, which, in any case, by now was out of the question, but it was exceedingly entertaining. With a wriggl-ing, happy, if frequently grubby, child in either arm, he was, he announced, in a state of perfect contentment: he only need-ed a bottle of Scotch to make him the happiest man in the world. Under his ministrations the quietest and most sub-dued child quickly became as noisy and self-assertive as an air-raid siren!

During the journey in the van, and later in the packed corridor of the less important train which crawled slowly over the moors and mountain passes towards Caernarvon Bay I talked—as also on the return journey—to at least a score of holiday-makers. Everyone with whom I spoke had endured a strain of work and monotony which five years ago would have seemed intolerable. What in the aggregate appeared to be an anarchy of selfishness, in the individual case reduced itself, when examined, into the salutary safety-valve demanded by human fatigue and limited physical and mental capacity in a country which still leaves decision in such matters to the individual conscience. No doubt among the crowds on the platform there were some who ought not to have been there and who were selfishly ignoring the Government's appeal not to travel. But every one of those with whom I talked—men and women alike—stood, or seemed to stand, in urgent need of a brief respite of rest, fresh air and peaceful surroundings. It was the measure of what civilian Britain has had to endure in the past five years.

* * *

XIII

The Final Act[1]

The long tragedy is entering on its final act. All over the world—in Baltic swamp and on flooded Dutch island, on the Polish plains and the Carpathians, in the wooded Vosges and the industrial fringes of the Ruhr and Saar, among the Apennine valleys and in the wild Balkans, in Greek islands and in the most remote solitudes of ocean and sky, in Burmese jungle and Pacific atoll—millions of men are gripped in remorseless, destructive struggle. Nothing except the destruction of earth itself can stop the struggle until one side is victorious and the other irreparably ruined. In all the annals of human war, there has never been so appalling a conflict.

The Germans are fighting desperately. The war they have twice in a quarter of a century loosed on the world is moving slowly and remorselessly into their own land. Millions of young

[1] *I.L.N.* 21 October 1944.

Nazi braves—the fanatic, blond savages whom Hitler and his henchmen have been schooling for battle for the past decade— are struggling to avert the inevitable. Beside them—terrified by the bludgeon and hip-gun of a police State—the dregs of the barrel are fighting too: old men from the factories, embusqués from offices and theatres, half-starved prisoners from the East, quislings and criminals, cripples and convalescents. And the arch-criminals, for whom all this bloody endeavour and sacrifice is being made, are breathing threats of new destructive weapons to mangle, torture and annihilate mankind, and are spurring on their scientists to evolve some suicidal devilry which will either save them at the eleventh hour or bring the pillars of the reeling globe crashing down on their own and the victors' heads.

It is not a scene in which any civilised being can take much satisfaction. To end it, our bravest and best—the flower of their generation—are giving their lives and enduring untold horrors and sufferings. Every day that it is prolonged means the loss of noble young lives that can ill be spared from the task of rebuilding and refashioning a broken civilisation. Yet there can be no turning back, for none is possible. There is nothing for it but to go forward whatever the cost, and win the victory which so many have given their all to achieve. The summit may still be far or it may be—as the writer suspects—very near. But far or near, we must go on till we reach it, till the foe crumples and we tumble, bloody, breathless but victorious, onto the bleak, windswept peak we have struggled so long to climb.

I have always maintained that, once battle was joined in the West, it would be the cumulative effect of the struggle that would bring Hitler down. For a few days at the end of August and beginning of September, it looked as though the very obstinacy with which the Germans had stood to their guns in the Normandy *bocage* would prove their undoing, and that the surge of British and American armour northwards and eastwards would pour unimpeded over the Siegfried Line into the Reich. But though nearly half-a-million prisoners were taken, the hard core of the German Army survived. Fighting close to its bases, while the victorious Allies raced forward at the end of suddenly elongated supply-lines and with inadequate port facilities behind them, it was able to hold before the Rhine. Only at Nijmegen, thanks to the heroism of our own and the American airborne divisions, was one branch of the river—the historic breastplate of the Reich —crossed.

Yet the check was only temporary. Once the necessary build-up had been made behind the new Allied lines, the gruelling, wearing battle to waste and destroy the German Army was resumed. The great bleeding process which the Russians began in 1941 is now continuing. It is not only doing so along a five hundred-mile front from Walcheren to the Swiss frontier, but in Italy from Ravenna to Pisa, in the Aegean and on the Greek mainland, in Yugoslavia, in Finland and on the immense Russian front from the Baltic to the Danube. All the while, whenever the weather permits, immense quantities of bombs—far greater than anything dreamed of in the days of German air ascendancy—are being showered on the industrial centres and communications of the Reich. It is only a question of time before the aggressors must break. The mills of God grind slowly, but they grind exceeding small.

Even then there will remain the enemy in the Pacific. That will be a war of a different kind, though one which will also, at tragic cost, have to be fought out. But I hope and believe the cost there will be carefully controlled. For once the initial bastions of the nightmare Co-Prosperity Sphere have been stormed, time will be wholly on our side. Closed in by sea- and air-power on a gigantic scale, Japan will be a blockaded fortress, utterly alone and without a friend in the world. The entire martial resources of the globe will be turned against her, and after five years of war and concentrated endeavour for war, they will be resources of no mean kind. By comparison, they will make Nippon's fearful earth-quakes seem like the tremor of a summer's breeze in the cherry-trees.

After that we shall have to begin to restore civilisation. That will be, perhaps, the biggest task of all. The habit of hating and abuse, the arts of killing and destruction, a scorched earth and charred cities are not comfortable or secure foundations for a Brave New World. And we shall be tired, disillusioned and sud-denly divided. We shall be tempted to turn our swords agains one another. That will be the moment for all our courage, forbearance and faith. The spirits of evil, malice and destruction, conjured up by evil men for their cruel ends, will still be loose in the world, and, when we have conquered their mortal champions, we shall have the still greater work to do of exorcising them.

CHAPTER 6

Brave New World

"O brave new world, that has such people in't!"
SHAKESPEARE

From 1939 to 1945, while writing 'English Saga' and the first volumes of my trilogy on the Napoleonic Wars, I continued to contribute a weekly page of commentary on the war and public affairs to the Illustrated London News. Simultaneously, as a Lecturer to H.M. Forces, I was speaking on military history and strategy, political science, and what is now called sociology, to units of all three Services. These ranged from search-light sites and small groups of private soldiers, ordinary seamen and air mechanics to staff colleges and command headquarters, both at home and abroad. The person who learnt most from this varied experience was the lecturer, whose visits to his countrymen in uniform took him to places as far apart as Baghdad and the Shetlands.

Students in Arms · The Needs of Social Man ·
The Rock of Human Nature

I

Students in Arms[1]

During the war an attempt was made by those responsible for the training and morale of the Services to provide forums of discussion in which the thousands of young men in uniform from factory, field and office could thresh out together the political and economic issues which concerned their future and that of the

[1] *Illustrated London News* 21 December 1968.

society to which they belonged and for whose survival they were fighting. Those who formed these groups had all the strength and weakness of modern democratic society. Their approach to political problems tended initially to be in one of three ways. Some, at first by far the most vocal, were highly critical of the organisation of pre-war society and in favour of radical and drastic change. Others, a smaller group, were conservative in feeling and were apt to be labelled by their more extreme Left Wing comrades as reactionaries or even sometimes "fascists". The largest group might have described themselves, had they attempted to do so, by the words, "Couldn't care less!" or "A plague on both your houses!"

Yet, as the discussion groups developed and the work of organising and providing them with factual material for debate grew, these divisions began to disappear. One found, particularly where the group was drawn from a unit which was static for any length of time, that it was becoming a miniature parliament of thinking individuals, arguing things out for themselves in the English way with a respect for fact and with growing courtesy and tolerance. Deep down, for all their differences of opinion, those taking part believed in the same thing. They believed in justice. By what method justice was to be achieved was a matter for dispute, yet what was accepted by all was the right of the individual to put his case to his fellows and receive from them, before judgment, fair play. One saw such men—comrades in a great venture—feeling their way towards that which the rest of the nation had still to discover, a common denominator for reconstruction. Unconsciously a meeting point was being sought and found between those who offered liberty without social security, and those who demanded what so many craved after the awful frustration of unemployment in the pre-war years—social security. And gradually one saw an, at first, almost imperceptible, but quickening, movement towards the inevitable British answer for which we have been striving as a nation throughout our history—liberty in a framework of discipline or, in economic terms, social security *with* liberty.

Being employed during the war as a lecturer to all three Services, I was able to watch what was going on in the minds of these warrior students. In the early days there was an angry, inchoate and, on the whole, negative antagonism towards the frustration and complacent defeatism of our pre-war economic system—a feeling, however unjust, that our rulers had been guilty of a kind of universal *non possumus*, summed up in the words, "Can we afford it?" Could we afford, in terms of money, to clear the slums, to give decent education to the majority of our people, to redistribute our population between our overcrowded cities and the vast spaces of our underpopulated territories overseas, to find employment to make the things of which so many stood in need. Even whether we could afford to arm against a foreign menace which every year had grown more obvious and to meet which the entire youth of the country had now had to take arms and suffer separation from home and loved ones, facing exile, wounds and death. And those with whom one was discussing these things had come to see the inadequacy of that question—an inadequacy made obvious by the events of 1940. They had seen a nation which, in the face of deadly danger, had stopped saying, "Can we afford, in terms of money, to do things which are necessary to save ourselves?" and had said instead, "Can we afford not to do them?" A nation which out of sheer necessity had discovered that what was physically possible and morally desirable could be made financially possible, and had learned the lesson that wealth and money are not necessarily the same thing. Real wealth, these Servicemen realised, could only be made in the last resort in one way, by human effort applied to the earth and its resources. Between 1940 and 1944 they saw what a country could do when it made up its mind to do it.

There came to these discussion groups a realisation of something else. It was not a totalitarian society which had made either the machines or the men who won the battles of Britain and Alamein and stormed the D-Day beaches. In spite of the immense material strength of the totalitarian countries and our own gradual recognition of the meaning of real wealth and of the way to create it, there was also a growing sense of the validity of that for which we proclaimed we were fighting—individual freedom. For it was seen that there was no use in making guns, tanks and aeroplanes, in whatever abundance, if one did not also create the necessary virtues in the men who were going to use them, and that there was a vital difference between a strong State and a strong people. Germany was a very strong State in 1940, Britain a very weak one; yet it was the strong people, not the strong State which ultimately won. And the men to whom I was privileged to lecture were trying to make themselves masters of certain virtues; of physical and mental fitness, faith and competence, courage, endurance and discipline, of the capacity for self-reliance, initiative and self-sacrifice—virtues measured, it is true, for the narrow and wasteful purposes of the battlefield, yet very real virtues for all that. And if it were true that, for the purpose of winning a war, human virtue was the highest form of wealth, the same must be true for the purposes of peace, and that the ultimate aim of society, and the test by which all institutions, political, legal, economic, should be judged, was the simple one, " Does it tend to create decent men and women?" For if it did not, however much it might pay in terms of money or serve the aims of some particular ideology, it would break down on the human factor in the long run.[1]

*   *   *

II

The Needs of Social Man[2]

Reconstruction is a clumsy word, but a very important one. The longer the destructive lunacy of war continues, the more important it is going to become, for, if mankind is to have a habitable house at all, the more there will be to reconstruct. We have already destroyed the achievements of decades; before long we shall destroy the work of centuries. We may end by destroying civilisation itself. Yet, sooner or later, the hour will come to

[1] I have always felt that it was a failure by Churchill and the Conservative leaders to understand what had been happening in the minds of the young men in the Forces that lost them so much of the Service vote in the General Election of 1945.

[2] *I.L.N.* 11 October, 1, 8, 15, 22 November 1941. These articles, based on what I was discussing at the time with groups of Servicemen under the scheme for Education in H.M. Forces, were written in the dark months immediately preceding Japan's and America's entry into the War.

rebuild. And the more carefully we prepare for it, the sooner we—or our children—will have a weatherproof house in which to live. As the tragic experience of 1919 proved, it is as necessary to be ready for peace as for war. Victory and the peace which follows victory are one and indivisible.

To rebuild society one must first ask what men and women want of life. For too long we have judged the worthwhileness of every activity from one of two angles. Half of us have asked, Does it pay? the other half have asked, Does it bring socialism and national ownership nearer? that is, a society in which all enterprise is initiated and controlled by civil servants for the common, or supposed common, good. I doubt whether many at the moment believe that either of these tests is wholly satisfactory. When one is groping through the dust and flames of a falling house, neither the Stock Exchange nor the Treasury can afford much guidance. Successful speculation in shares and commodities is not the answer to humanity's need. Nor is the perpetual rule of a bureaucratic big brother in Whitehall. Neither a capitalist nor a socialist organisation of society provides the complete answer. We have to seek further.

For the social needs of man are many and complex. He needs enough to eat, not only in quantity but quality; food, as our mediaeval ancestors used to say, that is "good and wholesome for man's body". He needs security of tenure and regularity of employment, not only to earn a living but because his nature prompts him to take pride and pleasure in his achievements. He needs security in his home, which includes decent conditions and education for his children. He needs security from war, the bubonic plague of our age. Yet the satisfaction of these material needs is not enough. Man needs something more if he is to be at peace with himself and his environment. He needs self-respect and status. He needs liberty or freedom of choice; freedom from irritating control and cramping interference—a satisfaction which Hitler's *Herrenvolk* seem incapable of allowing their neighbours, and whose lack, even were there no resisting Britain in his way, would sooner or later bring all his plans for a New Order to frustration. On the satisfaction of this need so much which gives life zest depends: love, adventure, even danger; the free choice of one's mate; freedom to dare and take risks, the gleam of the un-expected.

There is yet a further need of man: the need for faith and an ideal. He must believe in something greater than himself or his soul seems to shrivel. And if his soul sickens, his body and mind sicken with it. When Churchill, like Garibaldi, offered his country-men sweat, toil, blood and tears, he based his appeal on man's response to this basic and ultimate need. Christ, in saying that he who gave his life for others should find it, was not thinking of the next world only. He was founding a creed for this world on the rock of human nature.

*   *   *

If the most elemental need of man is food, the second is social security. By this I do not mean the kind of security that denies life, that tries to shut out adventure and change and danger and death and all the natural inevitable processes which are part of the human heritage. The young men who dive with their glitter-ing wings of the morning on the German fighters, or guide the bombers through the *flak*-stabbed darkness, are not seeking that sort of security. But there is another kind, vital to all healthy growth and progress. It is the security of love, of the cradle and home; the kind of security associated in the past with the English countryside, with its centuries-old tradition of wise farming and wise living; which gives a man faith to sow that he or others may reap and assurance to pass into the darkness knowing that the light will continue to shine.

All life is subtly compounded of these two: adventure and safety. "Out of this nettle, danger, we pluck this flower, safety." When he used Hotspur's great phrase, Neville Chamberlain—like many of us who followed him—had mistaken the time. Yet he was true in the end to his saying, laying all on the altar of sacrifice when the hour struck and dying as much as any man on the battle-field that his country's life might continue, and that the peace he had vainly sought to give the world by one surrender might be assured by another greater.

It is here, I think, the common denominator lies for those two contending schools of thought which have so long been fighting for the body and soul of modern society. Leaving aside those actuated solely by selfish motives—those who defend capitalism merely because it enables them to enjoy superior riches, and those who advocate socialism because under it they will be in greater positions of power and responsibility—we are confronted with the spectacle of sincere men like Sir Ernest Benn, who maintain that human liberty and happiness depend on every man being left completely free to find his own economic level, and equally sincere men, like Dr. Harold Laski, who maintain that they depend on all economic activity being planned and directed by the State; that is, by disinterested civil servants. Yet the more one examines these two creeds, the more one realises there is much to be said for both of them, and even more, from what one sees of their operation in practice, to be said against the abuses to which each gives rise. The first is too apt to make bad men, and the second to penalise good ones. Leave the economic career completely open to the talents, as our great-grandfathers did, and, before long, one has profiteers living at Monte Carlo and children being brought up in slum conditions which preclude them from ever becoming contented or satisfactory citizens. Shut the career to the talents in the name of some high-sounding corporate "ism" or "ology", and every idler and wangler seeks to pass on to society at large the cost of his idleness and dishonesty. Parasites flourish just as readily under Socialism as under Capitalism: in fact, more so, because in practice, being more numerous, it is harder to dislodge them.

Yet some measure of social security has come to stay, and is palpably needed. Men will not suffer the kind of insecurity which involves a perpetual threat of loss of livelihood through economic causes beyond their control. Mass unemployment is only a shade less intolerable to human instincts than total war. It was their realisation of this that gave the totalitarian demagogues their chance. It was no accident that Hitler's early successes fluctuated in ratio to the rises and falls in the German unemployment figures. He rode to power, like other dictators, on the back of the small man—petty-bourgeois or proletarian—who wanted a safe anchorage in the economic blizzards which were sweeping the world. Men out of work are on the way to becoming men in coloured shirts. Security in some things—the things that affect a man's continuing life, his love, home and family—is dearer to him even than political freedom. If he is denied it, he will sacrifice political freedom to obtain it.

We should make a grave mistake and imperil the very existence of democracy if we repeated this error after the war. The wise course is to recognise that, till we have secured the average man in possession of his home and a decent chance for his children, liberty will remain in danger, almost as much as it is with an undefeated Hitler—himself the political product of mass unemployment. Little though one wishes to see the world made safer for loafers and ne'er do-wells, the punishment of their failings should not be allowed to poison society and penalise the unborn. That was the flaw of laissez-faire, which, in rewarding some individuals and punishing others, injured posterity. There are some things of which a man's folly or misbehaviour cannot be permitted to deprive his children, who are not, after all, his personal property, but belong to themselves, the nation and the future. If we are to be a contented society after the War we shall have to use the power of the State to ensure for every child the stability of home, education, medical care and nutrition, without which it cannot easily become a good citizen.

* * *

If man needs social security, he also needs status. By this I mean those things that give him self-respect: which make him feel his work is worthwhile and his life of service to his fellows. The consumer as such possesses only one sort of status: that of purchasing-power. A world based solely on the satisfaction of the consumer is one in which only the fellow with plenty of "brass" can feel satisfaction. In a free society men cannot all be equally rich, but, in relation to the quality of their work and character, they can be equally respected by their fellows.

How often between the present war and the last one heard a man say, "Those were good days in the Army!" On the face of it, there was little to endear a man to a soldier's life in the trenches: there was danger, vile surroundings, death and wounds, torture of nerve and body amid mud and rotting corpses, twisted ruins and universal desolation. Those who merely read of these things could never understand the demobilised soldier's occasional yearning for the old Army life, with its companionship, its clear purpose; above all, its trust. So my old friend, Edmund Blunden, wrote in his noble Undertones of War[1]:

> When will the stern fine, 'Who goes there?'
> Meet me again in midnight air?
> And the gruff sentry's kindness, when
> Will kindness have such power again?
> It seems, as now I wake and brood
> And know my hour's decrepitude,
> That on some dewy parapet
> The sentry's spirit gazes yet,
> Who will not speak with altered tone
> When I at last am seen and known.[1]

It is this desire to be recognised for what he is at his best that constitutes man's need for status.

In the corporate England which grew out of the Christian polity of the Middle Ages there was more scope for the satisfaction of this need than in modern society. Poor though his standard of living, the ordinary man was something more than a nameless number in the national statistics: he was a member, however humble, of the society of his craft, of his parish church, of the local community. He took his turn in their offices and his place in their festivals and commemorative rites. But the gap between the traditions of the rural seventeenth century and those of the industrial nineteenth century were so great that the memory of that older England has been obliterated for the vast majority of our people.[2] Such social status as the ordinary man enjoys today is largely the creation of the last fifty years: of a process, not of restoration, but of new creation to fill an almost complete void. The growth of the modern Trades Union, with its insistence on special legal privilege and its immense and solemn *amour propre*, is an example of an attempt to recreate status for a status-starved

---

[1] E. Blunden *Undertones of War*, p. 137. Cobden Sanderson.
[2] See Peter Laslett's fascinating book, *The World We have Lost*.

"proletariat". The simple, often nameless heroes who worked in the teeth of every odds to build up the early Trades Unions were unconsciously reaching back to a great English tradition. The well-to-do employers and politicians who opposed them in the name of laissez-faire had lost their historical bearings.

Yet a Trades Union is scarcely an adequate substitute for those small and more intricate affiliations in which our remote past was so rich and which meant so much to our humble ancestors. For all its great economic and political service to the working-man, it touches such a small part of the rich complex of human life. Man is not only a wage-earner, a consumer, or even a voter; he is a craftsman, a worshipper, a father, a lover. He wants to feel that what he does, and is, matters to the community: to attain to an ideal and to be judged by a standard. In the days when I used to produce pageants, I was often struck by the pathetic eagerness with which unemployed men and women, who, in the eyes of the State, were only dole-drawers and economic encumbrances, assumed self-respect and dignity which the petty responsibilities of the pageant conferred on them. It has convinced me that the ideal State is one in which the largest possible number of citizens enjoy some special importance and responsibility. The ant-heap ideal of the egalitarian community fails to appeal to free men because it denies a fundamental human need. "Unlike the levelling equality of modern days," wrote Disraeli, "the ancient equality of England elevates and creates. Learned in human nature the English constitution holds out privilege to every subject as the inducement to do his duty."

* * *

Sir James Barrie described courage as "the lovely virtue", because on courage all the other personal virtues ultimately depend. On political liberty depend all the other social virtues. Its existence is the condition which enables them to grow and flourish. When we say we are fighting for freedom, we mean we are fighting for the coping-stone of our social order. There is no such coping-stone in Hitler's. When Ambassador Henderson looked round the allegorical paintings on the walls of Goering's palace, he remarked that he did not see patience among them. In the political gallery of the Nazi New Order for Europe, one looks in vain for liberty.

The essence of political liberty is that a man should be free to criticise those set in authority. Its social value is that only by such criticism can the institutions, ideas and practice of the State be kept aired. Despotisms which deny the right of criticism live in a hothouse. After a time, for this reason, they cease to live. The free air of human needs, conviction and vitality no longer inflates their lungs. That is why rigid despotisms always ultimately decay and, when the rot sets in, decay quickly. The Spain of Philip II and the Inquisition, the France of Louis XIV, the Turkey of the Sultans and Grand Viziers all suffered rapid decline and became the prey of healthier organisms. The sanity bred of our temperate climate and long immunity from invasion have made our race instinctively aware of this truth. We regard as unhealthy all political practices which tend to shut the mouths of opponents. We feel about them as we do about sleeping in rooms with the windows shut. The Anglo-Saxon instinct, after a glimpse of Gestapo-ridden Germany or Fascist Italy, is to exclaim, "Ugh, what a fug!" We are fighting not only for our own free air, but to open the windows of Europe.

It is a paradox that at the moment when we are fighting for the freedom of the world, our own freedom seems in the greatest danger. Powers are entrusted to the Government to crush freedom of speech and criticism that would never be tolerated in ordinary times. Such powers are necessary in a time of national danger: they were used by Elizabeth when she was fighting Philip of Spain, by the Whig Government of 1689 when it was fighting Louis XIV, and by William Pitt when he was fighting Revolutionary and Napoleonic France. Yet this does not mean that we should not be on our guard against needless excess of authority or imagine that the liberties our fathers fought for throughout the ages will return to us without a little struggling and perhaps, in some quarters, a little reluctance. It is natural for rulers and popular majorities to wish to suppress those who say unacceptable things. But centuries of experience have taught us as a people that the moment one yields to this kind of instinct trouble begins for everyone. Start silencing or imprisoning someone merely because you feel angry with him, and you end by getting knocked down or imprisoned yourself because somebody who dislikes your viewpoint is stronger or more popular than you. It is wholly contrary to our tradition of freedom to gag the objector. In ordinary times objection is, indeed, the very salt of English political life. Even in extraordinary ones like the present, it is best to ignore it—the classic English response to wrong-headed criticism—so long as it does not endanger the State. We have a tradition very precious to preserve and keep alive in a violent world. The old Adam in all of us that wants to suppress what it hates to hear, is too strong, even in free England, to be given a temporary licence. The price of liberty, it has been said, is eternal vigilance.

No British society worth the name will ever endure which does not preserve the right of every Briton to criticise and, within the limits of legitimate criticism, to oppose the Government. This is a maxim which all would-be planners and reformers will have to bear in mind, whatever the shape of their fine New Order to come. When a free parliament was restored to the English people after the iron tyranny of Cromwell's Saints and Major-Generals, a wise statesman said it was as natural to them as food and raiment and that Englishmen without Parliament were like creatures without their proper air. This instinctive feeling for parliamentary institutions is partly the result of long usage, but it also arises, like Parliament itself, out of a fundamental trait in our national character. Englishmen make their own parliaments wherever they are; there is a parliament in permanent session in every pub, just as Westminster Abbey is the national parish church. The popular English resistance to the more extreme temperance reformer did not arise out of any approval of drunkenness and its squalid accompaniments, but from a deep-seated instinct that the ale-house bar was the forum of a free people, and that when tongues were loosened and familiars brought face to face in regular fellowship, tyranny and repression could not flourish. It explains why G. K. Chesterton, the great man who wrote this page before the present writer, named his epic of English freedom

"The Flying Inn". And when Hitler's final history is written, it will be found that his doom was fixed on the day that the average company in the average English pub decided the fellow had gone too far and had got to be stopped.

* * *

III

The Rock of Human Nature[1]

"O brave new world," cried Shakespeare's Miranda, "that has such people in't." Is it, she might have asked, the world that makes the people or the people who make the world? The question is not academic. For it concerns our plans for reconstructing our broken planet when the hurly-burly is over. It affects us directly and materially. Philosophically, the answer, of course, is both. A decent world makes decent men and women. And decent men and women make a decent world. And if the latter be true what are we to say of the men and women who made the unjust, crazy, tyrannical, hate-ridden world we live in today? Why should we suppose that when the nightmare we have created on earth comes to an end, we shall do any better with the next chance? For unless we suffer a notable change, those of us who survive will still be the same men and women.

As the world will not grow better of itself, it is up to us, as individual men and women, to make it so. The planner alone cannot make it for us. "Give us the tools," said Mr. Churchill, "and we will finish the job." But when that particular job—that of freeing the nations from the menace of the Teutonic lust for power—is done, another as great will remain. Those who take from tired hands the task of social reconstruction, will also need the tools to finish the job. Those tools are men and women. They are you and I and every man. If they are cruel, greedy, filled with hate and blind to the sufferings of their fellow-creatures, the new world will be like the old. It will be worse if men are more of these things, and better if they are less. World improvement or deterioration will vary in precise ratio to human improvement

[1] *I.L.N.* 20 December 1941.

or deterioration. It is impossible to escape this natural law, which
works with the inevitability of a mathematical proposition. A
slum is bad for mankind, not merely because it makes its dwellers
uncomfortable, but because it tends to breed bad men. The man
who by greed or selfish laziness makes a slum is helping to make
other men, living and unborn, as greedy or lazy as himself. The first
step to abolishing slums is the self-improvement of the individual:
that is, of ourselves. I cannot see how any scheme of reconstruction
can succeed unless men and women reconstruct themselves.
Otherwise it will break down on the old rock of human nature.
Men will be persecuted because other men who happen to have
power allow themselves to hate those who disagree with them.
Men will be poor and wretched because other men are thought-
less, selfish and idle. Apply the test to Communism, Capitalism,
Fascism, or any other "ism", and the same truth remains. Apply
it to democracy; it still remains, and, turn as we may with our
theorising, we can no more escape it than a mouse can his tail.
Therefore, if we deplore persecution and blame Hitler and his
horrible New Order for it, we have got to rule out hatred and
intolerance from our own hearts. If we deplore waste and poverty
and the human suffering which springs from these things, we have
got to keep watch on our own idleness and selfishness and use
every hour of our day to leave our little corner of the world
better and richer than we found it. There will be no brave new
world for any of us without hard work, not by the State—which
cannot work of itself—but by the citizens who comprise it.
Without their efforts the State is only a façade—an elaborate
stage-effect, like Hitler's New Order, with nothing behind but
graft, corruption and injustice.

We take pride in the thought that we are a democracy. It is not
enough to be a democracy. The only democracy worth fighting
and living for is a good democracy: that is, a democracy of men
and women with standards. The real case for democracy is that
more than any other form of government it tends to foster the
development of such citizens. There is no virtue in numbers by
themselves. If there were, we should have to honour the Nazi
hordes who voted for and acclaim Hitler's evil actions. Ten
million men clamouring to kick a defenceless minority or remove

a neighbour's landmark are just as morally evil as one man doing so. And they are far more harmful.

If I were asked to define the virtues of a good citizen—the only kind of citizen who can bring about a good State and a better world—I would suggest that the attributes required are these. That he should be tolerant and kindly; that he should do to others as he would be done by; that he should scrupulously refrain from hatred and intemperance of speech as something that may injure his fellow-men; that he should speak the truth, and, without violence towards others, follow that which his conscience tells him is right, and be prepared to sacrifice himself for it, whether the world is with or against him. This is no easy precept, least of all in a half-educated democracy which inevitably, not knowing the premises, often jumps to wrong conclusions. Yet it is as well to remember that almost every form of humanitarian progress of which we are proud was due in the first place to the courage and resolution of some individual citizen—a Clarkson, a Shaftes-bury, a Plimsoll—who, seeing a great wrong, could not rest until he had done his best to right it. Above all, the good citizen is one who endeavours to put into the world more than he takes out of it. The young men who are giving their lives today that their country and civilisation may endure are giving so much more to society than society can give them that those of us who survive the war will owe it to them to serve the commonwealth in every way we can. Those individual virtues, which by and large are those of the Christian Church, are easy to state, hard to practise. But they are within the reach of every man; and if only enough of us can bring ourselves to observe them, we can look forward after the war to a better society than we have yet known, whatever outward form our new order takes. But if not, our brave new world will be no better than the old, and possibly a good deal worse.

CHAPTER 7

Back to Dear Old Blighty

"Take me back to dear old Blighty,
Put me on the train for London Town,
Take me over there, drop me anywhere,
Birmingham, Leeds or Manchester,
Well I don't care."

Popular Song of First World War

It was not to a brave New World that the Servicemen returned after 1945, but to what a popular song of the first World War called "dear old Blighty". Here, in the chronological order in which they appeared, are a few of my memories of the immediate post-war years.

"O, Listen to the Band" · The Gateway to Wales ·
"Champagne as much as the Sea" ·
The Mumbles Lifeboat · Pilgrimage to St. Andrews ·
In Darkest Kensington · London Clubs ·
St. George's Day in Purbeck

I

"O, Listen to the Band"[1]

In the old days—sadly tarnished by the erosion of the first German War and now almost totally obliterated by the devastation of the second—London was a city of pleasure. I suppose there are still young people who find it so today, though where in its shabby, paintless streets, its airless restaurants with austerity menus and impatient waiters, its non-stop buses and taxis, and its intermin-

---

[1] *Illustrated London News* 10 August 1946.

able preparatory-school taboos and restrictions, they succeed in finding such pleasure, only the very young in heart—who will always somehow find jewels in dustbins—can guess. But I and my generation are no longer young in heart; two world wars and their consequences have been too much for us. Like the old cars rattling and wheezing about the streets, the most we can hope to do is to keep going until a less-battered generation is ready to supplant us; the more glittering manifestations of pleasure are beyond us. Even the Proms, now held in the sound-deadening Nirvana of the Albert Hall, are thronged with ghosts; while the spick-and-span London of our youth, with its gleaming polish and hurdy-gurdy gaiety, constantly rises before our glazed eyes to reproach us as we shuffle down a seedy-looking Pall Mall or dodge between the cars at Hyde Park Corner. Lord's and the Oval themselves are mines whose rich treasures for us have been exhausted:

> For the fields are full of shades as I near the shadowy coast,
> And a ghostly batsman plays to the bowling of a ghost,
> And I look through my tears on a soundless-clapping host
> As the run-stealers flicker to and fro,
>   To and fro,
> O my Hornby and my Barlow long ago!

Yet there is one pleasure left to me in the summer London of 1946. It is to take my dog of an afternoon or evening and, crossing the Park amid a barrage of angry barking and crude canine insults hurled by my irrepressible companion at all and sundry—for, though biscuits are short and chocolates almost unobtainable, there is nothing old or tamed about his heart—make my way towards the bandstand. For here some beneficent public authority dispenses free music to the populace. And here once or twice a week, when my occasions permit, I sit, as a member of that sovereign body, and for a quarter of an hour listen to the band. By doing so I feel I am getting back some minute but comforting fraction of the money that the powers-that-be extract from my earnings. I am become for the moment a public beneficiary instead of a mere contributor. The enjoyment costs me nothing except twopence for the chair upon which I sit, and even then only when somebody takes the trouble to collect it.

The pleasure of listening to the band derives, I suppose, from several sources. It is only partly musical; for much of the fare provided seems scarcely music at all. It does not matter; so long as the sun is shining, the warm sheen on the faded chairs, the gleaming instruments and gay-shaped pavilion, the lovely green of the chestnuts and the contentment of the audience all provide pleasure enough. It is not, I admit, much fun for my dog whose musical and æsthetic faculties are negligible and whose only satisfaction during his enforced sojourn by the bandstand is to strain at his lead and bark at passing members of his species. On the other hand, there is for him the immense pleasure of leaving the place—a pleasure expressed so audibly that I can never depart before the end of a piece, even if it happens to be one I detest. Indeed, if I get away without being involved in a dog-fight, I count myself fortunate.

My fellow auditors—though auditors seems scarcely the right word—afford me particular enjoyment. They are so impervious to the world about them, so much creatures of the occasion, so firmly and stably seated on their ancient chairs of pleasure that I never cease to wonder at them. For them, as for me, in that escapist hour, the atom bomb, bread rationing, income tax, the omnipresent official form, the crowded train or bus, the thousand-and-one worries and frustrations of present-day life are non-existent. They are back, presumably, as I am myself, in the timeless world in which one visited the bandstand nearly half a century ago, with one's mother or nurse. Judging by the expressions—and these never betray the slightest sign of any musical appreciation or, indeed, of any awareness of the music at all—those around the bandstand fall into two categories. There are the quick and the dead. The former are family groups, lovers, newspaper-readers and relatives or friends of the performers. These carry on an animated and delicious social life of their own; replace, with proud and loving eyes, their young in the chairs or perambulators out of which they have noisily climbed or fallen; squeeze one another's hands, gaze into one another's eyes and titter over the absurd but infinitely exciting things which people in their happy state confide to one another; or make proprietary and unanswered signals to the patiently blowing artists on the bandstand. But the dead are, if possible. even more fascinating to watch. For they appear to be men and women in a trance: they sit gazing at the musical pavilion with unseeing eyes, half-open mouths and an air of motionless imperturbability. What is going on in their minds it is impossible to gauge. I am inclined to suspect nothing at all: that, in a world where the conscious is mostly pain, they have achieved complete unconsciousness:

> *We have triumphed: this achievement turns the bane to antidote,*
> *Unsuccesses to success,*
> *Many thought-worn eves and morrows to a morrow free of thought.*
> *No more need we corn and clothing, feel of cold terrestrial stress;*
> *Chill detraction stirs no sigh;*[1]

This, however, is no more than a surmise: their expressionless faces may only be a mask. They may be dreaming dreams and seeing visions: visions, perhaps—for they are mostly the old and faded—of a world where the band also played under the chestnuts in the Park, but where eyes—their eyes—were bright and full of hope, and life of grace and gaiety. I do not know, but hope it is so. Indeed it may be this—the accumulated atmosphere of it—which makes the bandstand such a delightful place.

All men, Wilde wrote, destroy the thing they love. I hope I have not done wrong in writing this and thereby imperilled my favourite metropolitan haunt in London. A little while ago I wrote of the satisfaction, not to say inspiration, I derived from watching the pre-matutinal bathers in the wintry Serpentine as I walked my dog beside its waters. Yet no sooner had my article appeared than barricades arose across the path by the lake; and it became no longer possible for me to take my morning walk there—a serious matter for me, for that particular path, having railings on one side and water on the other, was about the only place in London where I could let my pugnacious companion off the lead without his flying off at a tangent in pursuit of some other beast. Will the result of this essay be a further intervention by Authority to deny me my last remaining pleasure? Will the bandstand be dismembered or turned into an official dumping-ground for unwanted war material like the delightful and once-

[1] T. Hardy, 'Friends Beyond': *Collected Poems*, p. 53. Macmillan.

public footpath-tunnels under the Serpentine bridge, the chestnuts be felled, the instrumentalists be expelled for ever from the garden by a high civil servant with a flaming statutory order?[1] If so, it will be my own fault, and will serve me right. However, for the moment, the honest lads in their gay uniforms from musical colliery or northern works are still with us, the summer sun is still—occasionally—shining, and the chairs are only twopence. The brass has struck up "The Bee's Wedding", the stolid but soulful gentleman at the piano is waiting to give his rendering of the "Warsaw Concerto", and the ticket-collector is making his circle of the sunlit, empty chairs. And "O, listen to the band!"

* * *

II

The Gateway to Wales[2]

We slipped away from the old grey house on the Cotswold uplands in the latter part of the morning. There was so much work to be collected, so many things to be fitted into the car and so much delay caused by an excited terrier who, in his anxiety not to be left behind, would sit desperately on everything that had to be loaded, that the first flower of the day was gone before we climbed out of the little valley and saw the tangled Stonesfield roofs of the seventeenth century homestead[3] vanish into the mists. The clouds, which all this summer have made it their rallying-ground, going out from our high woodlands to drench the neighbouring counties and then returning as if to their home, were already gathering for some new atrocious act of aqueous aggression. We sped under them before they could break and subject us to the usual soaking, and then, gliding between battered fields of barley and the high, blowing grasses of the uplands, came to the great road the Romans built to bridge the hills. It was the first time we had taken a holiday since the war, and, as we opened out the engine,

---

[1] This has since happened.
[2] *I.L.N.* 14 September 1946.
[3] In the wooded Cotswolds north of Cirencester where, whenever I could escape from London, I lived in the immediate post-war years until my return to Dorset in 1948

our hearts began to sing and the dog to bark. For six days we knew the telephone could not ring, for where we were going there would be no telephone, and we, the world forgetting, would be by the world forgot. And one of us had the excitement of going to scenes wholly unfamiliar and the other to scenes once dearly familiar, though long unvisited.

The view from Birdlip was hidden in mist; the serried ranks of the far hills through which we were to pass were still unseen. The last Stonesfield roof fell away behind us as we ran off the wooded slopes, while the road gathered the raw debris of modern industrial development around it. The environs of Gloucester vividly contrasted the products of the age of Faith with those of the age of Frustration; on the one hand, the tower of that glorious cathedral, aerial in a slant of pale light from the heavens to which it half-belonged; on the other, a clutter of mean, shabby, industrial dwellings which recalled Burke's dictum that "to make men love their country, one must make their country lovely." I do not know what are the politics of the poorer inhabitants of modern Gloucester, but, if they are friendly to established wealth and order, they must have more than the ordinary share of human patience. My eye travelled again to the tower of the cathedral. The men who built it knew more of the nature of man and of the architecture of human society than we.

Then we crossed the Severn and were in another land. West of the river those who in the last two decades have levelled half England's trees seemed to have stayed their hand; as Gloucestershire merged into Herefordshire, the landscape was still almost as Cobbett and Constable knew it, with timbered cottages and mellow red-brick houses set amid cohorts of noble trees. The day seemed to be lightening and the sky growing more lofty, and from the higher points of our route we could catch glimpses to the west of soft blue hills whose spaciousness held a hint of mountains behind.

We did not anticipate our pleasures, but ran mostly to the northward fringing the outposts of Wales with Shropshire still before us. We crossed the border into that richly satisfying shire a mile or two south of the Teme. Ten minutes later we were climbing the steep ascent of Ludlow, with the castle of Milton's

Comus on our left and the high-reared head of Clee on our right. Lunch at Ludlow on an August Sunday in 1946 was as unobtainable as coal at Christmas, but a few miles on, in a Victorian redbrick hotel, we found, after a little preliminary hesitation on the part of the management, an excellent meal served by a friendly and capable woman dressed—shades of 1900 and the prim Sabbath Shropshire of my youth!—in mechanic's overalls. Yet neither her manners nor her face were the worse for that, and, like the other passing inmates of her house, we blessed her.

The dog was barking when we came out, and, having comforted him, we turned the silver nose of the car westwards. The tree between Craven Arms and Clun, which I first saw bedecked with flags a generation ago, still carried its bright, if faded, pageantry of bunting against a green background of foliage, and the wooded hills of that quiet valley, though a little denuded in places, still wore their ancient beauty. Clun was as sleepy as ever; from the appearance of its winding street, Victoria might still have been on the throne and the long English security of the nineteenth century unbroken. As we left it and turned to the high hills, we saw our first mountain river. Ten miles on, we were in Wales, and fifteen hundred feet above the sea.

The Fates were very kind that day. Behind, England was still in cloud. But, though the alien softwood trees of a State department had already half-obscured the noblest view in the Marches, we could see from the left of the road, untroubled as yet by the Forestry Commission, the whole mountain range from Cader Idris to the Berwyns, with Snowdon's peak untouched by cloud. Between us and them, fifty miles away, stretched the green vales of central Wales, a patchwork of emerald and gold, with white clouds casting transient shadows on sunlit fields. I know no view so uplifting. For more than an hour we stayed taking it in, while our dog sought for invisible rabbits among the peat and rushes of that high, pure place.

We were thirty miles inside Wales when we stopped again. A notice-board outside the wooded drive of a private hotel arrested us; we looked at each other, decided to chance it, and a minute later were enquiring in a cool, tranquil country house whether we could be given tea. Outside was a lawn, a waterfall and, beyond woods, a green hillside. To our amazement, we were not turned away, but welcomed with open arms, the proprietor, recently returned from the Forces to make this new venture in the ancient and almost forgotten art of quiet hospitality, waiting on us himself. We found ourselves sitting in a framed window, bathed in sunshine, in a room panelled from floor to ceiling in early-seventeenth century oak, with the benison of generations of peace about it. We lingered there so long that the valley road before us was bathed in the vivid green of a Welsh summer evening when we drove westwards again.

Presently we turned into the north, past white-washed cottages nestling under mountains. Wordsworth's eternal lights and shades marched and counter-marched upon the hills in glorious apparition, and half-a-dozen steaming, boiling charabancs from Birmingham panting up the pass could not disturb the quiet of Dinas Mawddy. As we reached the summit, we saw couched on the skyline between Cader and the Rhinogs a bowl of gleaming gold. It was the sea, twenty miles away, beyond the bar at Barmouth. An hour later we were sitting in the parlour of an old Welsh farmhouse, with the unbroken culture of a thousand years about us. Behind us were the mountains, around us mountain ash and the sound of running water, and before us the western sea and the great sweep of Caernarvon Bay—

the olden, the golden sea of Wales
Where the first star shivers and the last wave pales.

Next morning the present with its familiar frustrations returned. The clouds regathered, the Army occupied the beach, the sound of gunfire resounded all day in the hills. But for a few hours at least, we had revisited the land of lost content, regaining something of the birthright of beauty and quiet which during the past seven years warring nations have done so much to destroy.

*   *   *

III

"Champagne as much as the Sea"[1]

This morning my eye fell on a headline which sounded like something out of the bad old past—from the days when the Prince Regent revelled with Lady Hertford in the Brighton Pavilion or the gilded youth of the 'sixties pledged Cora Pearl in the shoes of the ladies of the ballet. "Champagne," it read, "as much as the Sea." On studying the passage I found it referred, not to the pages of history nor to the democratic hospitalities of the Kremlin, but to the current voyage of an austerity Britain's greatest pride, the Britain-can-make-it ship, the *Queen Elizabeth*. And it was one of our leading actresses speaking—speaking over the telephone, which most of us find so difficult to get installed in our humbler homes or offices but which is apparently available for all in the *Queen Elizabeth*. "Champagne?" she said to an enquiring reporter, "There is as much of it as the sea."

Now the interesting thing about this passage, which commanded headlines on the front page of my newspaper, is that it was obviously not inserted with the idea of arousing envy, hatred or disgust among its readers, few of whom can even procure enough pallid beer or watery milk, let alone champagne, for their modest needs. It was put there with a quite different object: to give pleasure and satisfaction. Judging by the number of similar references in the Press during the past week to the sumptuous delights of the *Queen Elizabeth*—"gay and opulent with the warm extravagance of a liner's luxury" was one description—the democratic public loves nothing better. Those who write and edit our newspapers know their business; they may not perhaps do much to elevate the public taste, but they certainly cater for it, such as it is. And the public likes to be told about the goings-on of the very rich. Only to please it nowadays they apparently have to be very, very rich. Feudal dukes, farm-busy country squires, the smaller and more respectable type of industrialist or merchant, well-to-do old ladies living on dividends in old-fashioned mansions in South Kensington, aren't good enough, as they were in

<hr/>

[1] *I.L.N.* 2 November 1946.

the days of our less fastidious parents. They are the enemies, it would seem, of democracy. But the kind who can afford to travel in the *Queen Elizabeth* or fly in luxury air-liners across the Atlantic are in a different category. For them nothing is too good; thousands of workmen can be deflected for months from making household fittings of a humbler kind, hundreds of acres of urgently needed agricultural land can be hastily concreted for their aerial occasions, even ancient and inhabited villages destroyed to serve their overriding travel needs without anyone, not even Communists, so much as whimpering a protest. Does not that great patron saint of Communists all the world over, good Mr. Molotov himself, travel by the *Queen Elizabeth*, guarded by armed detectives against the homicidal tendencies of his fellow-voyagers and, presumably, enjoying the democratic fare so lavishly provided? What, one wonders, can be the meaning of it all. For back here, on the common level of everyday life, most of us, though we come of an unenvying race, are so frustrated for lack of common necessities—adequate housing, decent clothes, palatable and sufficient food—that we are inclined to be resentful about anyone who appears to be the least bit better-off than ourselves. We think—and sometimes even speak—of such, however unjustly, as profiteers and parasites, unworthy comrades who have dodged the column or jumped the queue. But not so with these far-off and glittering ones in the luxury liner or transatlantic clipper. They have outsoared the shadow of our night. They are like the fabulous beings from sunny Hollywood whom we gloat over in the cinema and whom common want or need can never touch. One does not envy one's gods. One merely worships them in their felicity.

One explanation which I have seen advanced is that this carefree, materially magnificent life of the very rich symbolises and is a heartening forecast of our own common future. The charming actress, in the interview referred to, gave expression to it; the atmosphere in the liner, she explained, was solemn, homely and dignified, "as if all the passengers were grateful for this wonderful glimpse into the future". But, though such hopes may animate the bosoms of the favoured few aboard the ship, I doubt whether they have any solid existence in the somewhat harassed mind of the common man or woman ashore. Most of us have about as much chance of travelling first-class in the *Queen Elizabeth* as of living in the Kremlin or Vatican. Our admiration and affection for the favoured creatures aboard is founded on some other feeling. And I am inclined to think it is the feeling, common to men and women in all ages, of admiration for success. The very rich are successful: they are the embodiment of our own most wishful dreams. For all our pretended passion for equality, we nearly all of us would like to achieve something far surpassing our own and the common lot. We may not any longer want to be a duchess or even a wealthy Kensington householder. But wouldn't we like to be Barbara Hutton or Betty Grable!

It would be idle to quarrel with this apparently ineradicable strain in human nature; in its unenvying adoration of a lot far out of its reach there is something rather touching. It may be silly, but it must be a very sour nature to whom it is wholly repugnant. It is an instinct, too, which, rightly directed, has often been instrumental in furthering human progress; some of the greatest and most enduring achievements of mankind have been fostered and supported by the existence of aristocracies— Chaucer's poetry, Michelangelo's paintings, Mozart's music. For aristocracies, whatever form they take, exist by virtue of this feeling.

What is disquieting about the present manifestation of this vicarious admiration is its rather uncritically materialistic direction. The spectacle of modern cosmopolitan millionaires in the mass does not inspire social confidence: they so often tend to be financial manipulators rather than producers, speculators rather than creators. Eighteenth century landowners and nineteenth century industrialists may have had their faults, but on the whole their aggrandisement and enrichment and the improvement of the world's material lot tended to go hand-in-hand. They got, indubitably, a great deal more than their fair share of the good things going, but they at least helped to get them made. One can't help wondering how under our present system of taxation any man can grow rich—or at any rate rich enough to excite our fastidious admiration—by any process of stable production. For the profits of such production, however great, are soon taken away by the State. One is left with an uneasy suspicion that the surest, even sole, road to wealth and influence today is the untaxed capital appreciation which comes from successful speculation in land, currency or commodity values—activities which may vary the distribution of human wealth, but seldom do much to increase it.

*   *   *

IV

The Mumbles Lifeboat[1]

On St. George's Day, 1947, William Howell, of the Mumbles lifeboat, together with seven other brave and devoted men, lost his life trying to save the lives of the crew of the steamer, *Samtampa*, in a storm off Porthcawl beach. He had himself suffered shipwreck after being torpedoed during the war and was implored by his relations and friends not to go out. His reply, like his action, is deserving of immortality. "I must go," he said, "they came to me when I was shipwrecked, and I cannot leave them out there." Another of the lifeboat's crew, Richard Smith—a thirty-five-year-old man who had just been demobilised—was to have been married two days later. He also, like his comrades, refused to allow any personal consideration to stand between him and the fulfilment of duty.

It is by such grandeur of spirit that a nation lives. These men were united in fidelity to their duty towards their fellow-men. Their action spoke, with an eloquence which no words could equal, for England, or, rather, for the spirit which the word England at its best stands for. They were animated, not by hatred or self-seeking, but by love, one without exclusion or exception at the service of all mankind. They did not ask whether those whom they died to save were politically or ideologically worthy of their sacrifice, whether they were richer than themselves or poorer, whether they were Britons or men of another race, whether they were brown or white, whether their shirts

[1] *I.L.N.* 10 May 1947.

were black or red. It was enough that they were fellow-creatures in need of succour. In doing so they followed, consciously or unconsciously, in the steps of the Founder of the Christian Faith. They made the name of their country glorious throughout the world and left to those who come after an inspiration and a faith.

Men who die thus, like those who died in the war, recall us to a remembrance of our duty. It is to serve England—the ideal for which they gave " the last full measure of devotion"—with heart, mind and body. Those who do that can have no quarrel with those equally ready to serve her. The bitterness and faction of so much of our political and economic life today scarcely bears scrutiny in the light of the selfless unity of the men of the Mumbles lifeboat. It is explicable only in the light of the weariness, malnutrition and nervous strain that so many are suffering at the present time. They explain our pettiness and ill-temper, but they do not excuse it. For, if we throw our minds back a year or two, there is so much to remind us of the bonds which bind us. The empty places in our midst should serve to reunite us. For unless we work together in brotherhood to solve the problems of peace as we worked to solve those of war, those who died will have died in vain.

In a democratic and parliamentary country it is right that we should dispute as to policies and ways and means. But when our whole existence as a nation and its contribution to the world depend on our united efforts to reconstruct a war-eroded economy, it seems suicidal to ascribe to one another base motives or label with opprobrious terms those who, in all sincerity, disagree with us. I am no Socialist, but every British Socialist is my countryman, and so is every British Liberal and Conservative. They were my countrymen during the blitz and on D-Day, without distinction of class, calling or viewpoint, and they are my countrymen today. If I disagree with their politics, it is still my duty at such a time as this to exercise restraint and forbearance in what I say or write about them. It may be my duty as a voter and citizen to expose the fallacy of their opinions, but it is also my duty to respect the feelings and dignity of those who express such opinions. For if I taunt, abuse or insult them, I create, not unity among Britons, but division and hatred. And that, in our present situation, though few seem to be conscious of it, is a kind of betrayal. By rocking a boat in rough water, one imperils the boat. And we are all in that boat.

After the last war we went through a period of similar bitterness and class division. At that time, though we could afford it more readily than today, it imperilled our victory and what we had fought for. That it did not bring us to civil war, as at one moment it threatened to do, or to a bitterness and division so great that we should ultimately have gone the way of France in 1940, we owe, in my belief, largely to the precept and example of one man, Stanley Baldwin. It is not fashionable to praise that statesman today, but, as many a member even of the Party which opposed him in politics knows and privately acknowledges, more than any other man in the post-war 'twenties he took the bitterness out of British public life. Whatever may be said against his foreign policy or lack of it, it will be for that achievement he will be judged by history. "No gospel founded on hate," he said in 1922, "will ever seize the hearts of our people—the people of Great Britain. It is no good trying to cure the world by spreading out oceans of bloodshed. . . . Four words, of one syllable each, are words which contain salvation for this country and for the whole world, and they are 'Faith', 'Hope', 'Love' and 'Work'. No Government in this country today, which has not faith in the people, hope in the future, love for its fellow-men, and which will not work and work and work, will ever bring this country through into better days and better times, or will ever bring Europe through or the world through."

*　　*　　*

V

Pilgrimage to St. Andrews[1]

My visits to Scotland—that proud, fierce, hospitable land from which I often receive indignant letters protesting at my occasional use of the forbidden word "England"[2]—have been, to my shame, very rare. During the war my occasions took me to Scotland three or four times, but even these visits enabled me to see little of the country: the night train to Edinburgh or Glasgow, a glimpse of the passing landscape through the windows of a naval car, a few hours flying over cloud-misted acres of forest and mountain or along grey, rocky shores, days among the islands of the north too crowded to see anything outside the confines of the camp or anchorage to which my visit was confined. But twice since the war the generous hospitality of a northern University has called me across the Border as a free man to receive an Honorary Degree.

Sleepers, grateful though I am for their relief, are wasted on me, for I seldom manage to sleep in them. No sooner have I got used to the rocking, jolting and noise and composed my restless thoughts into drowsy quietude than the train stops and I immediately awake. Just as I am once more dragging myself up the elusive ramparts of sleep, it starts again and I become more wakeful than ever. After three or four hours I generally give up the idea of sleep and settle down to work, grateful at least to be lying on my back in the privacy of a well-upholstered cell. So it happened on this occasion that I saw not only Durham Cathedral in the October moonlight and the lights of unsleeping collieries, but was awake when the train crossed the Border and saw the dawn come up over Berwick and the sea. It is a noble and ample gateway, worthy even of a kingdom so rich in noble prospects as Scotland. The air, as the northern air always seems to be, was full of invisible music;

---

[1] *I.L.N.* 25 October 1947.
[2] "I console myself by recalling that Sir Walter Scott used it in the same context. Four fifths of our island's population are English, and they have a right to their name."

music born of courage and knuckle-bone hardihood, of purity and
of a kind of eternal youth which springs from the rocky soil of
this ancient northern land and gives her sons and daughters their
vigour. For a few blissful minutes, as the train sped beside the
road that Cromwell and many another long-suffering English
invader had laboriously travelled, it even lulled me into something near sleep.

Edinburgh never fails to astonish and delight. No other city
receives a train into its bosom in so dramatic a manner. At one
moment one is looking at the outline of rocky hills that might be
fringing Sinai; at the next one is in a great smoky chasm, peering
up at the gigantic outlines of what appear to be two separate and
sky-towering cities, one on either side of one, out-topping Babel
in fabulous silhouette. One ascends from the station to the outer
or, rather, upper world by a series of lifts and tunnels, broken by
occasional caverns, emerging at the end through a vast revolving
glass door on to the splendour of Princes Street. This is not quite
correct, for it is not Princes Street itself that is so splendid, but
what one sees from Princes Street. For there, silhouetted against
the sky and adjacent mountains—if mountains they are and not
merely titanic pieces of stage property erected a century-and-a-
quarter ago by Sir Walter Scott—is the majestic and haunting
vision of Auld Reekie. No Reinhardt, dreaming of a back-curtain
for some superlative performance of *Die Walkürie*, could have
conceived a more majestic and fantastic setting. It is almost like
a blow across the eyes: a violent and magnificent repudiation of
the conventional idea of the sober, matter-of-fact, prudent Scottish
lowland character, so well, if a little drably, represented by the
average Scots lowland town. For there is nothing drab or prosaic
or matter-of-fact about the skyline of Edinburgh; it is as daring
and romantic and wildly improbable as an Elizabethan voyage
or a Chesterton novel. And this is equally true whether it is seen
from the windy, tram-littered promenade of Princes Street or
from across the Forth or from the Lammermuir hills. Of all the
cities I have seen, Edinburgh is a challenge to unadventurous
living and an appeal to all that is imaginative, unresting and
heroic in men.

Perhaps it is because I have never been able to stay there for

more than a few hours that I feel this.[1] On this occasion I had only
minutes in which to gaze at the shadowy outline of the mediaeval
roofs and pinnacles silhouetted against Arthur's Seat. Then,
having eaten a hurried breakfast in that vast, mysterious and
wonderful hotel, I again descended through caverns and tunnels
to the station. The keen, friendly eyes, rosy cheeks and busy
vigour, and good manners, of the crowds on the platform contrasted strangely with the strained, pinched, undernourished
countenances and nervy, short-tempered ways of war-battered,
weary, shabby 1947 London. Soon my train was gliding through
suburbs and gardens and little fields towards the north, running
along the southern shores of the Forth towards the great bridge
that spans it. Remembering the naval bustle of the war years and
comparing with it the solitary aircraft-carrier now anchored in
paintless dereliction below the bridge, I could not help reflecting
on how quickly Britain discards her armour when victory has
been won.

Yet there is something greater than the ships which ride the sea;
there is the sea itself. All through the busy landscape of Fife, half-
rural, half-industrial, it was never far away. At one moment it
was lapping—grey, imperturbable—at the foot of the railway
embankment; at another it was invisible, but still palpably
present a few miles away beyond the low-cambered, green fields.
One thinks of England as a land wedded to the sea, but Scotland
is almost part of the sea itself. Its very breath is of gulls and fish.

Presently the train bore me to the little grey university city
which was my journey's end. I glanced up from my writing and
suddenly saw it, and the sight—so strange, so un-English—almost
made my heart stop. There were the green and low sandy links,
the most famous in the world; there the eternal sea; there, rising
out of green and grey, the resolute, towered town, defying time,
tide and tribulation. As many another man must have done, I
fell in love with it at first sight, and every hour I spent there made
me love it more; the cold gentle wind that ruffled the trees in the

---

[1] "Since writing this I have been privileged on several occasions to stay at Holyrood-
house during the General Assembly of the Church of Scotland—and once was even
called upon to address that formidable and historic body—and I now feel Edinburgh's
magic even more strongly."

streets; the ancient houses lit by lamplight, standing valiant, uncompromising and four-square as John Knox himself; the sculptured archways and towers reaching back through Renaissance and Middle Ages to the first Christian missionaries; the scarlet gowns making their brave show against the grey and green. And it was not only the living of whom I found myself made company in that place; of the valiant youth—now, its sword laid aside, *in statu pupillaris*—who had lately made the name of Scotland honoured and feared in every land from Alamein to Lübeck, from the Chindwin to Ultima Thule. Here, too, was the invisible legion of all who had fought and wrought and studied throughout the ages to make Scotland a by-word for courage, learning, wise frugality, hard work and sanity: virtues which have charted civilisation on its voyage through the storms of the past and can still chart it through the troubled seas of the present.

> *St. Andrews by the northern sea:*
> *A haunted town it is to me!*

* * *

VI

In Darkest Kensington[1]

Often, in the course of my work, I have occasion to walk through darkest Kensington. The great houses built by the Forsytes a hundred years ago rise in long cliffs on either side of the monotonous pavements, their unpainted surfaces peeling scabrously and their vast Italianate lower windows staring uncurtained on unfenced, neglected gardens. There was a time when the guns thundered nightly and the skies above them were pierced by shifting arrows of light; then the houses were empty of all but shaken ghosts. But now, at least in the daytime and in official office hours, they teem with living occupants. Even in their richest days, in the golden, curtained, gas-lit past, when they were staffed by a dozen housemaids, a butler, a boots and a brace of footmen apiece, and when even the wealthiest families were raised

[1] *I.L.N.* 8 Jan. 1949.

in decimals on a patriarchal system, they cannot have had half as many occupants as they boast today between the hours of nine and five. For Officialdom has fastened its tentacles on Kensington, which must now rank with Llandudno and Bath as the mightiest of Whitehall's suburbs. In every house, as the winter twilight draws on, the windows blaze with unshaded electric lights, and shabby clerks and typists, and scarcely less shabby porters and messengers in official uniform, shuffle to and fro with pots of tea. As they pass one another they sometimes smile wanly or exchange looks of recognition and, in this Christmas season, crack little jokes, for humanity will take root and blossom somehow in the barest crevices. Here is the great brain, or, to be more precise—for the brain is in Whitehall—the great hindquarters of modern British democracy, sitting massively on the unborn Britain of the future. More clearly than by any statistics showing that one out of every ten wage-earners is now a Government clerk checking up on the others—or whatever the correct figure may be—the titanic scale of our bureaucracy can be realised by a casual walk through once residential Kensington. It is like the sight of the Grand Fleet steaming out of Scapa in the first World War or the starry, throbbing gonfalons of Bomber Command passing over-head in the last—something which impresses the mind, and more than the mind, with the sense of an all-pervading, unchallenge-able phenomenon. Here is a hundred years of radical political endeavour made manifest. Here, as big and clear as the Devil's hoofmark on the downs and heathlands of legend, is the seal and stamp of the Fabians on history. The pale bookworms have triumphed; pallid and spectacled like them, we are all clerking or clerked upon today.

"And what good came of it all?" asked little Peterkin. A famous victory it certainly was; the massed phalanx of rich Victorian individualists who half a century ago, with their prudent wives and rentier cousins and aunts and their frock-coated and lace-capped retainers, inhabited these mansions, are today as though they had never been, their tax-doomed and attenuated descendants directed into factories or enrolled, like miserable Starkey among the Indians, in the ranks of the clocking-in, tea-drinking clerks. In my own brief lifetime I have seen the army of the vanquished

Forsytes in all its strength and glory, have heard the tinkle of its delicate, massed tea-cups, and seen the broughams and victorias assembled in their proud hundreds in Prince's and Queen's Gate, and now, still apparently the same person, see the barbarians solidly encamped among their sacred shrines and temples. The victory is complete and overwhelming; any return of those who a few decades ago owned the earth is utterly unthinkable. The negative side of the triumph is obvious, but what of the positive? Who owns the earth now, the glory and fullness of it? Or have the glory and fullness vanished with the vanquished? And, if so, what real purpose has the victory served?

For men and women are flesh and blood, with the pride and fire of flesh and blood, and cannot be content with a paper kingdom alone. Nature abhors a vacuum, and, unless the triumphant army of the clerkly can create a real kingdom of men in the place of that which they have destroyed, their triumph, for all their present apparent power, will inevitably be short-lived. Some new destroyer and conqueror, impelled by the returning surge of human hopes and aspirations, will pour over Kensington and many another place and expel the sterile clerks and counters. Their realm is too colourless, too bloodless to endure. A saucerless cup of tea and a filing-cabinet are not enough. Humanity will demand some more alluring symbol; the trumpet and tucket will sound once more, and the human multitude, glorious and absurd with banners, will set off on the march again towards the unattainable illusion, scattering the clerks and their fluttering pieces of paper into oblivion.

For, though the Fabians have accomplished much, they have not satisfied the soul of man. Thanks to their patient and methodical resolve, the worst of the horrors and black reverse of the Victorian individualists' brassy kingdom have been eliminated or, at any rate, brought under rational control. The squalid drunks no longer dance and fight outside the gin palaces on Saturday nights, the ragged sweepers and homeless waifs from the slums and back-alleys no longer flit like shadows under the varnished, unscalable area railings and tightly closed front doors, the processions of pallid, desperate unemployed no longer struggle with truncheoned policemen at the Park gates. The poor are better

clad, better educated and infinitely better cared for in sickness and
adversity than they were when I was a boy. But they are no longer
on the march. They are listless and waiting, unless my reading of
my contemporaries' hearts and minds is at fault, for something
that will fire their enthusiasm and satisfy their inexpungeable
desire for the illusion and grandeur of this imperfect, ever restless
world. In the meantime they crowd in their millions into the
picture-houses to gape at the celluloid ghosts of a synthetic
romance, or, deaf to the appeals of their political leaders, shower
the potential savings with which our corrective fiscal and administrative system—at such an enormous expense of actuarial
labour—endows them, into the pockets of pool-promoters, wide-
boys and gambling emperors. And while they do so, purposeless
and spiritually sick, the great governing army of the clerks, as
listless as they, count and recount, enquire and record, measure
the measureless and painfully number the dust of a community
growing ever more eroded for lack of faith and purpose. For all
this counting and checking up on other people's activities is not
performing the only function that ultimately justifies and
redeems the constraint of man by man—the harnessing of human
energies to creative and, therefore, satisfying and ennobling
purposes. It is creating neither spiritual nor material wealth,
and, with a dwindling and now almost extinct culture, is merely
living, on the crumbling wealth of a creative past, just as it half
inhabits, for the sterile purpose of counting, these empty husks
of what were once human habitations. Because of this, for all its
designers' good intentions, it cannot hope to endure. Over the
great houses in Kensington I can still see, caught in the gleam of
the pallid winter afternoon's sunrays, the sinister inscription:
"Mene, mene, tekel, upharsin." "God hath numbered the kingdom
and finished it. Thou art weighed in the balances and found want-
ing. Thy kingdom is divided, and given to the Medes and Persians."
In fifty years' time the power and presence of their present con-
trollers will be as much a thing of the past as their predecessors'.
For the manner of this world changes, and, whatever form the
next revolution in this country takes, it will be no stranger than
that which I have seen in my lifetime.

* * *

VII

London Clubs[1]

All along either side of Pall Mall, up St. James's Street and scattered about the northern escarpment of Piccadilly, are the historic clubs of London. They belong to a world that has gone, but, by a strange paradox, they have probably never been so full and so much used as they are today. This is natural, for they are among the last strongholds of dignity and spacious comfort surviving in England, and there are still tens of thousands of Englishmen who, having grown accustomed to dignity and this kind of comfort in their happier youth and middle age, cling to what vestiges of it remain. Whenever they can, they slip away from the crowded prison and the tumbril, and, momentarily forgetting the revolution through which they have passed, glide through the great glass and mahogany portals and disappear into the quiet, nostalgic fragrance within. No inspector or tax-gatherer follows them; no wireless blares or politician bawls; the sounds of the outer world are respectfully deadened, and the sights of it, glimpsed through the huge, aloof, plate-glass windows, are telescoped into a kind of remote distance. There are no chores to do, no jaded, resentful wives with armfuls of dirty plates, no shoes to clean, no boiler to light, no milk bottles to carry, no baker's boy to let in, no cat to put out. Mrs. Miniver's husband has for a moment got right away. Here are colonels and high Civil Servants, learned doctors and men about town, landowners from the shires and sportsmen from the happy hunting-grounds of memory, moving in leisured state about princely rooms where no dis-respectful word has been uttered or menial task been performed—except by those paid to do them—since their first construction when George III or William IV or the young Victoria was on the throne. Here, in the world of Molotov and Aneurin Bevan—whom, now I come to recall it, I have sometimes seen, an honoured guest and here much resembling a Roman senator, peacefully and harmlessly browsing in one of these paradises—are ivory towers

[1] *I.L.N.* 19 March 1949.

for the males of the once ruling class. Even the prices, toned down by substantial annual subscriptions and entrance fees, are reminiscent of the carefree past. It is surprising that, once inside them, their inmates ever depart. They have every incentive, one would have thought—except the irrational desire for female company—to remain perpetually inside.

It is difficult to define exactly in what the charm of such places resides. I think it is principally in their atmosphere. Their carpets may not be as thick, their lights as glittering, their food as rich, their liveried servants as numerous as those of the more luxurious kind of hotel, but they are infinitely more imposing. They have been the sheltered abodes of men of polished dignity and assurance for so long that it is almost impossible for anyone entering them to behave in a manner inappropriate to them. They impress themselves on their inmates like the interiors of Gothic cathedrals. They resemble the sanctums of archbishops or those of the more rarefied kind of commissar. As such they cannot be shouted in or whistled in or treated in any way but that of respect. They command instantaneous and instinctive obedience to their unspoken conventions and give out, as automatically, the strength and assurance which derive from an unalterable and ordered fellowship. I know of nowhere, not even the officers' mess of a great regiment, where the secret power of England is so clearly revealed. Hitler, who never entered one of these ancient temples, had already—though he knew it not—met his doom in them before he crossed his Polish Rubicon. The English, in their aggregate and silent disapproval, are a dangerous lot.

It is curious to think that a few years ago these great rooms rocked and trembled to the crashing of bombs and the staccato fury of guns. I remember taking lunch in one of them—a military and naval establishment—during the flying-bomb summer, when nearly everyone responsible for directing Britain's war effort, except those already in Normandy, seemed to be eating at the same moment in the room. No one took the slightest notice of the chugging and whistling overhead or of the periodic crashes; the enduring atmosphere of normality within was far more powerful than the temporary atmosphere of abnormality without. I have heard it said that, when the bomb fell on the Carlton in the first great blitz, several members continued asleep in their armchairs.

There is a passage in that most delightful and impressive of portrayals of England at war, written by the then American ambassador, *The Life and Letters of Walter Page*, describing an air raid in 1917, which well conveys the atmosphere of a London club at such a time:

"I was at a dinner of old Peers at the Athenæum Club—a group of old cocks that I meet once in a while and have come to know pretty well and ever to marvel at. I think every one is past seventy —several of them past eighty. On this occasion I was the only commoner present. The talk went on about every imaginable thing—reminiscences of Browning, the good years of good vintages of port, the excellence of some court opinions handed down in the United States by quite obscure judges—why shouldn't they be got out of the masses of law reports and published as classics? . . .

" 'Call in the chief steward. . . . Here, steward, what's that noise?'

" 'A hair raid, milord.'

" 'How long has it been going on?'

" 'Forty minutes, milord.'

" 'I must be deaf,' said the old fellow, with an enquiring look at the company. Everybody else had heard it, but we've learned to take these things for granted and nobody had interrupted the conversation to speak of it. Then the old man spoke up again.

" 'Well, there's nothing we can do to protect his Excellency. Damn the air raid! Pass the port.' "

The types who haunt these institutions may have changed with the times, but not, I think, the atmosphere. It seems time-proof.

There are clubs and clubs even in London's comparatively small West End, from eighteenth-century survivals like Boodle's, White's and Brooks's—that chaste and distinguished establishment which someone once likened to a duke's house with the duke lying dead upstairs—to the vast, late nineteenth-century, semi-political concerns in Northumberland Avenue, which are slightly and agreeably reminiscent of well-conducted railway termini in Paradise. And outside that charmed mile radius from the bottom of St.

James's Street there are countless other clubs: almost every English-man, it may be said, belongs to some club. But these, apart from the provincial capitals' prototypes of the West End clubs, are mostly clubs of a different kind, even though these more magnifi-cent concerns originally grew out of them—clubs, that is, where clubable men mix in unrestrained social intercourse rather than monumental designs for a certain kind of living. It is these last that inspire my Muse tonight—Turf and St. James's, Carlton and Reform, Travellers and Boodle's, "Rag" and "Senior", Oriental, United Universities, and a round, rolling dozen more. They may be escapist, they may be snobbish, they may be an an-achronism, they may be an affront to an egalitarian age, but, whatever they are in current ideology, I wish them well and ad-mire their strong capacity for survival. May they continue forever or, at any rate, until the first atom bomb!

*　　*　　*

VIII

St. George's Day in Purbeck[1]

St. George's Day, 1949—now ending as the last light glows pink against the jagged contours of Gad Cliff and over the silver waters of Weymouth Bay—has been indescribably beautiful. I spent most of it in a garden surrounded by old grey walls on which the advancing green tendrils of wistaria were casting thick sprays of deep mauve and where the first glory of magnolia and forsythia were already half-passed. The yews and ilex at the garden's foot were veiled with the nearer shimmer of pink and white blossom and with fountains of vivid green; the tulips along the border mingled their colours against brick mellowed by the suns of three centuries; and the stone of the deep-moulded, Renaissance-carved windows and door-frames of the old house glowed pink in the sunshine. Here, hour by hour, in the checkered patterns of shade and sunbeam, while the sound of distant gunfire reverberated, I sat on the lawn at my labour, collecting descriptions of England as she was in the aftermath of the Napoleonic Wars while I tried

[1] *I.L.N.* 7 May 1949.

to repaint that England I had never seen for the information of those who had also never seen it. But for all the beauty of the scene and the appropriateness of my day and task, my heart was sad—sad at the thought of so much that was lovely in England lost for ever, of her people imprisoned for so long in mean streets and amid mean, ignoble surroundings and subjected to a thousand mean, vulgarising influences; of the dangers which face her in a world she once controlled but which has of late passed beyond her control and where fierce, destructive forces simmer and threaten all that Englishmen have been taught to love and value. It was foolish and ungrateful—it was certainly idle—to have such thoughts on such a day, but, though I tried to banish them, they persisted. The woodland trees which encircle the old house and garden, their plumes still half-pink, half-green, trembled in the soft sea-breeze; the tawny downs and their dark clumps of firs, glimpsed through the iron gateway, glimmered in the distant haze; thrushes and blackbirds darted among the garden foliage under the Kremlin-like eyes of a watching cat.

In the afternoon I took my dog for his customary walk—or, perhaps, it would be truer to say, since in these matters his is the initiative, my dog took me. We climbed the down and struck westwards, a blue sea on one side, a lonely valley with a minute church tower flying the flag of St. George on the other. For a few hundred yards I skirted a cornfield, the vivid green rippling in the wind, while the little white terrier, with his brown cap and back spotted like a rocking-horse, darted ahead, snuffling the rabbit-scented air. Then I came on to the bare, open down, with its springy turf beneath my feet and the wind from the Channel flying past. There was no human in sight or any likelihood of one—only the grass and sky and a solitary white sail in the bay, the first I had seen since the winter. Deep in my thoughts, as idly deep as the dog scampering ahead was in corridors of scent, I passed through the broken fences and only realised after some minutes of walking that I was in one of those no-man's-lands which Englishmen of my generation first encountered in Northern France and Belgium in the first war to end wars more than thirty years ago, but which now, with the march of human progress, have become, in so many formerly quiet and beautiful places, a permanent part of our landscape. Indeed, so crowded and over-populated is our country that it is difficult to find any area not already given over to houses and urban or semi-urban development, where the quietude and surviving pastoral loveliness are not apt at any moment to be broken in upon by the vestiges and sounds of mimic warfare. I was reminded of this at the moment by the vicious whistle and kick of a shell making seawards high overhead. Realising that I had unwittingly wandered into the outskirts of a battle area, I retraced my steps. But, instead of returning along the knife-edge of the down by which I had come, I made my way back through the lower ground between the down and the sea. And here, a few hundred yards from the border of that little corner of England now for ever forbidden to Englishmen, I found an old house in a little wood. Its doors and windows were nailed up with black match-boarding, its stone roof was overgrown with creepers and brambles, owls and bats nested in its ivied trees, but its beauty, made by successive generations of English craftsmen through four centuries, still survived. It was strange to think that mine might be one of the last appraising eyes ever to see that beauty, loved by so many and now doomed. A few more years of the present neglect and nothing will remain.

Gazing at it, it seemed ironical that the reason given by the Government for its breach of faith to the people who once lived in this ravished corner of England was that the capital cost of the wartime military "installations" made it impossible for the Treasury to authorise their removal elsewhere. I could not help wondering about the capital cost of the ancient home and breeding-ground of good Englishmen now sealed off for ever from the use of present and future generations. Unlike the builders of these far more temporary installations, which in fifty years' time will be both out of date and, judging by the rate of deterioration of most modern buildings, worn out, the men who built the doomed manor-house of Tyneham, its ruined church, farms and cottages, built for the centuries. We have not only robbed our own generation of their handiwork, but generations still unborn. The economic arguments we use to justify our barbarism are false arguments, for our economy is based not on enduring wealth—the wealth that enriches men from generation to generation—but all too often on the opportunities it offers for the quick exploitation of the passing hour: for the contractor's profit, the middleman's rake-off and the labourer's job shuffled through as quickly as possible for the maximum cash return obtainable. Our values are awry.

It was this loss of ancient English values that made me sad on this most beautiful of St. George's Days. And then this evening, as the slanting light of the setting sun transmuted the garden in which I was writing into something scarcely of this world—grass, trees, blossom, flowers, even the very weeds under which a long military occupation had smothered everything and nine months of ceaseless battle have as yet failed to eradicate—I regained my sense of proportion. The loss is there, though we may ignore it, staring us in the face: tragic, feckless, eroding. Yet side by side with it is something which redeems and transcends it. I thought, in the glorious twilight of this St. George's Day, of the great company of Englishmen who during six bitter years gave to their country and the high cause of man all they had to give, who battled in these skies, endured the blitz, suffered, wrought and triumphed in desert, ocean and jungle, who went out—some of them from this very garden—and crossed the seas on D-Day to inscribe on England's shield an imperishable glory, and died, many of them, that their country and all it stands for might continue. Because of their sacrifice and greatness of heart and soul, that which is lost shall be found again, that which is broken shall be repaired, that which is grown old and worn shall be made new. For a nation which can breed and inspire such sons is undying and has the power to renew itself from the ashes of its own past.

PART II

Avons of the Heart

In Avons of the heart her rivers run.
RUPERT BROOKE

CHAPTER 8

The Country Habit

"The country habit has me by the heart."
V. SACKVILLE-WEST

If much of my life has been spent in London, more than half has been lived in the country. For twenty years I have farmed and bred cattle, and at one time owned—though I do so no longer—a few hundred acres of Wiltshire valley and woodland. I like to think that, if my books outlive me, the beeches I planted there will live as long or longer.

The Cornfield · England's Lovely Counties ·
Norfolk Dumpling · Forester's Memories ·
Lord of Many Acres

I

The Cornfield[1]

All afternoon and evening we worked in the cornfield, stooking the crop which was to feed our little stock, and so, indirectly, man, during the coming year. The machines for cutting and binding had arrived late, and several days of a week of sunshine had been lost waiting for them; the air was translucent and the distant horizon of cliffs and sea so beautiful that the thought of rain was never far away. We therefore worked urgently, following close in the sweeping tracks of the binder, moving slowly in from the wide circumference towards the narrowing heart of shimmer-

[1] *Illustrated London News* 20 August 1949; 29 November 1958; 17 February 1962.

ing corn. None of us, save the men on the machines, were very
experienced in the art, but, knowing what depended on it, we
worked with a will and with that steady unceasing compulsion
which all work with living nature seems to necessitate. The goal
in our minds was not the hour at which labour ceased, but the
completion of the work, the last stook stacked, the field clear and
garnered. Even the beauty of the scene was incidental. Only
occasionally did we raise our eyes from that high, slanting field,
sparkling and rustling in sun and wind, to take in the wonderful
panorama below: the old grey house, with its William and Mary
red brick chimneys rising out of the trees, the green clay pastures
stretching to the margin of the sea, and the tawny downs, the
jagged cliffs of shale, limestone and chalk spread in fantastic
panorama from Broad Bench to Ringstead, the blue of Weymouth
Bay and Portland lying like a distant giant floating on the bosom
of the Channel, the high, white clouds driving like solitary
galleons out of the west. No more beautiful setting to the husbandman's business can have ever existed, and, as the shadows
lengthened and the rooks began to wheel home, its loveliness and
peace surpassed the human power of description. Our throats and
lips were parched, our feet battered by the iron, uneven ground,
our bodies pierced with innumerable spear-points of oats and
barley, but, as the corn vanished and the stooks rose, in sunlight, twilight and, last of all, in moonlight, a feeling of aching
triumph and satisfaction overcame weariness. We had been all-
day participants in a battle and it was nearly over. The enemy,
next winter's want, on our little piece of the farming front—all
that we could see and experience—was in retreat. A victory had
been won.

But battles with Nature are never done. Next day the wind rose
and swept with gale force out of the bay, and many of the stooks
we had so laboriously raised were laid low. I was forced to spend
two more afternoons away from my work relaying what I had
helped to lay, while the wind cunningly shifted to east from
west—against which quarter we had been buttressing—and then,
after we had relaid our stooks, back again to south and west. Yet
what Nature takes with one hand she gives with another, and
the wind which demolished dried what it had torn down when

the rain ceased and the sun shone again. Whoever farms in this land of ever-changing sea winds has constant anxiety but as constant compensation.

In England climate and soil vary so much that no one, however great his previous experience, can hope to farm land rightly until he has known it for a season or two. In the little corner of the Isle of Purbeck where my own agricultural experience began, the local farmers used to tell me that all who farmed there fell into initial mistakes because they made assumptions and used methods applicable to the rest of the neighbourhood but unsuited to that particular spot. Everything there was a little different. The sun shone when it rained on the other side of the hill and *vice versa*; the wire-worm which attacked my crops and would have ruined them anywhere else proved innocuous because the woods that sheltered the fields in that treeless moor attracted every bird from miles round. The grass seeds, the fertilisers, the methods of cultivation that were right in the valley between the limestone and chalk hills only a mile away were not necessarily so in that secret pocket of Kimmeridge clay between the outer downs and the sea.

It is this baffling diversity in nature's rule which makes English farming so fascinating. A man has perpetually to pit his wits, knowledge, skill and experience, as well as sinews, against that wily, infinitely diversified, yet rewarding teacher, our island weather. He has to farm as a sailor has to sail, with one eye cocked at the changing skies. Nor, though he has many anxious moments, has he ever a dull moment. When Michaelmas brings the old farm-year to an end, there is the thrill of seeing the land ploughed for the autumn, the beauty of a fine tilth, the excitement of a new ley showing green against the October woods to give the cattle a last bite of grass before they turn to their winter's diet of kale, hay and silage. Every month brings its special problems, its disappointments, anxieties, struggles, and its sense of something accomplished—though never all that had been hoped.

Until I had some experience of farming I used to regard February as the dullest month in the calendar. Now, it seems to me the most exciting, as well as the most anxious. For with cows and livestock to feed, the earliest growth of grass becomes almost a matter of life or death. At this time every dairy farmer in the West is on tenterhooks over the race between the coming of spring and his diminishing stocks of fodder; now that kale has been finished, how long, he asks, will the hay and silage last and those interminable bills for winter concentrates? And at some moment in February there will suddenly arrive a day when all nature is lyrical with happiness—a warm wind from the south, softness in gently drying soil, birds singing in the hedges, a red glow over the young larch plantations, the first delusive promise of spring. On such a day even more than in the real spring I feel like Chaucer, unable to remain at my books and driven out by some irresistible force to walk in the fields—

> *When that the month of May*
> *Is comen and I hear the foulys sing,*
> *Farewell my book and my devocioun!* . . .

And the joy of early spring when, despite cold March winds, the cows can file out from the dispersal yard and climb the hill to their first bite of rye grass is something life in a town can never offer. After the incessant chores and worries of keeping a yarded herd fit and fed through the winter, the only satisfaction comparable is that of the scholar, artist or scientist who, grappling in solitude with the stubborn realities of his material, stumbles suddenly on the means of overcoming them.

It is this constant testing of hopes and effort against reality—the infinitely diverse and ever-changing, yet eternal, reality of nature—which gives the farmer his satisfaction and makes a seldom financially well-rewarded and, for the small working farmer, exceedingly arduous calling such a worthwhile one. Many farmers have bad luck and some are broken by it. Yet few willingly abandon the struggle to make a living out of raising from earth and its plants and beasts a livelihood for themselves and sustenance for their fellow-men.

* * *

II

England's Lovely Counties[1]

England has thirty-nine counties—forty if one counts Monmouth-shire—and I do not know which is the loveliest. There is not one of them which has not some claim to be beautiful and whose sons and daughters would not be ready to champion her above her thirty-eight sister shires. Even those which are largely urban and industrial—Lancashire and Staffordshire, for instance, have beauties which have no parallel in any other county. Warwick-shire may have Birmingham, but she has also Stratford-on-Avon and the noble parklands of the Vale of Warwick. Leicester may be an uninspiring city to those who do not look on her with the eyes of love and long familiarity, yet what hunting man can see the green, rolling pastures and neat quickset hedges of the countryside round Harborough and Melton and not feel he has reached the celestial fields? And the least exciting counties by guide-book standards are often the most satisfying to live in. In that delightful book, *England Have My Bones*—the kind of eccentric, individualist, unclassifiable book that only an Englishman would write—T. H. White wrote of his own county:

"One can't say that the Shire is a better place than anywhere else. Among other things, the place itself would scarcely appreciate the compliment. It would be against its nature to compete. It would lose what reality it possesses if it were made in any way to outstand. There are certain counties which once had outstanding qualities, and which have been overwhelmed for that reason... But their loveliness makes them provocative, and their day will come. The invaders will top the skyline, marching under petrol pumps and curiosity shops and corrugated iron roofs ... The Shire has protected itself against these things by a non-committal policy . . . It has concealed its individuality in order to preserve it. We have a few loop-ways, a few yellow signs, a few corrugated iron roofs, a few thatched ones, nothing very definite: so that the invaders pass through,

[1] *I.L.N.* 26 November 1955.

as Oliver Cromwell did before them, looking for somewhere
else."

One can only write about what one knows. I was born in
Norfolk, bred in London, schooled in Kent and what then was
the rural part of Middlesex, taught the use of arms in Sussex and
Norfolk, Yorkshire, Hampshire and Kent, and given a university
education in Oxfordshire. At one time or another I have worked,
lived or farmed in Cambridgeshire, Buckinghamshire, Hertfordshire, Gloucestershire and Dorset. And I own a tiny corner of
Wiltshire, close to the Dorset border, the county in which I first
learnt to love the English countryside; that is to say, under our
mid-twentieth-century definition of ownership, I am responsible
for maintaining some of its fences and ditches, farm-roads and
water-courses, for preventing some of its trees from falling on
anyone's head and for keeping down a little section of its community of rabbits and vermin. I also own—to use the same misleading word—the source of one of its rivers and the site of one of
its many prehistoric camps.

Yet, like others, my knowledge of England and her shires—so
small and easy to know even in a single lifetime—does not end
with these familiar counties. I have walked on the Roman wall in
Northumberland and enjoyed the sense, rivalled only in England
in the lovely hill shire of Derbyshire, of being on the roof of the
world; have climbed mountains in Westmorland and lost myself
on the Durham moors; have looked down from the heights on
Sheffield and bathed in Robin Hood's Bay, and gazed from the
high garden at Haigh over smoking Wigan, beautiful against the
October sky, at the silver flashes beyond. I have spent long happy
summer days in one of Cheshire's great parks, seeing across the
"vale royal" of England, the Derbyshire skyline on the one hand
and the hills of Wales on the other. On my way to and from Wales
I have motored over almost every road in Shropshire, certainly
one of the most beautiful of counties, and over those of its lovely
neighbours, Herefordshire and Worcestershire, whose beauties I
once had carefully pointed out to me from a conveniently-
situated hilltop by no less a Worcestershire worthy than Stanley
Baldwin. I have stayed in one of Northampton's noble palaces,
which with its spires and Collyweston roofs are its peculiar glory,

and walked, with my shoes covered with buttercup gold, down its majestic avenues. I have bathed in Cornish coves and got soaked to the skin in Devonshire mist, and have wandered, exploring, from tower to tower in that land of splendid churches and orchards, Somerset; have walked all day on Gloucestershire's limestone hills and through her high, cold beech woods; and paddled a canoe from high noon till moonrise down a slow, meandering, sedgy stream, with Berkshire on one bank and Oxfordshire on the other. I have seen Harrow's spire rising above its white, wintry drapery and encircling Middlesex elms, and lived twenty happy years in that gentle, rolling North Buckinghamshire plain which even now, though I seldom see it, is still more home to me than anywhere outside Wessex. I have produced a pastoral play in a glade in Hertfordshire and a pageant in an Oxford College garden and another on the Cambridge Backs; have ridden on the Surrey downs and searched for flints on a hill-camp in Kent and for Chanctonbury Ring in Sussex in a thick November fog, and even once, as a very small boy, fallen over the edge of a quarry in Hampshire! And of each of these counties I recall scenes that are part of my picture of England, beautiful, kindly and haunting, and which I shall carry with me to the grave.

It is in its astonishing variety that the glory of the English landscape lies and in the rapidity with which one passes from one beautiful scene to another completely different. I was reminded of this a short while ago when, at the end of a crowded and tiring day, I was collected from a little town on the southern edge of the Bedford Level and driven through Cambridgeshire, West Suffolk and Norfolk to stay with some old friends on that mysterious coast which looks out across marshes and wide sands onto the sea of the old Northern legends, and out of which, bearing terror and new life for England, our first Anglo-Saxon forebears came. A chance encounter with a wartime acquaintance and his wife turned a brief halt at a wayside inn into a long, leisurely meal, and by the time the journey was resumed and the low, rolling uplands between Swaffham and the coast reached, it was nearly midnight, and country Norfolk, which keeps early hours, was fast asleep. Crossing the wooded Breckland there had

been a good deal of drifting mist, and on the higher ground
beyond Castle Acre I got out to wipe the front of the windscreen.
As I did so I became aware, as so often in returning to Norfolk—
but never so clearly as at that moment—that I was in a different
world, as remote in its own way from the clayey soil and air of
Middlesex and the Home Counties as, say, the peak of Ararat is
from the Basra flats. The air here was like one's youth suddenly
restored, sharp as the finest blade of steel and so clear that the
stars appeared as jewels; the trees, already almost bare on that
windswept but now windless and utterly silent upland, silhouetted
in exquisite tracery against the starlit night; the whole atmosphere that of some enchanted region, half of this earth and half
of some other, in a flash remembered:

> *Bring the cap and bring the vest;*
> *Buckle on his sandal shoon;*
> *Fetch his memory from the chest*
> *In the treasury of the moon.*

Duncan noticed the same phenomena as he approached Macbeth's
castle, where the delicate air "nimbly and sweetly" recommended
itself to his senses. It is so along the sea-approaches to all the
eastern coasts of England and Scotland from Norfolk to Cromarty.
Even the most insensitive traveller, returning to them after long
absence, feels the sudden change in the tempo of being as his lungs
fill with that light, electric air. It is perhaps most strongly felt
in the Borderland between the Tweed and the Lammermuirs
which gave birth to the great heritage of anonymous song and
ballad that is the British equivalent of the Homeric legends: the
land where True Thomas, lying on Huntlie bank, saw his vision
of the three ferlies "down by the Eildon Tree".

The changes wrought by science and what is called Progress
may, I suppose, ultimately reduce the buildings and what bureaucrats term "installations" of our island to a monotonous and ugly
uniformity. Yet they can never wholly eradicate its subtle
differences of soil, climate and air. It is these that endear us above
all else to the places we love, from which our earliest memories
are formed and out of whose earth our bodies were compounded.
"Make me content," wrote Edward Thomas,

With some sweetness
From Wales
Whose nightingales
Have no wings—
From Wiltshire and Kent
And Herefordshire
And the villages there—
From the names and the things
No less.

And at the last we go back to them, if not in body, then in heart, and become again one with them, for in "our end is our beginning".

* * *

III

Norfolk Dumpling[1]

By chance of my father's occupation, I was born in the little woodland village of Dersingham on the shores of the Wash. I am, therefore, by birth, though in nothing else, a Norfolk man. I was stationed in Norfolk for a short time in the First World War and once produced a pageant during a few crowded, happy weeks in the Cambridgeshire fens close to its western boundary. Occasionally, too, I have visited the East Anglian county on business or pleasure, seen Holkham's noble arch and drive, and stood on the ancient cobbles of King's Lynn and in Borrow's glorious market square at Norwich, and lazed and bathed away the hours of a summer's day on Bird Island or on Brancaster sands. Yet though I have spent only a tiny fraction of my days in the county of my birth and know at least a dozen English counties better, something in a man's blood or lungs responds to the nature of his birthplace; it was here he first breathed the air and awoke to consciousness, and I was Norfolk born. So whenever chance brings me to the coastline where the Sandringham woods keep their wedding with the grey North Sea and the winds from the Danish flats, the years drop away and I am back where I began, a

[1] *I.L.N.* 22 September 1951.

spirit of air and earth and water before the heavy, indigestible weight of flesh and experience made me what I am.

It is a noble coast. It has none of the romantic splendour and Celtic poetry of the Dorset seaboard: the fantastic cliffs and precipitous bays where the rocks of the primæval world play out their eternal drama of conflict with the southern sea. There the sea is an enemy; a magnificent but inhuman force which has no commerce with the land but battle. But here in Norfolk, land and sea blend so that at dusk they merge and become one; sand-dune and whingrass, wave and white horse have "curtsied here and kissed". When Shakespeare wrote "Come unto these yellow sands," it may have been the Norfolk coast on which he was drawing from experience; did Lord Leicester's company visit it, I wonder, after it played at King's Lynn in the hot, summer, pestilence-ridden months when it quitted London and went on tour? It is a far cry from the Forest of Arden to this pure, bleak shore.

Here the Anglo-Saxons, who are the dominant strain in our long, mixed ancestry, landed and became seized of the land which bears their name. The wild duck, straining in a trembling V across the moving waste of waters that forms the sole horizon to the low hedge behind which I am writing, are the prototypes of that remote sea-folk out of whose loins we spring. They came fiercely, facing and bringing death, but creating, even as they slew and fell, life which was to endure and far transcend their own simple beginnings: the free, courageous life of England that has gone out into every corner of the world and infused on both shores of the Atlantic the love and institutions of freedom. The Count of the Saxon shore—some stern Roman or dark Iberian or African —must have cursed these newcomers for flaxen, pestilent barbarians as he marched and counter-marched his glittering, dusty cohorts from Brancaster to repel first one, then another, of their unpredictable, turbulent invasions. They came like the wind out of a cold sea on to a cold shore, but, as their swords flashed, they bore the sea which was their real home into the heart of England, so that she and it were to remain for ever one. It was not for nothing that Nelson was born on this coast: Nelson who transmuted sea, grey sea, green sea, blue sea, wherever he sailed, into something English, so that to this day the waters which wash the Spanish shore at Cape Trafalgar and Cadiz and those which flow into Aboukir Bay seem as familiar to Englishmen, and are as impregnated with the spirit of England, as those of the Solent or Bristol Channel. A boy who is to become a sailor should grow up on such a coast as this, where sea and land are one: must lie, as Raleigh lay on the Devon beach at Budleigh Salterton, with his eye level with the beckoning horizon and the unseen immensities of ocean beyond.

Driving along this coast one sees an England as different to that of the South and West as chalk from cheese. It is a land of little, wide-open, wind-swept harbours, where tiny yachts and sharpies tack up and down between sandbanks and mud-flats; of quiet, narrow-streeted little towns whose houses appear to be built largely of cobble-stones; of men with sturdy red faces and broad shoulders equally at home in a boat or a bar; of lush meadows filled with grazing cattle, and sweeping woods appearing between low, bare, windy uplands; of fast-moving grey seas flecked with white; of proud little churches with splendid towers; of air like the finest vintage champagne, crisp and invigorating yet light as thistledown. It is a land to make a man brave, resourceful, independent; good, I should think, for golfers' handicaps, and the kind of place in which children, with brown faces, grubby, fishy hands and rolled-up pants, assembling here each autumn for their holidays, grow up to be explorers and commanders of motor-torpedo boats and the mothers and wives of such types. It is a land, above all, of a settled, unobtrusive and apparently unshakable competency and prosperity: the glories of Lord Leicester's Holkham and that wonderful estate originally founded out of sandy rabbit warrens are its crowning symbols. If there is a better-farmed county in England—I cannot speak of Scotland and her proud Lothians—I have yet to see it: in a day's travelling I noticed only three thistles, and those on a golf-course. Summer ends early here, but summer or winter, Norfolk is a land for the sturdy and fearless. It has been made the dearer to me and thousands of others by the books which my friend, Wyndham Ketton Cremer, has written about Norfolk neighbourhood in the eighteenth century and by Mr. Mottram's classic studies. I am proud to be a countryman, if only by accident, of Nelson and Borrow, of old Crome and Walpole, of Turnip Townsend and Coke of Norfolk who "loved husbandry". Long may the great county stand watch over the Wash and England's eastern gate, her "Holy Boys" fight for her beyond the grey seas whenever danger threatens, and her shrewd, indomitable "dumplings" of plough and tractor continue to raise the nation's finest crops!

*   *   *

IV

Forester's Memories[1]

Every few weeks I escape to the country and spend a day or two in a valley of beeches made dear to me by memories of early life. The Nadder rises in the ancient monastic park below my windows, and the beechwoods rise in a solid wall of green above it, the horseshoe they form encompassing the house and farmlands and opening eastwards—where the little stream flows towards its junction with the Avon—on a sweeping view of distant woods and downland. I know of nowhere in southern England more peaceful or more remote from the busy world around it. A mile or two to the south the main London-Exeter road bears its unceasing load of traffic, and at night, standing on the terrace above the sleeping woods and lakes, I can hear the far rumble of great lorries speeding westwards or towards the capital, while from the other side of the protecting trees and hill to the north comes the sound of a train on the main Southern Region making its way under the Pole Star and pointing Bear towards the wide Vale of Marchwood and the Somerset meadows. But in the hidden Wincombe woods one can walk for an hour and never see or hear another human being. One is alone with birds, foxes and badgers and the innumerable company of small, creeping things whose universe is confined to these lonely slopes and dells. And here, whenever my work is finished and I can escape, I slip away with a sickle in one hand and a swing-cutter in the other and become for a few hours a solitary amateur forester. My place is on the lowest

[1] *I.L.N.* 21 June 1958; 14 December 1968

and humblest rung of the forestry ladder, but it is an entirely
satisfying one and I would not change it for any other in the
world. In a minute I am out of view of the house and far out of
sound of telephone or questing voice. The great trees surround
and close round me like the walls of the tunnel down which Alice
fell into Wonderland and I am back where I walked and dreamed
as a boy fifty years ago. But now I dream no more of imaginary
personal triumphs or schemes of human improvement; I know
that the material world offers nothing better than the absorbing
task before me.

Presently I come to the clearing in the woods which is my secret
destination, throw my tools across and climb the wire fence that
shuts it in. Below me and the path I have been following lies a
steep southern slope thick with bracken, laurels and brambles
and, rising among them, thousands of larches and little beeches
whose weeding I have reserved for myself and whose future is my
particular charge. The lives of the other trees I plant each winter
are only mine to order and care for by proxy and process of
accountancy, but these few thousand plants on this remote slope
are as much mine to tend and care for as though I were their
mother. Whether they live or not and whether some of them will
one day become giants of the forest, like the great trees around
them, depends on unpredictable factors, both human and divine,
far beyond my control. For the moment their future is in my
hands. A false slip of the hand, a glancing blow with sickle or
swinger, the failure to remove some encroaching bush or bramble,
may mean death to an arboreal infant which might otherwise
outlive me by a couple of centuries and give shade, solace and
timber to generations unborn.

Much of the work has to be done on one's knees, pausing to dig
and prop up the earth under the shallow roots of trees which had
been pressed down the slope by bracken, deer or weather. And
here, until dusk falls and I can no longer see the tiny trees I am
tending, I continue, aching in leg and back and with blistered
hands, but happy and released from all thought or care but that
of the delicious life of the woods.

Summer and winter the magic never fails; I return to the same
place and, there, lose myself in the woodlands of which I am for

this short while a minister and servant. In winter I attack the laurels and furze which are indigenous to the few acres I have taken under my protection and which, without this winter's campaigning, would soon overrun the whole of this fertile area. In summer, apart from brambles, my war is mainly against the bracken which, though by now out-topped by the larches, still towers, in July and autumn, over the tiny young beeches. But whereas in December and the first leafless months of the year one need think only of attack, in summer one has to proceed with great circumspection and guard carefully against damaging the delicate-growing trees hidden in the undergrowth. One has, too, to remember that bramble and bracken, though one's enemy if allowed to get out of hand, can be an ally, wisely used, against other foes of little trees—scorch and sun and those shy, lovely marauders, the roe and fallow deer, who haunt my glades. Rabbits one can fence out of plantations and, though burrowing badgers are constantly digging under the wire, the prevalence of myxomatosis has for the past year or two kept the former at bay. But against deer, who can jump all but the highest and most costly fence, there is no protection except extermination, and that, in these wide woodlands, where they can travel for miles unseen through brackeny glades and thick undergrowth, is virtually impossible. And the damage which deer can do to little trees, particularly to slender, willowy young larches and poplars, has to be seen to be believed. For one who regards trees as almost the first of man's friends in the plant world—the protector and harbinger of all the others—the sight of hundreds of ringed and ragged infant trunks is one of the saddest sights in nature. Once the bark is completely ringed, death for the tree is certain, and all one's labour, and Nature's, is in vain. For this reason I am convinced it is wise at one stage of their growth to leave round young larches a thick protecting ring of bramble. Where this is lacking in the first few years after planting, deer, if at all prevalent, can easily account for one out of every two or three trees.

Deer, squirrels and rabbits are not the only enemies of trees. High among them are to be numbered men, who all too frequently treat them, not as the allies they are, but as useless and expendable encumbrances of nature. The destruction of wayside and hedge-row timber in England during the past decade, both by farmers and by the officers of local authorities, has been terrifying; the whole character of our countryside, once so superlatively beautiful in its summer foliage and winter tracery, is being changed, and for the worse. Only in the outer suburban areas around London, where vast numbers of poplars, horse-chestnuts and flowering fruit trees have been planted in the last thirty or forty years, and in the great forests of the Forestry Commission, has the old thickly-wooded appearance of our countryside been preserved. In London itself the massacre and mutilation of fine trees never ceases—often in the name of an illusory safety which is almost completely disregarded where the needs of fast-moving traffic conflict with the security of human life and limb.

Happily for me, the threatened trees of London's parks and squares, though I love them dearly, are a long way from the quiet woodlands where I spend so many fugitive hours weeding and tending my little trees. It is probably an idle dream that they will ever come to maturity in such a destructive and suicidal age as ours, but in the meantime they are there to be guarded through their first perilous years, and it is release and happiness to be allowed to tend them. "I like very much the society of woodmen," wrote Disraeli of his Hughenden plantations. "I don't know any men who are so completely masters of their business, and of the secluded, but delicious, world in which they live. They are healthy, their language is picturesque; they live in the air, and Nature whispers to them many of her secrets." It does so even to those who are only amateur woodsmen like myself. Often when, as night falls, I return through the darkening beechwoods with blistered and bramble-pricked fingers and a heart at peace, I recall his words: "A forest is like an ocean, monotonous only to the ignorant."

*   *   *

v

Lord of Many Acres[1]

Somewhere, in one of those passages, rescued from faded family letters, which illuminate the dry-as-dust past with the light of living humanity, the great Lord Halifax, writing amid the turmoils and perils of the Popish Plot and Exclusion Act debates, wrote, "Our world here is so overrun with the politics, the fools' heads so conceited, and the knaves so busy that a wasps' nest is a quieter place to sleep in than this town . . . I confess I dream of the country as men do of small beer when they are in a fever." Lying in bed in London for the past ten days in the company of some malignant germ, this phrase of that most human of seventeenth-century statesmen kept running through my head, and I found myself doing exactly the same thing. Only my thoughts, being like his purely personal thoughts, turned, not to his great Nottinghamshire abbey amid the glades of Sherwood Forest which lay at the secret and inner core of Halifax's heart, but to a valley of beeches formed by the infant Nadder, and beyond them, where the woods widen out to the south-east, the line of the downs,

"so noble and so bare".

So it has always been with men of our race, ever since the days when our remote Saxon ancestors first broke the stubborn clay-lands of the shires with their deep ploughs. We may, most of us today, be townsmen, just as Carolean Lord Halifax, by virtue of his trade of statesman and courtier, had become a townsman. Yet, wherever we have country roots or can put them down, back we reach to them whenever the need arises for refreshment of body or soul.

Suspended as my home is on the very borders of Wiltshire and Dorset, so that I am domiciled on the beechy slopes of the one, yet look on to the tree tops and downs of the other, I belong in heart to both. Forced by my calling and obligations to spend much of my time in London, I find myself, as I grow older,

[1] *I.L.N.* 7 March 1959; 3 November 1962.

repeatedly day-dreaming of those two dear counties, each so different yet so entangled with my life and memories. Journeying frequently from town to country, from metropolitan scurry and uproar to woodland quiet and solitude, I realise I have many compensations. It never fails to make my heart leap to see, each time with the thrill of surprise at its perfection and beauty, the spire of Salisbury Cathedral rising from the cup of the downs as the winding London road descends from the Plain into the valley of the Avon; to glimpse, from a distant hillside, the woods of my deep western coombe and the silhouette of barns filled with hay borne home on summer evenings, to hear the rooks cawing in the beeches as I stop to open the gate before entering the descending tunnel of trees at whose far end lies home—the low white Regency house with its painted verandah and rambling grey stone walls and chimneys, the lawn poised above space, the enormous multiple rhododendron which for three weeks in the year flowers in half-a-dozen brightly contrasted colours, and between whose shade and that of the little rough-fenced paddock, where the young heifers snuffle and graze in the darkness when I go out after putting down my work at night, my old dog, Jimmy, lies in his casket of ashes. It was here that he always ran, wild with excitement, on being released from the car to lift his leg before, amid triumphant barks and unavailing cries from his human guardians, he disappeared in the direction of the rabbit warrens in the valley below. And following him in imagination, I enter the woods, stopping at each familiar beech and chestnut, whose ancient trunks and vast spreading branches I have known for more than half a century. All round me is that other world of beasts and birds, to whom the woods also are a sanctuary; at night from my window I can hear their cries and movements as they go about their nocturnal business, seeking their food and mates. I love to think, amid the sound of the London traffic, that this life of theirs and of the living vegetable woods around them is going on at this very moment and will continue to do so though I am far away, just as it did before I was born and will continue to do after I am dead.

I have other country resorts to which my heart repairs when my body is imprisoned in London. There is the beautiful house

by the southern sea with which I struggled, trying to restore its
war-ravaged beauty and order, for eight seemingly wasted years
until the whole of its vast stone roof had to be taken down to
renew its death-watch-beetle ridden timbers. Yet the sight of its
mellowed mauve stone and of that peaceful garden, first a wilderness full of snakes and rabbits, strange weeds and discarded army
junk and later a measured pleasance of trim lawns, bright
flowers and formal trees, is something which neither time nor
absence can take from me: that and those incredible cliffs, amid
whose scenery the house and its quiet gardens and surrounding
pastures were set. Hay-making on those romantic slopes on fine
days, when the sea was sparkling blue and the sleeping giants
towards Lulworth and Ringstead the colour of deep sapphire
was like something out of an Italian primitive. Here, too, my dog
was—and is—always with me; nosing for rats' nests and snakes
in the, for him, ecstatic days of the garden before it had been
made tame and dog-dull, or racing wildly on the down edge
high above the house, scattering rabbits in every direction and
inhaling the wild sea wind. Sometimes we would walk together
as far as the two stones on the lonely cliff that marked the spot
where a former Lord Chancellor and his dog used to gaze out on
the incoming breakers, sweeping in from the west beyond Portland and its race, and meditate on the proud fleet of Britain on
which his country's security and his own wealth and power
rested. Lord Chancellor Eldon and his dog Pincher, my dog Jimmy,
proud, unchallengeable fleet of England, Britain's security, all
are gone. But the wild cliffs and the Dorset seas and the thyme-
scented salt air are unchanged and there as heretofore, at this very
moment, my heart is there with them, made free of that lonely
beautiful place for ever. As it is, too, of the Cotswold sheep-walks
above Colesborne and the deep coombes that slope southwards
from mysterious Elkstone; of the huge expanses of golden sand
and marsh that is the sea-coast of the holy land of Walsingham;
and, most of all—for it is so rooted for me in ancient content—
the clay buttercup meadows and hedgerow elms and red-brick
and half-cast seventeenth century cottages of North Buckinghamshire where I had my home for nearly a quarter of a century. To be
free of so much loveliness and able to revisit any part of it at

any hour of the day or night is to be lord of many acres, and it is as such that I lie here, amid urban sights and sounds and unfinished manuscripts and chewed pencils and elusive pieces of india-rubber.

CHAPTER 9

Creatures Great and Small

> "He prayeth best, who loveth best
> All things both great and small;
> For the dear God who loveth us,
> He made and loveth all."
>
> S. T. COLERIDGE

Keats, in one of letters, described the world as a vale of soul-making. If men possess potential souls, it seems that, with their capacity for love and courage—the qualities which appear to create souls in men—animals can possess them too.

A Dog that Chose · Camberley Kate ·
A Good Biter · The Lioness and the Badger ·
Sammy the Cat

I

A Dog that Chose[1]

Jimmy was a rough-haired English terrier. He had a snow-white coat which, when brushed and washed, was almost dazzlingly white; large and well-proportioned brown and black spots, a short, stuggy brown-tipped tail that usually, like his aspiring spirit, pointed perkily upwards; long, graceful legs which with his stout heart could carry him swiftly as any deer or race-horse; two satiny brown ears that sometimes lay in repose and at others pointed upwards like the pavilions of a mediaeval

[1] *Illustrated London News* 16 Feb 1946; Christmas Number 1959.

army; and the most beautiful eyes I have ever seen. He may not have conformed to the pedantic requirements of any Breed Society but, viewed purely as a dog, he had everything proper about him.

He entered my life on a Cornish cliff at the darkest moment of the war. It was soon after our defeat at Knightsbridge, when the victorious Germans were hammering on the gates of Alexandria and Stalingrad, when the position at sea was more grave than at any time of the war and when the Japanese tide in the Pacific and South East Asia had still to be turned. I had just been given a fortnight's respite from work I was doing for the Services and had taken the opportunity of spending ten days in a farmhouse on the North Cornish cliffs. It was my one wartime holiday and during the afternoons my wife and I made the most of it; sometimes picnicking on the beach and at other times taking long tramps over the cliffs. On one of these we walked to Boscastle, about six or seven miles from the farmhouse where we were staying. And there we encountered the waif who for the next fourteen years was to dominate our lives. In a backwater of immeasurable quiet—the quiet of long rollers and surge and heather cliffs—the dog found us.

We were eating sandwiches at the time on a small promontory overlooking the west side of the harbour. I had thrown a few crumbs to some gulls who were obviously old habitués of the place and who, voraciously soaring and diving, were taking their toll of the picnicking few—honeymoon couples, old people and Service men and women on leave scattered about the cliff. Suddenly I became aware that we were no longer alone. Sitting very silent and intent by our side was a white, shaggy terrier with brown cap and ears and a stump of a tail, gazing at my sandwiches with a look of infinite reproach and longing; he was obviously grieved that such largesse should be distributed among undeserving seagulls. Though food in those days was not plentiful and I was hungry, I was unable to resist the look in those large brown eyes, and my last two sandwiches, bit by bit, were handed over to this obviously expert and, as it turned out, professional beggar. What was so remarkable was that, though, as we subsequently came to realise, he must have been half starving, he made not the slightest attempt to snatch the proffered food but took it so gently that it seemed to leave one's hand by an imperceptible process of suction. Never had I known a dog with such a soft mouth or with more gentle winning manners—not even the great-hearted, graceful, deep-ruffed Alsatian who for seven years formed the background to my life and after his death left it, for many months, desolate. This soft mouth was one of the dog's distinguishing traits and always remained so. A connoisseur of food, especially, as we discovered later, of the rarer and more expensive kinds, he was never greedy. He merely showed, as only he could, that he needed it, and then waited patiently for his need to be satisfied.

Owing to his half-starved condition, he seemed at the time to be an old dog: thin, matted, mangy, with a pink hairless underneath on which black spots showed like skin eruptions. We took him to be the property of some poor family who could afford him little food or attention. Yet before he had been with us many minutes he gave us a taste of his quality. A hundred feet beneath us was an estuary, with scores of gulls resting on the sand. These the dog obviously regarded as enemies, for he suddenly jumped up, dashed down the precipitous rocks and, barking wildly, drove them, squalling and wheeling, out to sea. Then he raced up the cliff to us, wagged his little stern ecstatically as he approached, and sat down again by our side, intently and wistfully surveying the sandwich-box. The whole exercise was carried out in double-quick time and evinced the highest degree of alertness, zest and savoir-faire. And yet, as I have said, he seemed an old, rugged, undernourished dog, and was unquestionably very mangy.

It was only after we had sat there for an hour that we realised he had no collar and that he belonged to none of the picnicking parties who had been sharing the promontory with us. And when, now alone, we rose to leave, the dog rose and followed us. Or, to be precise, he preceded us, for from the start of our association he took the initiative. He did so in a manner that made it clear that there was now a bond between us and that he regarded us as his property. Whenever we paused he paused, and when we sat down—which we deliberately did to see what would happen—

he sat down too and regarded us with a look of deep interest and affection. He seemed, indeed, for all his shaggy and disreputable appearance, the soul of amiability, for we noted particularly the friendliness with which he greeted the dogs in the outskirts of the little town through which we had to pass, wagging his tail in a frenzy of welcome at their approach and lavishing upon them those attentions which seem to endear dogs to one another. There was never the faintest hint of a fight in his manner; he positively loved his fellow-dogs, all of them, the motion of his quivering tail seemed to say. Not even the churliest cur could have picked a quarrel with a creature so imbued with the spirit of universal charity.

After that, passing through the town, we lost him—or rather, he lost us. We were relieved, for the prospect of a stray dog on our hands so far from home, and at such a time, naturally dismayed us. Yet some days later, just before my brief holiday ended, we walked over the cliffs again to pay our last visit to the storm-battered estuary where we had encountered the little creature. In the intervening days we had spoken of him and his inexplicable charm, and had half-wondered whether we should ever see him again. But we were not thinking of him at all when, just as we were finishing our tea in the local hostelry, we found him once more sitting quietly by our side.

It was inevitable, I suppose, that we should have offered him cake, and inevitable, too—though we were not expecting it—that he should again have followed us. This time, as we climbed the steep hill out of the town, it became clear that he was following us in earnest. Remembering that we had a six or seven miles' walk over the cliffs before us, and that we should have to retrace our steps next day if we were not either heartlessly to abandon him or adopt him for life, we were greatly distressed. We were still on a main road, and to all the people we met walking towards the town we explained our plight and asked them to take the dog back to where he belonged. But from them we also learned what we had guessed—that he belonged to nowhere; that he was an inveterate runaway for whom the police were seeking a home and who had been eking out a summer's existence rabbiting on the cliffs and begging largesse from picnic parties. And though two or three of them did their best to lure him back to the town, he refused to be caught and persisted in following us.

A mile or so out of the town our way left the main road and struck across the cliffs. After that, we knew, we should meet no other travellers. We accordingly did our best to persuade the dog to return. But he appeared to regard our gestures and pointings as a species of game, cocked up his ears and watched us for a time, then lost interest and sat down, awaiting our pleasure. In the end I was reduced to threatening him with a stone, which I threw, miserably and feebly, in his direction. When the dog realised that what I was doing was no game, but a deliberate attempt to get rid of him, the confidence in his bearing vanished in a moment and he became a broken, forlorn, abject creature, with drooping tail and tragic eyes. He slunk away, and we hurriedly resumed our path towards the cliff, daring neither to speak nor look at one another. I felt as though I were a murderer.

But we had not done with the dog; that loving heart was to redeem us. For suddenly my wife gripped my arm and said, "Look," and, turning, I saw him following, miserably, far back from the underside of the hedge. That was the end or, so far as we were concerned, the beginning. We let him come up and thereafter he took charge of us, trotting ahead as though everything was now arranged, as indeed—though we did not know it—it was. But, as we discussed him, I agreed that, if the farmer and his wife with whom we were lodging would let him stay for the next two nights—our last in Cornwall—I would telephone the police in the morning and offer him a home.

At the farm we were successful in obtaining permission for the dog to stay with us. When, after our supper, we returned to the room where we had left him on the floor, we found him, to our horror, curled up on one of our landlady's armchairs. It was symptomatic of what was to come: the quiet assurance of it, the luxurious comfort, the air of full proprietorship. Consigned for the night to a barn into which he was inveigled with a bowl of bread and milk—a dish for which, for all his recent hunger, he showed considerable contempt—he was waiting at the door to be let out when early next morning my wife went to release him. I can still see that eager, slightly offended, little white figure emerging like a bullet from his place of confinement and greeting his rescuer on the top of the stone steps that led to it.

During that day the dog was constantly disappearing and re-appearing, as befitted the incorrigible rover he so clearly was. And yet the curious thing was that, just as he took food so gently and with such irreproachable manners, he was perfectly house-trained. A good home he must have had at some time, and now apparently wanted another. Yet in all other ways he was a wild dog, used to complete liberty and impatient of the slightest restraint. In the course of the morning, while we were bathing, he attached himself to at least half-a-dozen other parties, and there seemed no reason to expect he would remain with us. When I telephoned the police to offer him a home he had already vanished, only to reappear unexpectedly soon after permission to take him had been granted.

Yet when that afternoon, after we had toiled up the cliff from the beach after his twentieth disappearance and my wife and I had agreed that if he rejoined us, as at that moment he did, I should walk him back to Boscastle and return him there if he would follow me—since it scarcely seemed a kindness to deprive one of his liberty who valued it so much—he turned his back firmly on me and persisted in following his mistress to the farm and a life of domesticity. He had chosen.

Next morning, when the car called to take us to the station, he had again disappeared—rabbiting—and it seemed certain we should have to depart without him. But just as the luggage was being put in, he reappeared. My wife had made him a collar of string, and with this round his neck—a symbol of his changed status—he accompanied us to the station. When he saw the train and realised he was to go with us he went mad with joy. And through all the long, crowded journey to London he remained quiet and gentle, curled up at our feet or in the corridor, patiently awaiting his future. Even Waterloo, with its to him bewildering turmoil and clatter, did not daunt that staunch little heart, though, when his mistress left the taxi and disappeared into a shop, he became wildly agitated. And when, late at night, we arrived after further train and car journeys at the old North Buckingham-shire house which for the next three years was to be his home, he trotted into the garden as though he had lived there all his life. By every muscle of his taut, alert body he made it clear he regarded it as his own.[1]

* * *

II

Camberley Kate[2]

Someone—a discerning bishop, I think, who had been urged to prohibit their presence in the churchyards of his diocese—once observed that Heaven must be largely peopled by dogs. Certainly if, as we are told, Heaven is love, these animals, who have so unaccountably attached themselves to the human race, would seem to possess for their limited natures a rather larger share of this divine attribute than most humans. The intensity of the affection they display towards those to whom they have given their hearts is something that never ceases to amaze; their loyalty, their humility, their capacity for forgiveness and complete freedom from resentment, even when they have been apparently forgotten or slighted by the objects of their devotion, are Christian virtues in which few can claim to equal them. All they ask is to be with those they love, to serve them and share as far as possible their joys and sorrows. Look at the eyes through which a dog watches his master and one can catch a glimpse of what is meant by the Kingdom of Heaven, for it mirrors the soul of a creature which, in its adoration for the subject of its love, has forgotten self.

I am always moved when I hear of a human being doing something more than ordinary in acknowledgment of the bond of love between man and dog—between, that is, two of God's creatures who have achieved understanding and mutual trust despite the immense differences in their natures and circumstances. Equally, I feel appalled when I read of acts of human

---

[1] The story of Jimmy's subsequent life is told in my book, *Jimmy*, Collins, 10s 6d.

[2] *I.L.N.* 22 February 1964. This article brought in more than £3,000 in spontaneous gifts for Miss Kate Ward, who with characteristic selflessness used it to create a trust for her own and other animals after her death.

cruelty and hardness of heart that betray and outrage that relationship. Of those who have shown by their deeds their awareness of
the value of canine affection and trust, there can be few who have
surpassed the record of an old lady now living in the little Surrey
town of Camberley. Anyone passing in the middle of the day
along its long crowded high-street, down which there forever
moves in either direction an interminable and noisy motorcade,
may catch a glimpse, if he is lucky, of an astonishing spectacle.
Preceded by a certain hubbub, he will see an elderly woman
making her way along the pavement surrounded by dogs of every
kind and species, pushing before her a small wooden go-cart made
of box planks, over the edge of which peer the proud and happy
faces of three or four privileged members of her canine flock,
while the remainder, tethered to the cart, wave their sterns in
enjoyment and appreciation of their two hours' regular walk to
the common behind Sandhurst. There can be no doubt in the
mind of anyone who sees them and has had any experience of
dogs that they are happy and well cared-for and that they are
completely devoted to their human rescuer, guide and friend. Yet
their benefactress is a poor working woman now nearing her
seventieth year, living alone on an old age pension, who for
nearly twenty years has kept open house for unwanted and ill-
treated dogs and who devotes her whole life and her all to their
maintenance. Obeying Christ's precept to "take no thought for
your life, what ye shall eat or what ye shall drink", this valiant
and tender-hearted woman, because she loves, understands and
pities these gentle, affectionate beasts betrayed and abandoned by
man, shares with them her home and food, refusing none that
are brought to her door, keeping them till she can find them
homes and, in the meantime, trusting that somehow Heaven will
provide for them. Some years ago, moved by the sight of that
valiant little figure as she manoeuvred her pack along the pavement and guessing what her self-imposed mission of love and
service to these lowly and trusting creatures must involve in
labour and sacrifice, I wrote to her out of the blue and begged
her to accept from a fellow dog-lover a small gift for their
Christmas dinner—for it was December. She replied, "When
people like you see them and understand what I am trying to do,

it helps wonderful. It's often been the last penny but I have known to be so up against it as to kneel down and ask at 2 a.m., and it's come." On another occasion she wrote—for we have become friends—"I always say they are His. I am just looking after them. I love to feel I am the unknown hand (never mentioned in the story) to get ready the stable for His coming on earth." I have one picture of her that I particularly treasure—with two dogs, too weak to sit up but huddled against her, who had been dumped from a car in the middle of last winter's terrible weather and whom she rescued after they had been wandering for five days, starving and shivering, round a local army training-ground. That lowly home in the London Road at Camberley, with the friendless dogs gathered round the winter evening's fire with their faces turned upwards to their benefactress as she sits among them, is about as near to the Kingdom of Heaven, I feel, as anywhere one could find in England today. When I think of Kate Ward—"a Yorkshire lass that has the guts left to love the unwanted," as she once described herself—I am reminded of the words, "Inasmuch as ye have done it unto the least of these, my brethren, ye have done it unto me." A dog is only an animal, but then so, for all his achievements, pride and acquisitions, is man, who need not feel ashamed to number these humble but devoted beasts among his brethren. "I can only do a tiny bit," this stouthearted Englishwoman wrote in a recent letter to me—she has twenty-nine strays in her home at the moment—"over three hundred saved, and now at 69 years with only my old age pension I will spend my last years in taking, caring and loving them." And that, when one comes to consider it rightly, is the spirit which made this country great.

*   *   *

III

A Good Biter[1]

Some pictures of a mongoose in a newspaper revived a memory I had almost forgotten. I once shared a house with one of these little creatures, and the recollection of its sojourn—it lasted several years—was quite nostalgic. It was purchased for a few pounds in a London store, for it is, or was, comparatively easy to buy a mongoose. What is much more difficult, at least in England, is to keep or dispose of one.

The one which shared my home was grey, bristly and at least nine-tenths wild. It regarded human beings rather as Russian Communists seem to regard their allies, as something to be borne with and used when necessary, but to be held in persistent, if occasionally concealed, suspicion and, when not otherwise inconvenient, to be well bitten. During the first year of its sojourn it bit almost everyone in the house two or three times a month, and it was a good biter. It enjoyed biting, but, having bitten, it proceeded with dazzling rapidity to turn its mind and its long, enquiring nose to some other object or activity. It plainly believed that a mongoose who bit and ran away would live to bite another day. In this assumption it was correct, for it continued to do so with complete impunity as long as it lived.

Attempts to cure it of the habit were unavailing. It is impossible to chastise a mongoose—one might as well try to chastise a mouse or a lizard—and one cannot reason with it. One must either accept its habits and idiosyncrasies or destroy it or part with it. In this also it had a resemblance to our Russian allies. Being as an Englishman unable and unwilling to proceed to extremities, one took it as one found it. And, after all, this was only fair, for the poor animal had no choice but to live with us.

Not that it did not try to get away. It made many attempts to escape, and, had it been able to write escape-stories, it could have earned enough by publishing them to purchase a daily grass-snake, its great love. I inhabited at that time a very old house

[1] *I.L.N.* 5 March 1949.

whose thick and uneven boards of elm and oak were riddled with holes. Though the mongoose used to pass its nights in a cage which stood in one recess of a large open fireplace, it seemed cruel not to give it all the liberty one could; so in the daytime the little creature was allowed to roam the room as it pleased—one in which all holes had been carefully stopped. Finding no egress, it spent most of its time racing up and down the back of a sofa, turning with a wonderful speed and agility, and uttering fierce, spluttering cries at anyone who attempted, out of affection or for any other cause, to obstruct its course. The rest of its time it spent in incessant and insatiable exploring, darting with intent, beady eyes towards some distant object, only to be deflected long before it arrived by some other object, towards which it would dash until again deflected. For this reason it seldom arrived anywhere, which was a good thing, for it must have tended to make the room more interesting for it than it would otherwise have been. Still, it plainly regarded its four walls as a prison, and, whenever anyone opened the door, it would make a dash for the passage beyond. Though the inmates of the house fell into a habit of guarding against this, sooner or later someone would forget the lurking quicksilver on the other side of the door, and the mongoose would be out. Where it went on these occasions was a matter of chance; it might dart upstairs, race round a corner or double back on its tracks. But almost certainly, sooner or later, it would disappear into a hole. After that everyone available would be summoned to keep watch, not only on that particular hole, but on all the others within reach. Yet as the intestines of the house were complex and manifold—a mysterious world of dusty caverns and mouse-haunted corridors unexplored since the seventeenth century—the mongoose, which was nothing if not an explorer, was often invisible for several hours. When the watcher's patience was at last rewarded by a glimpse of a little twitching grey nose and the scrutiny of two minute, shining eyes, as likely as not the quarry would again withdraw, like Villeneuve before Nelson's watching frigates, and all would be to do again.

Curiosity was this mongoose's predominating trait—a vivid and unresting curiosity. It wanted to roam and it wanted to climb—and a cruel fate, in a hostile climate, kept it confined within the narrow haunts of man. I often thought it should be released and allowed to sally forth into the Buckinghamshire fields, but the cold northern clay and the guns of my poultry-keeping neighbours would have soon brought its days to an end. It was never really happy until it had ascended to the highest point of whatever room it was in, whence, standing erect on its hind legs, it would pirouette round, peering intently into every corner of the horizon. For this reason it was always glad—even in its angry and tempestuous morning course up and down the back of the sofa—to leap on to my proffered shoulder, and thence to the top of my head, where it would rear itself up and, taller than man, its jailor, survey the landscape. On summer days I used to take it round the garden, or occasionally down the lane, so poised.

Its name—for little originality went to its christening—was Mongy. In appearance, when quiescent, it resembled a grey rat. I shall never forget bringing home a seafaring acquaintance who was assisting my researches in some naval enterprise—a convivial soul who liked his liquor as deep as the seas he had so long and honourably sailed—and witnessing his sudden perturbation at the sight of what appeared to be a large grey rat lying, very much at ease, at full length in front of the fire. The poor creature's greatest joy was an electric fire; before such it would preen itself in a rich jungle luxuriance, bristling out its fur so that the hot, sunlike rays could reach its little inner hide. In the evening this was its invariable place: there, or in the warm, companionable lap of some brave man or woman. I say brave, because as often as not its approach to such a haven was up the inside rather than the outside of one's clothing. Affected by a spasm of evening affection —in the morning it had none—it would suddenly insinuate itself into skirt or trouser-leg and start to ascend rapidly. I can still experience the hot, tickly sensation of its taut, pulsating body, and the terror in my guests' eyes when they, too, were similarly honoured.

It died long ago and was buried, not in the soil of its fathers, but in alien clay. The photographs in my newspaper were so like it that, looking at them, I almost felt that twenty years had lapsed and I should find my old friend lying once more by the fire or racing up and down the sofa back.

*   *   *

IV

The Lioness and the Badger[1]

Few lions—or, rather, lionesses—can have had a more distinguished career than Mrs. Adamson's "Elsa", not even the well-known lion who allowed a Roman citizen of Nubia to extract a thorn from his foot and years later, recognising his benefactor in the arena, refrained from devouring him—a tale from which generations of British schoolboys suffered in that, now I suppose discarded, educational exercise called Latin Unseen. She has even been made the subject of a learned treatise by Sir Julian Huxley, entitled "The Importance of Elsa", full of phrases like "personal involvement", "emergent animal personalities", "fully integrated", "psychological development", "enlarged mammalian ethnology", which any author would be proud to find in an article devoted to his work. It seems sad to think that "Elsa" herself is not alive to bask in this autumnal glow of scientific recognition. One hopes, however, that it is appreciated by her children who, thanks to Mrs. Adamson's dedicated labours and those of the House of Collins, are repeating their mother's literary achievements and success. The three cubs, as Julian Huxley points out, have developed very diverse temperaments, and it is perhaps too much to hope that the jovial and exuberant extrovert, "Jespah", who "roamed through the tents and nibbled at human toes", would keep abreast of the latest articles in the Press or even read the letters about him in the *Sunday Times*. Just as a fox-hunting squire who inherits a famous library can spare little time to its shelves, so, one supposes, Jespah must miss the finer points of the scientific analysis of his mother's personality, while enjoying her well-earned royalties in pursuit of the wholesome, if philistine, pleasures of a normal lion's life. But I like to

[1] *I.L.N.* 23 September 1961.

think that Elsa's shy daughter and namesake, "Little Elsa"—
"so timid that she could never approach the human circle"—is
the kind of girl who develops into a serious reader and always
has a copy of *The Hibbert Journal* and a work, say, of Jung's in
her lair to read as she meditatively eats her evening haunch of
gazelle. If so, she must be gratified by Sir Julian's recognition of
her mother's significance.

Yet though I have never studied "the science of animal
behaviour" or ethnology, as Sir Julian tells us it is called, and am
no more qualified to write about such matters than I am to do so
about the principles of nuclear fission, I have seen enough of
animals in my limited experience to endorse his conclusions.
When he writes that "the story of Elsa demonstrates the wealth
of potentialities in higher mammals waiting to be drawn out"
and that "the best and perhaps the only method of eliciting them
in any fullness is through emotional but intelligent involvement
by way of . . . understanding love," I know what he says is
true. Animals, like human beings, have a strong, spontaneous
capacity for fear; nor, without it, seeing what a predatory world
ours is, could they continue to exist. Yet, if only it can be brought
out, they have also a strong, and deeply moving, capacity for love
and trust, "love that casteth out fear". Indeed, if one wants to
test the truth of the Christian philosophy of love one can hardly
do so with quicker results than by adopting an animal and treating
it with persistent consideration and understanding because one
loves it. For what one will see, within the conditions of its animal
nature, is the development of what, for want of a scientific word,
one can only call a soul. The animal will, in fact, transcend its
physical limitations by its love for a fellow-creature, not of its
own kind and bound to it by no natural or reproductive relationship. The mysterious force or spirit of love will inform not only
its actions but its features, so that, just as with a human being
possessed by love, its expression will become transcended. One
can see this most easily in a dog—an animal which, having, by
some astonishing process of racial evolution, adapted its nature
to human domestic existence, is in an exceptionally favoured
position to enlarge its personality through interchange of love
with a human being.

What, as Sir Julian Huxley points out, is so peculiar, though by no means unique, in Elsa's story and Mrs. Adamson's achievement, is that the development of her personality through her personal involvement with a human being was effected, not in the artificial conditions of domestic captivity, but in those of her natural wild existence to which her human friends had deliberately restored her. She was, as he says, "fully integrated with the life of the wild," sought out a wild mate, brought up her cubs in the jungle, killed her own prey, received fearful wounds in fights with rival lionesses, "yet the human attachment remained unimpaired." All this is intensely moving and revealing, yet—apart from the formidable and dangerous strength of a lioness—there is nothing unique about it, as, for instance, Gavin Maxwell's charming book about otters shows. Recently I have had the privilege of watching the growth of a similar relationship between my sister-in-law and a female badger, the shyest of the larger denizens of the English woodlands, who was deposited on her doorstep by a farm boy whose friends had dug the trembling creature and her family out of their sett. I happened to be at my Wiltshire home on the night of its arrival and I have seldom seen anything more pathetic than this defenceless, bereaved little creature surrounded by the most dangerous of all its hereditary foes. With infinite compassion and patience my sister-in-law taught it to take nourishment at human hands and to share the daily life of her own domestic animals—a young Alsatian bitch, three Pekingese, a cat and several kittens, a pair of budgerigars and a garden full of hens. Within a few weeks one could witness the astonishing spectacle of a badger, with her long-pointed white and black-striped head, tiny human-like hands and round, bearlike, shaving-brush posterior, gambolling ahead of her adopted human mother and her dogs and engaging in mimic warfare with the Alsatian, as this unconventional group made its way through the curious cattle in the park or proceeded along the paths in the beechwoods, themselves full of wild badgers' setts into which "Brookie", as she was christened, would periodically disappear, only to emerge and scamper, or rather glide, with astonishing velocity after her companions when they resumed their walk without her.

After a month or two a far more remarkable thing happened. For, as the badger grew, her existence in a small, overcrowded cottage presented almost insoluble problems, and, out of sheer necessity, restrictions had to be placed on her liberty. Her habit of rising in the middle of the night, breaking into the larder and eating everything there edible by badgers—and nearly all food appeared to be—proved too much even for her human custodian's seemingly inexhaustible charity to animals. In the end, after two or three ineffectual attempts to bar her out—for a badger can open or climb over almost anything—the larder was made impregnable. But badgers are nocturnal animals, and this interference with the freedom of her home hurt her deeply. That night she vanished. All my sister-in-law's attempts to find her proved unavailing until two days later, walking past a disused sett in the beechwoods with her Alsatian, she was greeted by Brookie with cries of joy as the latter suddenly emerged to rejoin her human and canine companions. Since then this astonishing animal has lived a life, half-wild, half-human, betaking herself every morning to one or other of three ancient setts on the wooded hillside above her human habitation and returning at tea-time, after which she joins in the normal life of the household for the rest of the day, expecting and consuming three full meals between then and bedtime. As often as not, when she leaves for her sett in the morning, she takes with her some object of household use—a hearthrug or a cushion which she endeavours, sometimes with success, to pull into her sett; on one occasion she was discovered trying to remove a deck-chair. This dual life seems both to satisfy and enrich her nature. During the past few weeks a look of great trust and gentleness, formerly lacking, has appeared in her eyes. Sometimes when a human being or a dog unknown to her appears she will withdraw hastily and in obvious agitation, but she has only to hear my sister-in-law's voice or the Alsatian sniffing at the door of her sett to emerge with welcoming cries.

*　　*　　*

V

Sammy the Cat[1]

It is a week now since my old cat, Sammy, went out with a lame leg into the long grass of the June meadows and ditches. He is still missing and I fear he will never return.

Sammy was—and perhaps still is—a red cat. He had a beautiful white waistcoat of great softness and four very white paws. Someone—probably a rival—had helped himself to a large slice out of his right ear, thus giving him a slightly battered and rakish appearance. A scar on his nose enhanced this effect: together with his enormous whiskers he gave something of the impression of an old-time German nobleman who had been very well and expensively educated. Nor was the sense of possessing a past, which Sammy conveyed even in his most dignified and domestic moments, wholly misleading. For the tiles, using the word in its metaphorical sense—since mine is a rural neighbourhood—was Sammy's spiritual home. His earthly one he shared with me. He did so with great grace and charm, conferring considerable distinction on a comparatively humble residence. For if Sammy was a rake, there was no denying he was also an aristocrat. His was the highest kind of aristocracy—the sort which makes one realise instinctively there could never be anything higher. It was not that he possessed anything in the way of a pedigree: a long line of village ancestors, all gingery and all small, was the most that Sammy could boast had it ever occurred to him to boast. Nor was there a trace of the Persian in him: like the great Elizabeth, he was mere English. Apart from the exquisite softness of his coat and the lithe grace of his movements, his supremacy— as marked in the world of humans as of cats—lay in his unspoken, unchallengeable assurance that he was welcome at all times and in all places. Never doubting this, he never made the least effort to exploit his personality. He did so without trying.

But the strongest of all Sammy's traits was his lovingness. Never was a cat with such a passion for affection: to receive it he

[1] *I.L.N.* 17 June 1939. This was written thirty years ago, but I have kept it in the present tense.

would even leave a plate of fish half-tasted. He was really devoted to the company of humans: would run eager and purring into their presence and go into an ecstasy of vibration if one pulled his tail the right way. His master, who had long mastered the exact art of this friendly exercise, was treated with a passionate devotion which was clearly as genuine as it was flattering. This faithful beast would gather up his elastic strength and hurl himself into my lap, sit outside my bedroom purring loudly for admission, and give little cries of pleasure when he discovered that I had returned home after absence. No dog—always subject to his cat's prerogative of proud independence—could have been more devoted or companionable. Even his habit of digging his claws deep into one's leg in moments of strong feeling arose from the intensity of his affections. He did not only lavish these on human kind. He had a strong affection for his own species—too strong a one. In the end, I fear, it was his undoing. His love-affairs peopled not only my own house but those of many other people: a whole world of cats sprang into being as a result of his widespread attentions. Often I have seen him drinking milk out of the same saucer as his children's children's children's children: and to all, if of the opposite sex, he proved himself, regardless of the laws of consanguinity, a husband as well as a progenitor. The loft was always full of kittens so long as Sammy was about. So were the lofts of my neighbours.

For, noble and rare creature though he was, there was nothing exclusive in Sammy's courting. Few cats can ever have had a pleasanter home or—not to put too fine a point on it—been more spoilt. But for the sake of some distant love he would always leave it, including his own half-dozen or more wives, and go adventuring again. In this respect he never grew old. I will not say that he answered such calls without hesitation or reflection: he would generally spend some hours, or even days, mewing a good deal and occasionally looking up at me with pleading eyes before leaving the comforts of his home and setting out across the milkless, fireless fields. I think he regarded it as a duty, and now that he is gone—if he has gone—I am inclined to agree with him, for it is a comfort to reflect that he left behind so many little images of his own comely self. Often he would be found miles

away, laying siege to some remote farm-yard Helen: on such
occasions he would generally return half-starved, blood-stained
and tattered after Homeric contests with what must have been
whole armies of local Toms. Occasionally, to execute his campaigns the better, he would put up at some neighbour's where,
on account of his trustful charm, he was always kindly received:
the district nurse was a particular friend of his and was sometimes
his hostess for several days. But a fortnight ago he returned thin
and limping, after a long absence, with a cruelly swollen leg. For
two days he was nursed and pampered back towards health: then,
as soon as he could stand upright, he disappeared again. Twenty-
four hours later he was found hobbling and mewing piteously in
a field a mile or two away. Brought back by car, he lingered sadly,
lapping milk and sleeping uneasily for another night and day,
and then once more he slipped out and vanished, limping, lame
and game, into the fields and woods.[1]

[1] He never returned.

CHAPTER 10

Forty Years On

Forty years on, when afar and asunder
Parted are those who are singing today,
When you look back and forgetfully wonder
What you were like in your work and your play.
Then, it may be, there will often come 'oer you
Glimpses of notes like the catch of a song—
Visions of boyhood shall float them before you,
Echoes of dreamland shall bear them along.

EDWARD BOWEN

Cricketer's Dreams · An Effervescent Fixture ·
Ireland Revisited · Enchanted Islands ·
Anne Carter her Book · London in October ·
The Veterans' Parade ·

I

Cricketer's Dreams[1]

The little inn by the West Dorset sea had a minute patch of grass
between it and the gaunt row of Edwardian boarding-houses
opposite, and on the grass stood a set of rickety cricket stumps,
with a single stump defiantly facing it about a dozen yards away.
I had not noticed this remote link with Lord's in my first impressions on revisiting the place where I used to be taken on holidays
in the early years of the century, when jovial King Edward VII
was on the throne and Marie Lloyd in the heyday of her fame.
But more than anything else it brought my past back to me—
more than the shingly, shelving shore where I learned to swim,

[1] *Illustrated London News* 23 September 1950.

with many a gulp of Channel water, from a boat off the end of a rope; more than the little harbour where, in that simpler age, coastal sailing-craft, manned by W. W. Jacobs characters, crowded together to delight a small boy's eyes and, with rich stink of tar and brine, luxuriously fed his sea-dog-haunted imagination; more even than the dreaming coastline circling westwards and southwards into Devon, past Golden Cap and the glimmer of far white houses that marked Jane Austen's Lyme Regis. For, though till that moment I had altogether forgotten the fact, on that identical patch of grass, though not, I suppose, with those identical stumps, I used to play the greatest cricket of my life. Never, in my long, laborious, unrewarded, inglorious cricketing career—not when, by A. J. Webbe's side, I saw on one occasion Archie MacLaren make a century and on another Trott take a double hat-trick; not when, still a fag, I kept wicket in my first house-match at Harrow and almost missed but actually caught, in a nervous spasm of snatching, a member of the school eleven; not when, during the First World War, by chance of temporary station but certainly not of desert, I played for one incredible afternoon in the same team as Hobbs—did the game assume for me the romantic wonder that it did in those early days of childhood nearly fifty years ago by the Dorset sea. The games I played there were, at their largest, impromptu matches between half-a-dozen or so children and a few grown-up relations. More often, when I could find no one to bowl for me or to face my own erratic but tireless bowling, they were played by myself alone, throwing the ball high into the air and then racing, bat in hand, down the pitch to receive it at first bounce and send it bounding high into the roadway and, occasionally, right across it onto the beach. But they were games lit by the light that never was on sea or land, games in which the imagination rode prince of the player, games which in my hopeful fancy were the forerunners of matches that would astonish the world. In imagination I was not a clumsy little boy with astigmatism and ill-co-ordinated hands and a congenital inability to play cricket as he wanted to play it. When I held the bat I was G. L. Jessop, crouching, with one eye on the roof of the Oval pavilion where I was about to send the ball flying and

Australia's till that moment well-founded hopes of victory. When I put myself on to bowl—as I unceasingly did—I was Barnes, and the straightest, artfullest trundler the world had ever seen. At cover-point I was greased lightning; in the slips as vigilant and sure as the Brigade of Guards. There was no limit to the wonders I performed—in imagination—and the delight I took in performing them.

Do other little boys, I wonder, living in the atom-haunted middle instead of in the Victorian-shaded beginning of the twentieth century, derive the same delight from the free play of their fancies? Or are such day-dreams forbidden them by enlightened parents and teachers as a form of indulgent wishful-thinking? I do not know. I only know that I could not indulge in them now. In my fifties I am aware of what everyone but I must have known in my boyhood: that my chances of playing at Lord's are non existent and always have been. The end, and beginning, of my cricketing career is a seat in the Pavilion, achieved not by athletic prowess but by virtue of the fact that a thoughtful and far-sighted father entered my name for candidature on the day of my birth. The glories of a late cut off Lindwall can never be mine. Nor can the spectacle of Nourse's wicket spread-eagled by my well-schooled cunning.

> *The eternal dawn, beyond a doubt,*
> *Shall break on hill and plain*
> *And put all stars and candles out*
> *Ere we be young again.*

And yet, as on that August afternoon of sun and wind, I looked at those diminutive stumps and that patch of ragged, salt-bitten grass, shining in the vivid Dorset air, I felt that with a bat in my hand I could still challenge the world. That I could still be what I would be: not Bryant the dry-as-dust, Bryant the scribbler, but Bryant the artful trundler, Bryant the slogging joy of the Tavern and Mound. And was that youthful dream of ambition any sillier than any of the dreams of ambition or human amelioration with which I and other grown men tease themselves? If I was a young ass in 1906, Stalin is an old ass in 1950. And for all his submissive millions, he will get no nearer his real ambition than I did with bat and ball. It is not in the nature of man to achieve dreams of glory, and, when he does, they are dreams no longer and have long ceased to be glorious, at any rate to him.

It was Robert Louis Stevenson who said it was better to travel hopefully than to arrive. All my experience of life confirms his diagnosis. I have had my little successes, and have enjoyed them, I dare say, as much as any man, but they have given me no joy to compare with those of sweet, romantic, unrealised anticipation. Indeed, I have generally found that at the moment when I have been reaping the reward of some long-wrought endeavour, I have been mentally employed in day-dreaming and preparing for some future and probably unrealisable achievement. It is only when the imagination is active that man takes wings. At all other times he is clogged, sluggish, earthbound—a dull, joyless creature. And it is the impossible that really inspires him most of all. As we grow older, we are drawn in memory more and more to those early hours of dreaming anticipation, when time was a beckoning highway, not a closing corridor to decay and the grave, and when life was given us, in our estimation, to achieve all our heart desired. And those who retain the secret of youth are those who continue to hope and dream greatly in defiance of all the gloomy phenomena of material realisation. I think if I could stand for an hour a day, bat in hand, on that wind-swept pitch on the sandy Dorset grass by the southern sea, I should still remain young by virtue of my dreams. For I should then inhabit, as I inhabited then, a world in which Ranjitsinhji was eternal and C. B. Fry for ever young, and I numbered among that glorious, immortal company, playing throughout an everlasting summer in fields of asphodel.

*　　*　　*

II

An Effervescent Fixture[1]

There is one cricket match I never fail to attend. For two days of
the year little matters to me except that Harrow should beat Eton,
or if it cannot manage to do that, that it shouldn't lose! There I
sit in a kind of trance transcending time, with my whole being
consumed with a passionate desire that victory should go, not to
the best, but to the right side. Sometimes it does, sometimes it
doesn't; more often, the match, being subject to the vagaries of
the English climate, it does neither. Yet for all my agonised
partisanship, I find this makes little difference to my enjoyment.
If I was out there in the middle of the ground, batting as I have
never batted or bowling as I have never bowled—for, with me,
desire on the pitch always far outran performance—I couldn't be
enjoying myself more.

In the days when I wore fourth-form coat and collar, "Lord's"
was a great social occasion. Every seat in the ground was filled,
while an enormous concourse, in which the fair sex predominated,
continually processed round the circumference, paying no attention whatever to the cricket. The fuss, starch and flummery of
dress was almost stifling; for days before the event even the
humblest fag was obsessed with such unwonted objects as patent-
leather shoes, white spats and tasselled canes, all of which were
de rigueur on the great day. Being by nature an untidy, not to say
slovenly, little boy, it was all, for me, rather terrifying. Yet I
would no more have missed it than, say, an ensign of the Guards,
in the days of the Regency, had he a chance to be there, would
have missed Waterloo! Though there was no actual compulsion
in the matter, I doubt whether a boy in either school would have
absented himself. He could never have held up his head with his
fellows had he done so.

Between the wars a laxer spirit prevailed. The match was still
attended by a large, fashionable crowd, though nothing like so
large and fashionable as in Edwardian days. The first faint
stirrings of a "permissive" society had begun, the "bright young

[1] *I.L.N.* 27 July 1968; 11 July 1936.

people" were breaking out of the close ring of convention and tradition, and the weekend habit had started to empty the West End on Saturdays and provide, like tennis, a rival attraction to Lord's. Yet the latter was still a major social event, though no longer an unchallenged and unchallengeable one. During the 'thirties to make one's way to St. John's Wood through its pro-letarian southern approaches wearing a top hat was to be made aware of a certain ground-swell of social resentment, even to find oneself the object of derisive and opprobrious remarks! The unquestioning acceptance by the Cockney world of a "toff's" cricketing gala day had become a thing of the past; the political puritanism of the "Waste Land" could be felt in the Long Room itself, where the then Conservative Prime Minister, himself an Harrovian like the great wartime Minister who was soon to follow him, could be seen swinging his legs under the table. There was a faint prophetic rumbling as of tumbrils in the air.

Yet curiously enough the Second World War, like a thunder-storm, seems to have blown all that away, for when it was over and "Lord's" after six years' interregnum was held again, all resentment at what remained of its ancient sartorial elegance had vanished. There was in those early post-1945 days a delightful alfresco air about the occasion, as though its devotees, now only a fraction of their former number, had just escaped, as indeed so many of them had, from the kitchen sink, while around such top hats as were worn after their long wartime sojourn in dusty boxes and cupboards there was an attendant nimbus, if not of moths, of mothballs. During the last few years clothes worn at the match have grown as diversified as those of the general com-munity outside, if not even more so. The men affect every kind of attire, from grey morning coats and top hats, worn by such scholastic Jacobites as myself, to that extraordinary assortment of garments of diverse and conflicting periods, apparently hastily selected and at random from a fancy dress costumier's box, which appeal so strongly and unaccountably to that section of male youth which wears its hair to its shoulders. Others attend unashamedly in nondescript everyday wear and the kind of hats that look as though a bus had been over them. As for the ladies, they come in all the sex's many guises, from the miniest of miniskirts to the kind of funeral finery worn by Victorian great aunts at church bazaars. And everyone is happy and utterly indifferent to what anyone else is wearing.

For the game's the thing. Though the attendance is only a shadow of what it once was—and here I feel, though one speaks of them with awe, the headmasters of both schools might do more to remind both boys and parents that a great traditional occasion is worthy of support—those who do come, both young and old, enter into the spirit of the game with a zest equalled in no other match of the year, not even a Lord's Test Match. The difference between this ever fresh and effervescent fixture and that of the ordinary county match is like the difference between champagne and a bottle of milk which has spent a weekend on the doorstep. Whatever happens to the fortunes of the game, sooner or later—and more often sooner than later—the excitement grows intense. Even before the match begins many of those making their way to the ground have a look in their eyes reminiscent of the gentleman in Coleridge's poem who on honey dew had fed and drunk the milk of paradise.

> *O cabby, trot him faster,*
> *O hurry, engine, on!*
> *Come glory or disaster*
> *Before the day be done!*

So sang Edward Bowen, greatest of schoolmaster poets, of the match in 1888 when F. S. Jackson captained the Harrow eleven. This year my "cabby" was a Barbadian who, when I asked him if he came from the Islands and explained what my errand was, entered into my hopes and wished me victory with a grin as wide and sunny as the Caribbean. What was more, I—or rather, Harrow —had it, and by as narrow a margin as anyone not suffering from heart disease could desire.

To the historian this match remains a sheer delight. It dates from the days when Lord's was a suburban meadow, and its coaches and carriages, which appear annually from heaven knows what forgotten mews or stable-yard, belong to the time when the spectators drove their vehicles on to the ground and sat in them in preference to the more plebeian grass, which was then the only alternative. The rival players are the beneficiaries of the pious Henry VI and a thriving Elizabethan yeoman—the Middle Ages pitted against the Renaissance—and the match between them was first played before Trafalgar. Byron took part in it, and Peel, Aberdeen, Palmerston, Gladstone and Rosebery, as in our own time Baldwin, Churchill, Eden, Macmillan and Douglas-Home—who also played in it—watched it as partisans. There is nothing more endearing to human nature than an annual festival. It exhilarates and it binds. It occurs sufficiently seldom not to lose the agreeable sense of being an occasion, and yet often enough to be reassuring and familiar. Creatures of habit in a world of change, our hearts cling to whatever gives an illusion of permanence.

For two days the hallowed field, tented no more save in its obscurer parts and encompassed now by stands built for more famous but scarcely greater matches—for it is the heart that measures greatness—is made the temple for an act of ritual. It is like the ritual of a great Continental cathedral, in which every comer can take his part when and as he pleases and never mar the strong harmony of the whole. Within certain clearly prescribed rules, which no one has any need to transgress, everyone can do exactly what he or she likes. The more perfectly the rules are observed, the greater the enjoyment and freedom of the individual. The women can stroll, gossip and fill the ground at each interval with kaleidoscopic colour, the watching boys loudly appraise every stroke, and the old men tell tales and see visions. In the Pavilion the gentlemen of England—an anachronism these thirty years but for this match—take their ease in their own peculiar Zion. Some place their hats on the seat beside them, some tilt them over their eyes, and others blandly consign them to the backs of their pates. Above, on the roof, others, untroubled by the thought of their female belongings and acquaintances far below, have taken off coat and fancy waistcoat and are unabashedly displaying to the heavens their braces and shirt sleeves. "Haaarow! Eeeton!" shout the boys. Nonchalantly at first, and then with growing fervour, the gods join in.

When the match was still young, Keats, who never saw it but was born into an England where rich and hallowed ritual in every ancient town and village was still the heritage of her people, saw with a poet's eye the truth and beauty inherent in the festival of a long-dead community painted on a Grecian urn:

> *Who are these coming to the sacrifice?*
> *To what green altar, O mysterious priest . . .*

Already the white-coated umpires are walking to the wicket and across the green field come the young eternal figures.

> *What little town by river or sea-shore*
> *Or mountain-built with peaceful citadel,*
> *Is emptied of its folk this pious morn? . . .*

Black and white, crimson and blue, light blue for Eton and dark for Harrow, the stands are crammed and the lists are set. And round and round the ground the deathless procession goes, pretending gravity, filled with delicious secret joy, chattering and shining in its finery.

> *What men or gods are these? What maidens loth?*
> *What mad pursuit? What struggle to escape?*
> *What pipes and timbrels? What wild ecstasy?*

*   *   *

III

Ireland Revisited[1]

When I was a boy Ireland was a source of ceaseless concern and controversy to all politically minded Britons. Like the poor, its problems, were always with us. Liberal-minded persons with high ideals, like Thomas Broadbent in *John Bull's Other Island*, ardently believed that an Englishman's first duty was to liberate Ireland, and grant her, if not independence, home rule, and highly civilised men and women, who would never themselves have dreamt of using personal violence against anyone, dreamed of the day foretold by the poet, James Clarence Mangan, when

> *the Erne shall run red,*
> *With redundance of blood,*
> *The earth shall rock beneath our tread,*
> *And flames wrap hill and wood,*

[1] *I.L.N.* 31st August 1968.

And gun-peal and slogan cry
Wake many a glen serene,
Ere you shall fade, ere you shall die,
My dark Rosaleen!

What was more, there were in Ireland itself dreamers who were prepared to do a great deal more than merely dream to put such libertarian and, for them, patriotic idealism into practice and, emulating the Fenians and moon-lighters of old, strike down with bullet and bomb British officials and soldiers and, if they happened to be in the way, even their wives and families.

Other Englishmen took a vastly different, and far less sympathetic, view of these Irish aspirations. They viewed them as a form of treason, or as the ravings of a small and unrepresentative gang of political agitators, and held that they should be sternly repressed by police or, if necessary, military action. Having in my family several much loved kinsmen from the "black North", large and shrewd Ulstermen of staunch Unionist convictions whose addiction to business and field sports made them impervious to the charms of romantic poetry, my earliest impressions of the Irish question had a strong Orange tinge. Indeed, one of the proudest moments of my boyhood was an afternoon spent paddling Sir Edward Carson round the trout lake in my uncle's Wiltshire home, while the great orator occasionally regaled my revering ears with oracular words which, if possible, strengthened even further my conviction that Britain's Liberal rulers, in their lust for votes and power, were only awaiting the day when they would sell their country to Irish incendiaries and murderers!

These early impressions were, however, presently much modified by personal acquaintance with Ireland. Apart from a couple of visits to Ulster, it was not till I was sixteen that I first set foot in the part of Ireland which is now called Eire and about whose political future so much heat was then being engendered on both sides of St. George's Channel. I can recall vividly the excitement of the journey from Wiltshire at the beginning of the First World War to stay with an uncle in County Galway: the thrill of waiting for the Holyhead mail at midnight on Crewe platform, the sight of the Dublin hills and distant Wicklow mountains as the boat steamed into Killiney Bay in the early morning, and the long slow journey across central Ireland into the remote west, a land of stone walls and flashing water and tiny whitewashed cabins.

During the next few weeks I saw something of the real Gaelic Ireland as I cruised with my uncle along the Atlantic fringes of Connemara, putting into tiny harbours, or moored against rough jetties built by the Congested Districts' Board, whose vast, poverty-stricken estates in Galway and Clare my uncle administered, combining his duties with a Lieutenant-Commander's commission in the RNVR as he supervised anti-U-boat detection measures on the Connemara coast. It was a dual trust which enabled him to exercise to his heart's content—and mine—his passion and genius for sailing.

In his company I visited the isolated peasant communities of Atlantic islands in their fever-stricken hovels, set among the most beautiful and romantic scenery I have ever beheld or imagined, and trudged or, rather, trotted, at his side—for he was very tall and, like Charles II, " walked at a large pace"—as he strode over the peat moors and mountains of the mainland on his fascinating business. I was thus privileged to glimpse something of the old peasant Catholic Ireland, with its despairing poverty and superstition and fatalistic inertia, and of the forces which were already beginning, little by little, to transform it and give it new hope and purpose. For, though he belonged to the Protestant ascendency both by marriage and unquestioning conviction and instinct—he was a high Tory who looked back to Arthur Balfour's Secretaryship as the golden age of Irish administration—my uncle was whole-heartedly bent on creating a thriving, independent and contented community in what had long been no better than a wilderness of human deprivation and, through grinding poverty and fever, degradation. No reforming landlord, no Coke of Norfolk, can ever have thrown himself with greater enthusiasm or determination into the task of making two blades of grass, or rather fifty blades, grow where one had grown before. With complete absorption in his mission and utter disinterestedness he was laying the foundations, in the distressed areas of the west, of a new country. And its people, the more politically-minded of whom were ideologically at the extreme opposite pole to him, loved him for it and welcomed him enthusiastically, hurrying out of their cabins to greet him as soon as the news of his coming reached them or his tall, striding figure appeared on the lonely horizon.

Recently I returned to Southern Ireland for the first time, save for a Dublin lecture before the last war, in just under half a century. My uncle was shot during "the Troubles" soon after independence, while trying to shield with his body two colleagues from a roadside ambush of whose existence he had been warned by Free State troops but which, with his usual fearlessness, he had chosen to disregard, believing that no Connaught man, whatever his politics, would harm him. He may have been right, for the gunmen who shot him were strangers from far away Donegal, but he died and, for the moment, his work with him. Yet the new Ireland to whose making he had given himself did not die, for all its bitter growing pains, but took shape, albeit politically of a very different kind to any which, with his old-fashioned imperial beliefs, he would have approved. Today Eire, to all appearances, is one of the most sensibly governed, peaceful and contented countries in the world. Looking back, it seems almost unbelievable that we could have maintained, as we so arrogantly did, that the Irish were incapable of governing themselves.

Indeed, the overwhelming impression on anyone revisiting Ireland half a century after independence is that they are making a rather better job of governing themselves than we are. No doubt, with their smaller population and greater comparative space, it is a good deal easier; they can feed themselves—and other people, too—and they have not saddled themselves, as we, with a vast immigrant population of other race and traditions to do the menial jobs which we are too lazy or greedy to do ourselves. One has only to compare the cleanliness, good order and freedom from confusion of Dublin Airport with the ill-planned chaos, discomfort and confusion of London Airport—or the fare offered by their respective bookstalls—to realise how little right we have to claim superiority over Eire in administrative capacity, culture or even good taste and decency.

As for Ireland's former poverty and squalor, though much still persists in the Dublin slums, the transformation wrought in the past half century is remarkable. When Shaw wrote *John Bull's Other Island* in 1904 it was true, as Larry Doyle said to Broadbent, that in Ireland one was either a gentleman or one was not. There was nothing in between "the gintry" and poverty. Today there is a large and flourishing middle class, both urban and rural. As for the Irish countryside, unlike England's—which has been subjected, and is still being subjected, to a waste and desecration of which it is hard to speak with restraint—it is as beautiful as ever and, freed from the miasma of poverty which formerly hung over it, a joy to be in.

It is true that in my brief visit I saw only the best of modern Ireland, for I was a guest in a little community where kindliness, good sense and a genius for creating order and beauty had made something as near to an earthly paradise as anything to be found in the modern world. I carried away from my sojourn the memory of a morning spent riding in, and walking behind, a dog-cart, along lanes lined with beautiful trees and unsprayed hedgerows, during the whole of which I saw only two cars, the drivers of which treated the elderly horse drawing it with the respect which in England is only given to giant carriers preceded by a police escort. It will be long before I forget that morning of blissful, ambling peace, the jog-trot of the horse's feet, and all Kildare, shading away into blue horizons to the south-west; and eastwards, where the Wicklow mountains raised their gentle crests to Heaven, "the fair green hills of holy Ireland".

* * *

IV

Enchanted Islands[1]

How vividly I remember Bridgetown, Barbados, and most of all my arrival there! It was on a January night in 1934 a few hours after sundown that I first became aware of the island. I had left Plymouth about a fortnight before, on Boxing Day, in a Biscay gale that continued all the way to the Azores. Normally a tolerable

[1] *I.L.N.* 10 April 1954

sailor, this was my Waterloo. Apart from the crew, only a handful of the passengers were able to appear on deck during those initial days, while the rest of us lay in our cabins in a state of unrelieved and unrelievable misery. The ship, judging by one's nightmare sensations, frequently seemed to leave the water altogether and perform a somersault, while the crashing and banging on the bulkheads sounded like the bombardments in Northern France in the closing months of the first German War. I cannot say I was frightened, for I was far too miserable to care whether I was drowned or not; all I wanted was to be still and for the eternal heaving and crashing to end. The first sign of returning life I can recall was of crawling on to the deck during an oily and slowly declining swell and gazing enviously at the rocky cliffs of the Azores and wishing I was lying there among the stony fields and little white houses. After that the voyage became suddenly and unexpectedly pleasant. The sea grew calm, the sun shone, and my fellow-passengers, the better as I for a five-days' total abstinence from food, appeared on deck, in the dining-room and at the cocktail-bar. Indeed, I can look back on few periods so restful as the next few days. There were no posts, no letters to answer, and no particular reason for writing any, since none, mercifully, could be posted. I did a little work in a corner of the deck out of the wind, swam two or three times a day in the ship's bathing-pool, played deck-tennis and enjoyed the company of those I had never met before, should probably never meet again, but who for a few days became the centre of my world. I had never before during my adult life enjoyed so complete a holiday, and probably never shall again.

A few days after passing the Azores we came to a delicious region—the latitude, I believe, of the Bahamas. The sea was a deep, calm blue, stirring so gently that the ship lay in it like a babe in its cradle. A warm sun shone all day without a break, yet so temperately as to cause not the least discomfort, while the horizon, indescribably beautiful, was hung with pearly clouds that never for a moment threatened the serenity of the great arc of blue overhead. An air of quiet happiness pervaded everything and everyone; for a day we were like Milton's "bright aereal Spirits" that

live ensphered
In regions mild of calm and serene air,
Above the smoke and stir of this dim spot
Which men call Earth.

We may not have looked like them as we played quoits or sat sipping our dry martinis, but we felt like them! And somewhere, just beyond the horizon, we were aware of islands—enchanted islands, with gardens made for immortals:

There eternal summer dwells
And west winds with musky wing
About the cedarn alleys fling
Nard and Cassia's balmy smells.

When we returned to the world—and it was the New World I had never seen before—it was at Guadeloupe we made our landfall. I was so happy on the ship that I did not go ashore, but sat all day and looked at this outpost of America while my fellow-passengers inspected its streets, houses and schools. But a day later at Martinique—no historian could resist a name so rich in memories—I stepped ashore for the first time on West Indian soil. I do not know if Martinique is still as it was then, or whether it has now been invaded, like so many other places, by American culture. I hope it remains as it was, a chattering, jostling, gay provincial French island where Latin Europe and transatlantic Africa mingled naturally and without inhibitions with a grace and exotic poetry of which colonial France alone had the recipe.

Then, to my delight—for I was by now wholly wedded to the sea and the life of the ship—we slipped away again through waters made famous by generations of British, French, Spanish and Dutch seamen. Before night fell, my sea pride had a fall. Out of the south there came, with a roll of thunder, a hot, whipping wind that almost in a moment turned the Caribbean into a mill-race of swirling water and great waves which tossed our 14,000-ton ship about as though it was a skiff in an April gale. In my confidence in my now well-found, as I supposed, sea-legs, I treated it at first as a thing of no account. But as I tried to pack my bags for Bridgetown in my hot, swinging cabin, the sea quickly had me on my back. Every attempt I made to get up and go on with my task ended after a minute or two in the same way, with a bang and a crash and an ignominious, dizzy crawl back to my bunk. Then the storm ended as suddenly as it had begun, and, as I felt my capacity to stand upright returning, I staggered on to the deck for air. Then I became aware of magic. From the direction in which the ship was steaming through the darkness there came, long before the first lights of land were visible, a faint, delicate aroma. It was like the breath of some lovely woman, coming out of the darkness of the semi-tropical night. So, more than three hundred years before, the company of the *Olive Blossom*, driven from their course, must have first become aware of the Atlantic island they were to give to England. "James K. of E. and of this Island," they inscribed on one of its trees after they landed on its leeward shore, and from that day to this, thanks to its people's loyalty and steadfastness, it has never passed out of British hands. Even in Cromwellian days it remained loyal to the Crown and was the first place, in all his dominions, in which Charles II was proclaimed king. "Little England" it is still called, and as "little England" I shall always think of it, with that first memory of being rowed in the stillness of the night from the waiting liner to its quayside, while the bells—like those Justice Shallow heard at midnight—sounded the small hours across the quiet waters of the bay. Long may it flourish, green and serene, between the Atlantic and Caribbean, with its seventeenth-century parishes, its ancient Anglican churches, its noble avenues of cabbage-palms, and rolling hills of sugar-cane, and its House of Assembly, the second oldest in the Commonwealth! And long may Barbadians, that loyal folk of two races, play the noblest and most English of games, treating their white-clad umpires with the same traditional reverence that they pay to the Speaker of their ancient Parliament!

* * *

V

Anne Carter her Book[1]

A good many years ago I bought at an auction sale a folio of old songs dating from the early eighteenth century. Three volumes had been bound in one, but all the songs had engravings at the top above the music and words, and flute accompaniment at the foot. Looking through them before the sale, I could not resist them. They have lain on my piano ever since, and occasionally, to while away a leisure half-hour, I have picked out the tunes, the best set by "Mr. Handel", on a single clumsy finger.

The book was given to Anne Carter in 1739, the year of publication of one of its volumes. "Anne Carter her book" runs the inscription, in a prim eighteenth-century hand. I have no idea who Anne Carter was, but I imagine a young woman at the time of the gift, and plainly of musical tastes. Perhaps many young men sighed dolefully as they turned the pages for her in the flickering candlelight, wearing the slightly glazed and idiotic look that young lovers wear; perhaps she had no lovers at all. Perhaps her heart was broken, as tender women's sometimes are, or perhaps she married with little sentiment and grew, as was the wont of those times, into the very soul of her husband and learnt to sign herself, as one of her contemporaries did, "Your faithful, fond, obedient wife." I do not know the answer to these idle conjectures, and never shall.

The pictures are the chief charm of the book. After a morning's invocation to a lark made by a very Hanoverian young gentleman in three-cornered hat, wig, long coat and waistcoat and lace ruffles, and bearing both a sword and a walking-stick, what time the merry ploughman drives his horses—on one of which sits, or, rather, reclines, his buxom wife—across the swelling field, the book proceeds to illuminate Georgian life. A village lord with a beguiling face but the most dishonourable intentions tries —I am glad to say in vain—to inveigle a country girl into his stately coach and splendid, formal palace; a country parson, in wig, neat white band and ample gown, sits filling a glass from a

[1] *I.L.N.* 13 July 1940.

jug outside his tidy cottage while he trolls how a light heart and
a thin pair of breeches will carry a brave man cheerfully through
the world—

> *No politic notions perplex me,*
> *The thought of ambition I scorn;*
> *No troublesome wife for to vex me*
> *With scolding from evening to morn.*

And a fair and somewhat tomboyish Julia, in flounces, hooped
skirt and ribboned mob-cap, pelts her adoring Strephon with a
snowball—

> *White as her hand the wanton threw*
> *A ball of silver snow;*
> *The frozen globe fired as it flew,*
> *My bosom felt it glow.*

The pictures tell one so much one did not know before, and
which no poring over manuscripts can wholly reveal: that gentlemen in taverns hung their swords and three-cornered hats on odd
nails scattered about the wall, which they adorned at varied
heights, like pictures; that night-capped young men shut themselves up for the night in half-tester beds curtained all round like
tents, and read by the light of a sconce on the wall bearing a
single candle in dangerous proximity to the curtains; that table-
cloths were laid at picnics; that men of middle rank dined in
their hats. They depict the shape of glasses and bottles, of garden
rollers, of common chairs—the kind that have long since vanished
—of the little hats that girls wore perched on the top of their
heads when they walked or rode in the country; of butchers'
stools, of wash-tubs and cottage fences. By turning over the pages
one can obtain a kind of moving-picture of a vanished age, set,
as it were, to music. In the candlelight, when the curtains are
drawn and the brocaded figures in the gilt frames on the walls
become human, with the aid of the old piano that looks like a
spinet and was made so delicately by Mr. Simpson of Sweetings
Alley in George II's reign, one can dream one is living in 1740.

*   *   *

VI

London in October[1]

How beautiful London can be in October! An indisposition having kept me out of it for nearly three months, I was astonished to find how much my heart warmed to it, sad though I had been at the thought of leaving the country. I entered it at the point which sets one in a flash at its very centre. A century and a half ago there were other as famous, and perhaps as beautiful, approaches; when Byron's "Don Juan", reversing the course of the Canterbury pilgrims, caught his first glimpse of London, he did so from Shooter's Hill, on the Dover Road:

> *A mighty mass of brick, and smoke, and shipping,*
> *Dirty and dusky, but as wide as eye*
> *Could reach, with here and there a sail just skipping*
> *In sight, then lost amidst the forestry*
> *Of masts; a wilderness of steeples peeping*
> *On tiptoe through their sea-coal canopy;*
> *A huge, dun cupola, like a foolscap crown*
> *On a fool's head—and there is London Town!*

Yet though that classic traveller's view of London has long been obscured by houses and the town's growth, the approach by rail from the south-west compensates for it. Between Clapham Junction and Waterloo one sees, in the course of a minute, the heart of the empire bared. There, beyond the river, are the Abbey and Westminster Hall, the Government offices of Whitehall and the silhouette of Big Ben and Barry's Houses of Parliament. Much has been said against English nineteenth-century Gothic architecture, and much of it justly. Yet though I was brought up to regard it without enthusiasm, I have come with the passage of years to admire Barry's *tour de force* more and more, and to see it, not merely as the embodiment in stone of our parliamentary creed and history, but as one of the great buildings of the world. Touched by sunset, floodlit at night, glimpsed as a vast, only partly visible wraith in rain or fog, seen in the most ordinary circumstances at any time of the working day, in whatever light

[1] *I.L.N.* 6 November 1954.

or at whatever hour, it is always magnificent and always uniquely itself. After St. Paul's it seems to me London's greatest building, unsurpassed even by Wren's glorious Greenwich and noble Chelsea, or by Kent's delicate and lovely masterpiece, the Horse Guards. Imagine it gone, and its true place in London's architectural economy becomes apparent. Whatever its interior absurdities, it confronts the world with the majesty and timeless dignity of the institution it houses. To see it from the train as one enters the imperial capital is to understand Pitt's boast, " We shall stand till the day of judgment".

Yet, however dear to us, her buildings are only part of London's beauty. She is a city of mist and atmosphere, a murky child of water commercing with clouds. At her heart lies the river, and one sees it, alike at its most majestic and magical, at Westminster. One does not only need to see it as Wordsworth saw it, as he crossed it on his way to France on a June day in 1802, wearing the beauty of the morning, "all bright and glittering in the smokeless air". It is as beautiful on a murky November noon, with the traffic roaring over Westminster Bridge and the water's dark surface turgid with the discharge of Europe's greatest city. It was another poet, James Elroy Flecker, who, a century after Wordsworth, recalled under Grecian skies the smoky gloom of Charing Cross,

> And with what sweep at Westminster
> The rayless waters run.

Yet even more than the river, more than the buildings of Parliament Square, the grave dignity of Queen Anne's Gate, the bright paraded autumn flowers in St. James's Park and the ceremonial splendours of Palace and Mall, the two things that give most delight to a returning Londoner are its sense of liberty in order and its all-pervading trees. We take the life of London so much for granted that we forget the miracle of it; the centuries of struggle and effort, human wisdom and even stronger human habit that have produced a city population so effortlessly ordered, so well-mannered, so tolerant and good-natured. Despite the restraints and regulations of our over-populated, war-vexed era, there is probably no place in the modern world where a man can

feel so free, so much the master of his time and destiny as in this
vast city. Provided he observes the easy and decent conventions
of the place—no more than are necessary for the preservation of
the liberty and happiness of others—he can go where he pleases
and do what he pleases without the least interference, or even
observation, by his neighbours. Perhaps it is because I have lived
in it, on and off, for more than half a century and feel so much at
home in it, despite its many changes, that I am conscious of this
atmosphere of liberty; a sense of its being at once intimate and
impersonal that is London's peculiar charm for all those who live
in and love it. "The character of its inhabitants," Osbert Sitwell
has beautifully written, "never changes . . . Royal in their polite-
ness, ostentatious—even the poorest—in their generosity, unequalled in their courage, unsurpassed in their originality. In
spite of the immense foreign influence brought to bear on London
for so many centuries, the people are the very essence of the
country. Rich and poor are alike in their courage, in the continuity of their conduct and in their determination. . . . City-bred,
they have the countryman's humour, identical, sharpened only
by an additional tolerance and quickness. An immense love of
liberty, a feeling for the best of life, inspires them. In their
humour there is a sort of wise gravity that no other people knows,
a consciousness, too, of the sacred idiosyncrasy of every human
being that is typically English."[1] It may seem presumptuous and
even a little absurd to generalise in this way about the people of
any city, yet the moment one's feet are on its pavements after
absence one feels the truth of Sir Osbert's eulogy. London is a
school of life where "manners makyth man": greater than
Winchester, greater than Eton, greater than any part of the
training that makes the whole.

As for London's trees, never, I think, have they been more
beautiful than this October—beautiful in their colour and
contrast, in their ever-moving, dancing grace, itself a mirror of
the human freedom passing in street and park below. On St.
Crispin's Day, which is also Agincourt and Balaclava Day, I
walked in Hyde Park to see the elms in their last summer majesty
before the fall of the leaves. The limes—rather uninteresting trees

[1] Osbert Sitwell, *Sing High! Sing Low!* p. 179. Macmillan.

in winter—were already bare, but the elms still retained the fullness of their foliage, softened and glorified by the myriad colours of autumn. Indeed, this tree is always beautiful, even in the depth of winter, owing to its great height and the exquisite tracery of its branches, while its dark trunk, made even darker by fog and soot, is perfectly suited to London's melancholy, yet gentle and kindly, pattern of misty light and shade.

It is an extraordinary irony that in an age when we permit a quarter of a million of our people to be injured every year by fast-moving motor-traffic on the roads, authority is everywhere cutting down these noble and most English of trees because of a million-to-one chance—for it is no more—that a falling branch in a winter gale may injure a passer-by. Trees, like men, must die, and where their usefulness as timber has alone to be considered, as every forester knows, they must be cut down in their prime. But their lives in the hands of nature are very long, and where, as in a London park, they are grown for beauty alone, their splendour and usefulness to the community can be continued by wise management for centuries. There can be few cases—even after such improvidence as the prolonged failure for many years to re-plant the yawning gaps in Hyde Park's avenues—where it becomes really necessary to break the skyline of a town park before sufficient successors have grown up to take the place of the trees that have to be felled. The beauty of London's parks is a priceless national asset which should be most carefully preserved. Those who hold that towns should be beautified only by small, flowering fruit-trees which blossom for a fortnight in spring and remain featureless for the rest of the year, are strangely blind to London's beauty. We can only be grateful to the men of old who gave her her dower of plane and elm, and raised, in Rotten Row and on the banks of the Serpentine, what is perhaps the noblest arboreal skyline in Christendom.

*　　*　　*

VII

The Veterans' Parade[1]

Every summer, within a few days of one another, two military parades are held in London to commemorate the unchanging traditions of the British Army. The annual Trooping the Colour on the Horse Guards Parade in the presence of the Sovereign is the high festival and ceremonial endurance test of the Brigade of Guards enacted by its picked élite. The perfection of the spectacle, watched by thousands, depends on superb training, unceasing effort and a last lap of concentrated endurance on the part of every officer and man taking part. It rests on generations of tradition and organic growth. Anything more satisfying to the eye would be hard to conceive—the foliage of the Royal Parks on an early summer day of sunshine and high, floating cloud, the exquisite line of the seventeenth- and eighteenth-century buildings of Charles II's and George II's Whitehall, the approaching columns of scarlet flowing with an even rhythm, like stately rivers, to the assembly place, the moments of flawless, co-ordinated colour, sound and movement when the massed bands of the Brigade of Guards, led by their drum-majors, move slowly forward across the parade ground to the music of *Les Huguenots*, or the Household Cavalry—a cascade of ebony, scarlet and silver —flow across the chestnut-framed horizon, horses, men and commanders moving in proud submission to an authority that has grown out of the English past and centuries of endeavour.

Yet as beautiful in its different way is the annual Founders' Day Parade on Charles II's birthday at the Royal Hospital, Chelsea— a parade which has been held in the same place every year for close on three centuries. It must be nearly forty years since I first saw it, and though I have witnessed it repeatedly the spectacle thrills me as much as it did on that now remote occasion. The perfection and simplicity of the ceremonial, the old men gently marshalled by their veteran officers in Wren's great courtyard, some in formal ranks, others seated on benches along the colon-

[1] *I.L.N.* 23 July 1950; 13 June 1959; 9 June 1962; 15 June 1957

nades, the scarlet of their uniforms against the mellowed red-brick and soft white Portland stone of that beautiful building; the white plumes of the Governor and Lieutenant-Governor fluttering in the breeze, the old Pensioners' gnarled faces silhouetted under their black Hogarthian tricorn hats, all combine to produce an illusion of timeless enchantment. There is a charming informality about the scene. The four companies stand at ease on the lawns in front of the long colonnaded façade of Chapel and Hall, while the spectators face them on chairs also set out on the grass. Every window of the flanking buildings is crowned with watching heads, and Grinling Gibbons's Charles II statue is embowered breast-high with oak leaves in memory of the day when "the surly troopers riding by" failed to detect the hunted monarch poised amid the foliage above their heads. A few of the older or more seriously crippled Pensioners sit in rows on chairs in the colonnades; they parade, like those in the infirmary, in spirit, even though they can no longer march or stand at attention. Kindliness, as much as military precision and pride, pervades the occasion.

Yet, though it takes place every year, the parade is witnessed only by a few hundred spectators, is scarcely mentioned in the Press and its existence is unknown to the vast majority of our people and to the hundreds of thousands of Commonwealth kinsfolk, Americans and foreigners who annually visit our shores. For every hundred who have heard of or visited the Chelsea Flower Show, held in the same grounds, only one has heard of the Pensioners' Founder's Day Parade. Those responsible for our national education and the tourist trade could well use this leisurely and unhurried evocation of a vanished age to make known something of the poetry and artistic wealth of the English past. For what this parade of old soldiers symbolises is the British Army's age-long talent for combining mercy with order, gentleness with courage, pride and easy and beautiful display with freedom from ostentation. Though it has no monopoly of the soldierly qualities, there is one respect in which that Army has been unequalled—in its gentleness and good temper, its discipline in victory, its modest and humane dealing with those who, as a result of its victories, have found themselves at its mercy.

This gentleness is mirrored in the parade: in the easy-going yet orderly tolerance of the old Pensioners' discipline, itself expressive of the spirit that governs their place of retirement and animates their officers. It is to be heard in the regimental marches played before and during the ceremony—marches curiously different from those of other armies, for they are based mostly on country airs of traditional rustic or humorous connotation, often of great sweetness and almost entirely without military bombast or bravado.

Every, or almost every, Regiment is represented at the Parade. It is, indeed, All Regiments' Day. For a regiment is a communion, hallowed by the love and sacrifice of successive generations, and the Founder's Parade is a commemoration enacted by the veterans of the Army's regiments. These old men, in their scarlet coats, spending the evening of their day in their humble Valhalla beside the Thames, have stood the test and proved true; there is not one of them who has not shown himself ready at one or more times in his career to give the greatest of all proofs of love by laying down his life for his comrades. That and the years of discipline and self-mastery have stamped themselves on each gnarled face. And as, in their Companies under their Captains of Invalids, and to the tune of "The Boys of the Old Brigade", they hobble past the saluting-point, every man in his scarlet coat and black Hogarthian tricorn hat, the fact is obvious to the most unmilitary eye. No less resplendent than the shining medals on every uniform, from the humblest to the highest, the look of duty performed and accomplished in the eyes of men who have never betrayed their trust is the hall-mark of this beautiful and intimate London occasion.

PART III

True to Ourselves

"Public life," wrote Burke, "is a situation of power and energy; he trespasses against his duty who sleeps upon his watch, as well as he that goes over to the enemy." He also held that we "should bring the dispositions that are lovely in private life into the service and conduct of the commonwealth: so to be patriots as not to forget we are gentlemen." In commenting week by week on public affairs I have tried to remember these maxims, hard though they are to reconcile in practice.

CHAPTER 11

Sinks the Fire

Far called our navies melt away,
On dune and headland sinks the fire
Lo! all our pomp of yesterday
Is one with Nineveh and Tyre.
KIPLING

Lest We Forget · Drawing in our Horns ·
Strategy and Survival · The Changing Atlas ·
Black Bees in White Bonnets ·
Can the Commonwealth Survive?

I

Lest We Forget[1]

Seventy years—the psalmist's span of life—is a very short time in
the history of a nation. And seventy years ago was the year of
the Diamond Jubilee, when Britain was at the summit of her
greatness with the rulers of the world and the representatives of
the vastest empire ever known on earth gathered in London to do
honour to the aged Queen Empress who symbolised and presided
over all this glory. The sage Lord Salisbury, with the help of his
handsome philosopher nephew, "Prince" Arthur, governed the
country from Hatfield, "Joe" Chamberlain was at the Colonial
office setting the bounds of empire "wider yet and wider", and
Cecil Rhodes—his auriferous and diamond studded-prestige only
a little dimmed by the scandal of the Jamieson Raid—was dreaming, and not only dreaming, in terms of Cape to Cairo. W. G.
Grace was still playing cricket, young Prince Ranjitsinhji, C. B.

---

[1] *Illustrated London News* 5 August 1967.

Fry and Archie MacLaren were flashing centuries to every boundary, and almost every English shire boasted a hundred or more stately homes, filled with the treasures of six centuries of aristocratic civilisation and staffed by a vast army of deferential butlers, footmen, maids, nurses, gardeners, gamekeepers, coachmen, grooms and stable boys. And tribute in interest, profits and commissions poured into London, the Mecca of global capitalism, from every country in the world. And a young Anglo-Indian poet, who in ten dazzling years of precocious success had made himself the laureate of Empire, wrote:

> *Far-called, our navies melt away;*
> *On dune and headland sinks the fire:*
> *Lo! all our pomp of yesterday*
> *Is one with Nineveh and Tyre.*

During my lifetime, everything predicted in those four pregnant lines has come to pass. With the announcement of its impending retreat from east of Suez—a decade has now passed since the retreat from Suez itself—a British Government has put the seal on the process of decline and surrender. Obsessed with "growth", profits, wage-claims, gambling, take-over-bids, fast air and road transport, sex and the repetitive habits and mindless amusements of teenagers, the people of Britain seem to accept the process much as they do the weather. Most of them, as Mr. Macmillan put it, have never had it so good, and, so long as such prosperity for the multitude continues, it is hard to take too gloomy a view of our abdication of global authority and responsibility. The question is, Will the prosperity last? At the moment the goose hangs high; teenagers can spend their easily-earned millions on pop, gear and kicks; official personages and business tycoons can live and travel like millionaires at the public cost or on high-powered expense-accounts; the manipulators of company sales and mergers can pay six-figure sums for fashionably situated luxury flats and penthouses that twenty years ago would have sold for a tenth of the amount. Ministers of the Crown, Whitehall mandarins and provincial mayors and councillors flit in limousines from one function and committee meeting to another in endless succession, freed from the necessity, and even possibility, of thinking by a perpetual shower of agenda and publicity hand-outs; while working class families fly in their hundreds of thousands to package holidays in the sun. Recalling the grim conditions under which British working men and women lived half a century ago, one cannot but be glad it is so. Only the old, living in an inflationary age on pensions or fixed incomes, suffer real privation. There seems to be a washing machine and a refrigerator in almost every kitchen and a car at every garden gate.

Yet on what is all this widespread prosperity founded? Like everything else in this world, on what preceded it, that is, on the past. The crowded island Welfare State of today and the swollen, unwieldy administrative machine that directs it and which it supports, owe their existence to that very different Britain of seventy years ago, with her world-wide commercial interests and immensely powerful naval forces protecting those interests with the aid of military garrisons in every continent. Sustaining this imperial edifice was a philosophy in which the children of my generation were brought up. It was a philosophy compounded of faith and voluntary subordination: of faith in Britain as a corporate conception standing for justice and honourable dealing in a world whose future happiness depended on the maintenance and defence of these virtues; of willing subordination of the individual to the discipline that multiplied tenfold the power of the individual. This corporate idealism and voluntary subordination were strongest in the possessing and educated classes, but they ran right through the nation, producing in the opening years of the First World War an army comparable in size to the great conscript armies of the continent and excelling them in morale—one composed entirely of volunteers who surrendered their comfort, liberty and personal safety because their ideal of Britain and the virtues for which they believed Britain to stand would have perished without that sacrifice. So in an earlier age the private soldier of Francis Doyle's poem—recruited from rustic hovel or the gutter of some grim Victorian city—when ordered to prostrate himself before his Chinese captors, died a martyr's death rather than betray his countrymen's code:

Poor, reckless, rude, low-born, untaught,
Bewilder'd and alone,

A heart with English instinct fraught
He yet can call his own.
Ay! tear his body limb from limb,
Bring cord or axe or flame;
He only knows that not through him
Shall England come to shame.

It was that spirit in her sons, that sense of "duty done and duty doing", which sustained the great imperial and commercial edifice and took the initial shock of two world wars, withstanding, by doing so, the march of aggression, only itself to crumble in the aftermath of victory from the blows it had borne.

Can the prosperity of the fifty-five millions of this small island continue now that they have discarded both the empire which brought them trade and tribute and the idealism and self-imposed discipline which kept that empire in being? This is the crux of the British economic situation in the 'sixties and 'seventies: a chief reason why our legislators of all Parties are seeking feverishly to enter the Common Market, at the cost of whatever humiliation and repudiation of former pledges, in the hope that, by doing so, some solution will be found for the apparently insoluble problem of maintaining and improving the living standards of a people who have ceased to control the sources and channels of communication through which their wealth formerly came.

It is said that the British Empire was made in a fit of absent-mindedness. This is untrue. It was made by the concentration, industry, self-reliance and self-discipline of countless individuals, even if the State itself, in the libertarian tradition of Britain, played only a subordinate and reluctant part in the process. What is true is that it has been discarded in a fit of absent-mindedness, and that we are now about to realise, almost certainly in increasing measure, the price which has to be paid for such absent-mindedness. What one hopes is that, as the price becomes more and more apparent, the people of this country, who inherit the instincts and aptitudes which formerly made her great and honoured, will again produce leaders, both in action and thought, who will re-inspire them with the sense of purpose and faith they have lost. We need an Aidan to re-teach us our faith and a Pitt and a Drake to show us what courage and confidence can do. Then, our time of contraction and self-defeat over, we can resume, under new forms, our ancient precedence of "teaching the nations how to live", becoming once more a source of strength and stability to ourselves and a beacon and guiding light to others.

* * *

II

Drawing in our Horns[1]

The road was called the Old Kent Road, but it wasn't on the Surrey side of the river. The simple, white English lettering on the name board recalled some quiet, suburban roadway in South London or Bournemouth, but the small, tell-tale Arabic inscription in the bottom right-hand corner disabused one. The trees and flowering shrubs surrounding the verandahed bungalows on either side of the road belonged to a sunnier clime than ours, and the sand that took the morning shine off one's shoes came not from English sand-dunes but the desert. Nor did the chugging of a steamer in the distance suggest Millbank or Rotherhithe. It recalled, instead, what lay between Suez and Port Said.

For I was among exiles. The British were encamped, as their fathers and fathers' fathers had so often been, among the palms and acacias. These young men in khaki battle-dress and dungarees were securing the vital interests of their country and ensuring the triumph of her legalistic idealism in a strange land. But, being British, they had built in the desert a little semblance of the villa-ed England they had left behind to which, when their work among the sand was done, they returned at evening. And here they practised their British customs, according to their respective stations, read foreign newspapers, printed and set out English-wise, over their porridge and marmalade, sat about the crowded tables at the Naafi or church hut, smoking their pipes and drinking pallid beer, or barged and charged in mimic conflict after the leather ball of their favourite tribal sport. Around them

[1] *I.L.N.* 15 February 1947; 1 July 1967.

a somewhat mixed community of human and canine native
satellites conformed to their unalterable routine, the former not
without a shrewd, calculating brown eye to the main chance and
the latter with the enthusiastic and idolatrous devotion of their
kind. To dogs, at least, the expansion of the British race overseas
had proved an unbelievable blessing. As my eyes turned from the
nostalgic lettering at the street corner, I caught sight of a white
and woolly one rolling ecstatically at the feet of a R.A.S.C. driver,
who was about to lift him into that paradise of African dogs, the
cabin of a British truck. A moment later, well-fed and superbly
arrogant, he was barking furiously at the inferior native world
about him. The khaki English—those godlike dispensers of food
and caresses—had raised that four-footed bundle of hot, pal-
pitating fur out of the starveling, bug-ridden dust and haunted
servitude of his forebears. For dogs, at least, things in the land of
Goshen were, after countless centuries, as they should be.

They are scarcely likely to continue so. The British are drawing
in their horns and, with shrill adjurations to do so from many
enthusiastic—and sometimes interested—parties, are withdrawing
from the distant lands they have been administering. The eagles
or, rather, lions, are going home. For dogs this is obviously
an unmitigated calamity; and not only, I suspect, for canine but
for human underdogs too. The whip, the kick, the louse—those
apparently eternal badges of the oppressed, whether four-footed
or two-footed—seem likely to resume their ancient ascendancy in
places from which the island administrators had temporarily, if
only partially, banished them. Will mankind be the better or
worse for that departure? The man for whom I was waiting in
that oriental Old Kent Road beside the Suez Canal gave me, on
our way to a neighbouring camp, his views on the Sudan, a
country in which he had lately been stationed. He was a Socialist,
and before the war a lecturer in economics to a Trades Union—
the last person from whom one would have expected imperialistic
sentiments. Yet, speaking out of the experience of four years'
Army service in the Middle East, he said, with passionate conviction, that to hand back the Sudanese to the rule of the
Egyptians would be a crime against humanity.

When, in the closing stages of the Second World War, I visited the Middle East, the British were in control of the whole of this vast area, from Cyprus and Damascus to East and Central Africa, from Benghazi and the Tripolitanian desert to the Persian Gulf. My host, General Paget—that Bayard among soldiers who had trained Britain's D-Day armies—was responsible for the peace and order of this huge military empire, and wherever I travelled, lecturing and talking to groups of Servicemen, a state of peace and good order existed, greater probably than at any time in this region since the days of imperial Rome. Military control, coexisting with the civil governments of a score of kingdoms, principalities and colonial administrations, there was, but it was military control at its most unobtrusive, without any of the panoply or outward signs of militarism. A milder, better behaved and more gentle armed presence could scarcely be conceived. It was an army at peace with itself and the civilian population which carried on its normal life almost as though no army was there.

The only political fly in the ointment was an underground campaign of assassination by young political activists from Israel. Just before I arrived at the Commander-in-Chief's headquarters at Cairo the British Resident Minister of State, Lord Moyne, had been shot; and I remember that after dinner on my first night in General Paget's Mess, my host sat silhouetted in the open window against the darkened garden outside as though tacitly challenging, by his serenity and fearlessness, the dark forces of political unrest to do their worst against the calm, majestic force of the Pax Britannica he represented. A few weeks later, staying with Lord Gort in Jerusalem, I listened to that brave, gay and modest man telling me, as we walked together in the garden of Government House, how he had told a delegation of Zionist leaders, who had warned him he would be shot if he persisted in going everywhere unprotected, that he had no fear of that, seeing that in such an event he would obviously be succeeded by a Governor far less sympathetic to their aspirations. I was reminded of the passage in George Santayana's *Soliloquies in England* in which he contrasted the easy-going nineteenth-century British hegemony of the Orient with what he saw was only too likely to succeed it:

"The Englishman is no missionary, no conqueror. . . . He carries his English weather in his heart wherever he goes, and it becomes a cool spot in the desert, and a steady and sane oracle amongst all the deliriums of mankind. Never since the heroic days of Greece has the world had such a sweet, just, boyish master. It will be a black day for the human race when scientific blackguards, conspirators, churls and fanatics manage to supplant him."

Since my wartime visit to the Middle East the pattern of its rule has changed as it has done so many times before. Yet its background remains what it has been for centuries: the primitive, half-rural, half-nomadic civilisation made familiar to us in childhood by the Hebrew Bible. Some letters I wrote home at the time recapture something of the impression this timeless world made on me.

"I was thrilled when the sun came out today and I drove to the Pyramids. The lights, the fashionable shop-windows, the pseudo-European population, the smart American cars made no appeal. But what went straight to my heart, incongruously mixed up with all this modern tinsel, were the little glimpses of an older, immemorial world: the camels by the Pyramids with their coloured jackets, the Arab sweepers shuffling along in their white robes on the airfield, dirty, miserably poor yet dignified; the idle figures squatting, as though for eternity, in the bright, healing sunlight; the little brown cows in the green fields, and the sight which moved me most of all—a shepherd driving a mixed flock of asses, sheep and goats through the traffic, trotting along much as they must have done when Joseph and Mary came along the road to Egypt to be taxed. . . . I suppose it is a foretaste of the real East: a world which I think must somehow be more real than our modern world, being closer to that other world, to which, though we forget it, we belong as much as to this and, perhaps, a great deal more. I wish I could talk in their own tongue with these people, so remote from our own folk. They have dignity, though I admit little else. . . ."

"At the moment I'm jogging, after an early start from Alexandria, in a *wagon-lit* full of rich Egyptians (I should like

to spoil them and divide their substance among the poor
peasants with the filthy clothes and speaking brown eyes)
through the rich Nile delta on my way back to Cairo, where I
stop tonight before going off tomorrow to the Canal area. It's
an extraordinary contrast to the desert road by which I travelled
to Alex.—that an empty, shimmering fantasy of rolling sand,
this a vast green plain of immense fertility, full of fascinating
sights: olive and palm trees, long gleaming ditches between
rich black alluvial mud, earthen villages moulded out of the
ground with holes for doors and windows and of an antiquity
that makes the Pyramids look almost modern gew-gaws;
women of great ugliness and magnificent bearing, carrying
water-urns on their heads; gangs of white-robed peasants, and
patient oxen and little brown cows with soft eyes, and grey,
long-eared mokes, like the one that carried Christ to Jerusalem.
Somehow out here in the country, purified by sun and air and
the benison of things growing, the filth and poverty of this
primitive people that so shocks one in the slums of Alexandria
doesn't seem to matter; it is a part here, instead of an outrage
on nature. . . . And, when one once gets away from the cosmopolitan modernism of the towns and the rich, it all reminds
one so much of the Bible and one's earliest imaginings. 'In my
dreams I stood upon the bank of the river. And, behold, there
came up out of the river seven kine, fat-fleshed and well-
favoured, and they fed in a meadow. . . .' "
A superficial impression, perhaps, but sometimes an ignorant
newcomer sees what a more accustomed eye may miss. And it was
on that primitive world, screened behind the ideological façade
of Nasser's cardboard armies and Russia's anything but cardboard
arms, that the full force of a highly modernised, super-efficient
Israeli army has since burst with such dynamic and terrifying
impact. For all our sympathy with and admiration for the little
Israeli State, so naturally insistent on its hard-won security and
place in the Levantine sun, the British people should also remember the rights and dignity of the simple peasant peoples of Egypt,
Syria and Arabia. For though it has been forgotten by everyone,
including the British themselves—and most of all, perhaps understandably, by the Arabs—it was we who won the Arabs their

freedom from the Turks, who gave Egypt her Sinai frontier and created the Jewish national home in Palestine and the genesis of Israel. All these were gained and sealed by British blood, as Kipling's lines recall:

> *The blown sand heaps on me, that none may learn*
> *Where I am laid for whom my children grieve . . .*
> *O wings that beat at dawning, ye return*
> *Out of the desert to your young at eve!*

Once we gave peace, order and justice to the Middle East, as to so many other places in a troubled world. We do so no longer.

*   *   *

III

Strategy and Survival[1]

Geography, it has been said, is about maps, biography about chaps. Strategy is about chaps contending for places on maps. It is not taught in schools and, though malice, hatred and treachery are only too common in international dealings, in the democratic countries of the West it has become almost an extinct art. The only people who still practise it regularly as an instrument of national policy are those heavily-armed apostles of world peace—the kind of peace that reigns in Budapest and will soon, no doubt, reign again in Warsaw and Prague—the Communist Russians.[2] For, whatever their limitations as politicians, the self-appointed occupants of the Kremlin are masterly strategists. They never miss a point in the game and are for ever trying to obtain some favourable vantage-point, now in one corner of the globe, now in another, for exerting armed pressure on their less astute and unexpansionist neighbours. "Wider still and wider shall thy bounds be set," has become, in these days of goodbye to Elgar and all that, a very inappropriate motto for Great Britain. But it fits Russian foreign policy like a glove. No nation in history—not even Napoleonic France or Nazi Germany—ever

---

[1] *I.L.N* 8 December 1956.
[2] Written after the Russian intervention in Hungary thirteen years ago. History has now repeated itself—and for the second time since the War—in Prague.

swallowed so much in so short a time as the armed hierarchs of the Kremlin in the past two decades.

There is nothing inherently immoral or anti-social about a sound national—or, for that matter, inter-allied or international —strategy, any more than there is anything immoral about being a soldier or a policeman. "It is lawful for Christian men at the commandment of the magistrate to bear arms and serve in the wars." It is equally lawful for them, and, indeed, today highly expedient for them to do so in order to avert wars. For the strategist's art is not only necessary for winning wars; it is equally so for preventing them. Many a war has been begun when the victim or opponent of an aggressor has been man-oeuvred through neglect or supineness into a temptingly danger-ous and unsound strategic position. Such was the position of Britain and France in 1939 when, as a result of leaving the strategic initiative in peace to others, they exposed themselves to an attack which proved fatal to the latter and all but fatal to the former. If those who led British opinion between the wars—the publicists no less than the politicians and administrators—had troubled themselves a little more about the country's strategic position and a little less about its moral attitude and protestations of peace, millions of lives could have been saved and the world would be a far more civilised place than it is today. It is always a disaster for humanity when those who seek peace divest them-selves of the means of enforcing it.

In the nineteenth century, as a result of our victories in the Napoleonic and earlier French wars, Britain was in an extraordin-arily strong strategic position. She used that position, not to con-quer and enslave mankind, but to preserve peace and enlarge the bounds of trade, and with it, of human freedom. There is not a democratic and parliamentary nation in the world, including the United States, which does not at least partly owe its liberty to the police services in the past of the Royal Navy. It kept the peace and extinguished the conflagrations caused by the ambitions of would-be tyrants for a hundred years. It also suppressed the slave trade. Its pacifying power rested on Britain's island situation athwart the European trade routes, the protection given her Western Approaches by Ireland, her control from Gibraltar,

Malta, the Suez Canal and Aden, from the Cape of Good Hope, Ceylon and Singapore, and from the West Indies and Falklands, of the great ocean routes to South and East. It depended, too, on the reservoir of disciplined military power in British India which, under the Navy's protection, enabled prompt police action to be taken in any part of the eastern hemisphere from the Levant to China. Never in human history was power exercised with less loss of life or more beneficently than by oceanic Britain in the nineteenth century.

With what celerity have we divested ourselves of that power! It was not taken from us; we gave it away. We surrendered it out of what we like to flatter ourselves were the highest motives, but for which no one gives us any credit, and we now justify our inability to keep the peace and preserve the liberties we once preserved—freedom of the seas, freedom from slavery, freedom from aggression, petty or large—by declaring that we have become a second-rate Power and can no longer afford the luxury of being strong. Yet the weakness we now suffer is the result of our own deliberate divestment of power. After our sacrifices and victory in the first German War we gave independence to Ireland, surrendered the Irish bases—for lack of which thousands of our seamen perished in the second German War—and surrendered our trusteeship in Egypt. After the Second World War we withdrew from India, Burma, Ceylon, Palestine, the Sudan and the Suez Canal and are now withdrawing from large parts of Africa. Most serious of all, we allowed our Navy—the guarantee of our liberty and very existence and the foundation of our national strategy—to dwindle to a fragment of its former self, leaving Russia the greatest naval Power in the Eastern Hemisphere. There is an old saying that it is foolish to undress before one is ready to go to bed. For a people with an intense love of political and personal liberty, a high standard of living and strong humanitarian ideals, the price of such unwisdom may prove higher than any of us realise.

*   *   *

IV

The Changing Atlas[1]

My *Times* Atlas, if atlases received pensions, would have qualified for an old-age one several years ago, for it was published in 1896, the year before the Diamond Jubilee. It has served me for the greater part of my life, is sadly torn and dog-eared and is, of course, out-of-date. Yet I cling to it with affection, for it mirrors, not only the physical geography of the earth's surface, which is unchanged, but the political frontiers of a vanished world. Here, in its pages, is the Austro-Hungarian empire of the Hapsburgs, an imperial Germany which comprised Alsace-Lorraine, a Turkey in Europe which extended from the Black Sea almost to the Adriatic, and a Poland which was only a geographical expression and still partitioned between Europe's three continental empires, with Russia holding the major share. Only Great Britain, the Scandinavian and Benelux countries, Spain, Portugal and Switzerland had the same frontiers as today.

Outside Europe the political differences in the map were even more remarkable. The most startling of all were in Africa. In 1896, just over two years before I was born, the southern borders of Egypt—still, like Tripoli and Cyrenaica, a nominal Turkish dependency—stopped short at the second Cataract, beyond which lay nothing but a vast political vacuum and the illimitable desert over which the Mahdi exercised a shadowy, blood-stained suzerainty. Imperial Germany, with her rod of iron, ruled over Ruanda and Unyamwezi, Ukonongo and Wangindo, Adamawa and the Cameroons, Damaraland, Amboland and Manaqualand. As for the area which is now occupied by what today is Zambia and by what was until recently called Southern Rhodesia, there is no vestige of either name on the map. Instead, in that then huge tribal wilderness, though faintly coloured red and already under a British Chartered Company's suzerainty, there is Marotse-Mabunda, Baronga and Bamangwato, Matebeleland and Makalaka, Mashona and Blantai. And to the south of them, wedged a little precariously between the deserts of British Bechuanaland and the

[1] *I.L.N.* 30 November 1968; 29 January 1966; 21 June 1969; 2 November 1968.

Indian Ocean littoral of Portuguese Lorenzo-Marques and British Natal, were the little independent Boer nations of the Transvaal— the grandiloquently described South African Republic and the Orange Free State. Nor, in the far north-west, beyond the Gulf of Guinea and the Biafra Bight, is there any trace on my map of what today, though riven by war, we call Nigeria. There was only then Sokoto and Bolo Bolo, Gando and Yoruba, Bornu and Borgu, Benin and Akpam, with a fringe of British administered territory along the Ibo coast.

It is strange to reflect that there must still be some living, little older than myself, who grew up in that far-away Africa— one which had a closer affinity to the Africa of the Middle and Dark Ages than to the Africa we know, or think we know, today. It has all changed so quickly that one cannot help wondering what it will be like, and how it will be depicted on the map of the future, when another seventy years have passed. Indeed, in this respect my antiquated *Times* atlas is more revealing than its modern counterpart. For it foreshadows change, and change is the essence of African history in the twentieth century. It is likely to continue to be so for at least as long as the century lasts. Nor can anyone begin to understand the African problem who does not realise this.

Africa is the supreme test facing British statesmanship today. It is of vital importance for two reasons. One is that in this vast and recently awoken continent there are 250 million men and women, most of them, compared with the inhabitants of Europe and North America, under-nourished and under-privileged and whose lot it is both our duty and interest to better. The other is that, so long as the present confrontation between the free and Communist worlds continue, it would be a strategic and economic disaster for the West if the Communist Powers absorbed Africa in their closed and iron polity. On Britain in particular a special responsibility rests, in view of the fact that until recently more than a third of Africa's population was under British tutelage and rule. Since then, except in Rhodesia, Britain has divested herself of direct responsibility for ruling Africans and granted independence to all those whom she has temporarily governed and over the years educated for democratic self-determination.

If, as increasingly appears, that education for democratic self-rule has proved insufficient to safeguard the happiness and welfare of the peoples concerned, it can be argued that her responsibility for their welfare still continues. In the economic sphere at least, this has been recognised by successive British Governments who have made available, at the expense of the British taxpayer and elector, the most generous financial assistance to the emancipated African nations formerly under her rule.

Of Britain's purpose and intent in Africa there can be no dispute. It is to raise the standard of living and level of responsible democratic rule in every African country, and particularly in every African country with which she has had special links. The modern Commonwealth, which grew out of the former British Empire, exists largely for this purpose, and all political Parties in Britain are agreed on the importance of fulfilling it. On grounds of religion, humanity, trade and strategic security alike, a rich peaceable, law-abiding and contented Africa is our goal.

Yet, in politics as in other departments of life, the wish can be father to the thought. In our desire to see Africans and African nations what we want them to be, do we not tend to see them, not as they at present are, but as we feel they ought to be? During the past few years scarcely a month has passed without some shock to our complacency about the capacity of the newly emancipated African States to govern themselves in a peaceful, orderly and democratic way. Elections have been cooked, electors beaten up and intimidated, politicians and officials bribed, imprisoned and even murdered, the Press muzzled, judges arbitrarily dismissed, military dictators set up with tyrannical powers of life and death, and democratic processes travestied by one-party States in which voting is nothing but an obligatory paper obeisance to authority. In wide areas of Africa the conception of one-man one-vote is not so much a practical mechanism for registering majority opinion as a totem or prestige symbol. At present it has little more real democratic validity than the traditional raising of a triumphant chief on his warriors' shields. And as a background to all this, in several of the new African countries, open civil or tribal war—never far under the surface of African life—has broken out.

To a historian with any knowledge of how Englishmen were governed in days before they were gradually weaned from violence and bloodshed by the rule of law, there is nothing surprising about this. Recalling what African life was like even fifty years ago, it seems unreasonable to expect Africans whose grandfathers were tribal warriors or slaves—governed, as their forbears had been from time immemorial, by the savage superstitions of mumbo-jumbo and the witch doctor—to be able to establish, in the course of a single generation, the kind of tolerant and law-abiding democratic self-government evolved in our rich sheltered island as a result of centuries of experiment, trial and error. When Zambia achieved independence there were only a hundred Zambians with degrees. In a land three times the size of the British Isles only a thousand had passed the school certificate.

There is no need to despair of the ultimate capacity of Africans to govern themselves in a peaceful, orderly and democratic way. "It is liberty," Gladstone said, "that fits men for liberty." Many educated Africans are already fitted for self-government, while some are exceptional and outstanding men, just as Alfred and the Venerable Bede were in days when the vast majority of our ancestors were ignorant savages. There is much in Palmerston's commonsense dictum that "if any nation should be found not fit for constitutional government, the best way to fit such a nation for it would be to give it them." It is only right, however disappointing the immediate results, that Africans in purely African countries should be given freedom to work out their destinies in their own way by the same processes by which we worked out ours. What is not fair, or sensible, is to try to reduce to ruin what had formerly been one of the most liberally governed, as well as most peaceful and prosperous, States in Africa, merely because its European-descended electors, who for the past forty years have exercised the traditional British right of governing themselves, believe, with some justice, that we are set on prematurely subjecting them to the majority rule of a still mainly primitive people. For, rightly or wrongly, they are convinced by what has happened in other parts of Africa that African native rule would be used to deprive them of their liberty and property. Because of this belief, they entrusted their government to those who repudiated, however unwisely, the nominal—for in Rhodesia it has never been more than that—constitutional authority of this country.

I have always felt it was wrong, as well as unwise, for the rulers of Rhodesia to make a unilateral declaration of independence instead of standing firm on their existing rights—which neither we nor anyone else could legally have overruled—and waiting patiently until the reason of what they were contending for had become apparent: that is, the injustice of denying to Rhodesia what we had granted to neighbouring African peoples far less capable of governing themselves by democratic and parliamentary processes. I have always felt, too, that the British Government, however justifiably angered by that intemperate act of UDI, made a profound political and moral mistake in taking a narrow, anachronistic and purely legalistic attitude towards their fellow-countrymen in Rhodesia by treating them as traitors in a state of rebellion against the Crown. Some words I wrote a few days after UDI was declared summed up my feeling:

"For these reasons reliance on law, and law alone, may not bring about the results that the British Government, out of the highest motives, is seeking. That insistence on law and the letter of the law which has been so beneficial an influence on our historical development has its dangers. For, in times when political passions run high, it is apt to be seen by stubborn Britons on both sides as an end in itself instead of what it is, a necessary means to the great ends of peace, justice and the common weal. It was English legal tit-for-tat in the eighteenth century which first broke the unity of the English-speaking nations. Some wise words used by Burke—unhappily in vain—at the crisis of the American War of Independence, or, as it was then called, the American Rebellion, are not without bearing on what might tragically become the position between those acting in the name of the law and constitutional propriety at Westminster and those defending what they regard as their liberties and rights of self-government at Salisbury. 'It is not what a lawyer tells me I may do, but what humanity, reason and justice tell me I ought to do . . . Show the thing you contend for to be reason; show it to be common sense; show it to be the means of attaining some useful end, and then I am content to allow it what dignity you please'."[1]

What I predicted has come to pass. In the game of legal tit-for-tat the leaders on both sides have failed not only in understanding of the other's point of view but in the most fundamental of all a statesman's attributes, political temperance. Each party has taken its stand on a proposition totally unacceptable to, and indeed impossible of acceptance by, the other. The British point of view has been, and still is, that, in the name of the arithmetical formula of one-man, one-vote under which Britain has governed herself—not yet wholly successfully, judging by results—for the last half-century of her long parliamentary history, the coloured numerical majority should be granted, if not immediately, at least well within the lifetime of the present generation of Rhodesians, the untrammelled constitutional right to exercise complete sovereign power over the lives, liberties and property of the self-governing white minority which has created a thriving, peaceful and progressive civilised society in what was formerly, and that less than a century ago, a massacre-haunted, disease-ridden and savage wilderness. This proposition, strenuously and repetitively proclaimed, overlooked two inescapable facts. One is that, as all experience shows, a one-man, one-vote constitution can only end in the oppression of the minority by the majority in any society where there is no common corpus of culture and belief—and the political, social and cultural background and transmitted habits of the British who have made their homes in Rhodesia and evolved the Rhodesian State are still centuries removed from those of the primitive tribal Africans who, as a result of that young country's success and prosperity, have poured into it to share in its material benefits and multiplied there as never before. The other fact is that the introduction of party politics on European parliamentary lines into the political and social life of native Rhodesia resulted in murder and intimidation of a horrifying kind in the name of Party solidarity, and that almost everyone in Rhodesia, including the still unfranchised native African himself, knows that such murder and intimidation would be multiplied tenfold if one-man,

[1] *I.L.N.* 20 November 1965.

one-vote rule were to be applied in the immediate future to a State at present more peaceful and law-abiding than any other in the African continent. For this reason neither the white Rhodesians, who for the past forty years have successfully governed Rhodesia under a British parliamentary constitution nor, so far as can be ascertained, the indigenous majority, most of whom are still outside that constitution, want a recurrence of the kind of electoral violence which the so-called liberation Parties introduced into Rhodesian politics.

It is unrealistic of those living in this country to assume, as many liberal and progressive persons do, that an early advance of Rhodesia's Africans to full democratic citizenship would necessarily make it a more civilised and happier land than it is at present. It might do so; on the other hand—*vide* Katanga and Nigeria—it might not. Idealists are not justified in overturning a peaceful society merely because they consider it would look ideologically better the other way up. Unless we are prepared to offer alternative homes and livelihood to our fellow-countrymen who made their homes in British territory—often at the express invitation of a British Government—under the protection of the British flag and in expectation of the preservation of British law, order and political institutions, we have no right to subject them to a fate to which we would certainly not be prepared to subject ourselves. To be altruistic at one's own expense is one thing, but to be altruistic at the expense of someone else is not to be altruistic at all.

Yet the contrary proposition for which the Rhodesian Government has contended was almost equally unrealistic. It was that Britain had no right to champion and concern herself with the supposed constitutional needs of the as yet uneducated and un-enfranchised indigenous native majority, and that this was exclusively a matter for the existing and, to this extent almost totally unrepresentative, Rhodesian Parliament to settle. Though the white Rhodesians, having no representation at Westminster and having governed themselves through a parliament of their own for nearly half a century, cannot be expected to accept the dictation of a parliament exclusively elected in this island, the British people and their rulers have a very real responsibility for

those who live in Rhodesia, both black and white. For the
Rhodesian State exists, not merely by virtue of its white settlers'
hard work, enterprise and intelligence, but as a direct result of
British history, civilisation and endeavour. Without Britain's
past command of the sea, British expenditure and arms, British
commerce and finance, British prestige and place in the world,
and, above all, British ideas and civilisation, Rhodesia, as we
know it today, could never have come into existence. It is perfectly
true that in both World Wars white Rhodesians voluntarily
fought for Britain with selfless patriotism and gallantry, Mr. Ian
Smith and several of his Ministers among them. Yet it is equally
true that millions of Britons who had never seen that country, or
were ever likely to, fought for Rhodesia, and for the kind of
global conditions on which Rhodesia's existence depended, in both
World Wars and in the Boer War before that. What is more,
though in their exasperation with her, Rhodesians, however
understandably, seem to have forgotten it, Britain's continued
existence—her prestige and place in the world—is of vital importance for the future, and a world without her is not likely to
be a world in which little white Rhodesia will have much, if any,
chance of survival.

Nor is it fair to overlook, as the Rhodesian leaders have done,
the world-wide responsibilities and problems of Britain which
cannot be measured only by the narrow reckoning of Salisbury.
So much has to be taken into account by the rulers of a nation
whose livelihood, existence and influence depend on factors which
are not merely national but global. It has never been possible for
them, and never can be, to treat the Rhodesian problem in isolation. And just as Britons in this country, if true to the historic
creed they profess, are obliged to recognise the potential right of
all men, white or coloured, to equality of political treatment,
Britons in Rhodesia inherit by birth and ancestry the same faith,
and base it on their own right to self-government. If we in
Britain are mistaken in supposing that the changes we have been
demanding of Salisbury in the name of racial equality would
necessarily be change for the better, so are the white Rhodesians,
who have denied our premises, wrong to suppose that change in
their country, nine-tenths or more of whose people are at present

outside its constitution, can safely cease, leaving the political and economic balance between the races as it is. In view of what is happening in the rest of Africa, change of some sort, and probably drastic change, either for good or bad, is almost certain. For the momentum of change that began about the time my atlas was published is not going to be halted. The tide is coming in from beyond the Zambesi, and can no more be permanently stayed than Canute could stay the North Sea waves. The course of true statesmanship must always be not to oppose tides, but to use and harness them. The object of all Rhodesians capable of thought and imagination should be to educate, civilise and endow with economic and political opportunity as many of their darker-skinned neighbours and fellow-countrymen as possible. More than that of any nation in the world, Rhodesia's long-term future is dependent on being a multi-racial society. What matters is that it should be a trustful, tolerant, hard-working, law-abiding and peaceful one. Equality of rights for all civilised men south of the Zambesi was the watchword of the man who founded Rhodesia and gave it his name. It is for his heirs and successors to create civilised men.

The most profound mistake a statesman can make is to try to bind the future. It is something that can never be done, for the future will be decided by those living in it, not by those envisaging it from the present. It was failure to recognise this—on both sides of the ideological fence that divides Britons in Rhodesia from those in this country—which, from the start, bedevilled the Rhodesian constitutional problem. It was stupid to imagine that binding and unalterable rules can be imposed for all time on a self-governing country at the other end of the world which we no longer police or administer. It was equally stupid of those who rule Rhodesia to quibble and contend, to the exclusion of a reasonable and realistic settlement, over phrases and formulas whose practical application in an unforseeable future would depend on their successors' interpretation of them in the light of events and of the circumstances and convictions then prevailing, and which seem almost certain to be different to those of today.

It is still only a century since the whole of Central Africa was a savage hell where massacre, pestilence, famine and slavery were the agelong commonplaces of man's lot. The transformation wrought by European science and technology and by British ideas of law and liberty has only begun. The advances in human well-being and understanding that could be effected in the next century could make the present dispute, and all the pettifogging points and safeguards about which the disputants have been arguing, seem, in the light of a happier and more enlightened age, utterly meaningless. If only those in Salisbury and Westminster could have the magnanimity to trust one another, and above all, the imagination and faith to leave it to those who come after to create, in the natural course of time, a multi-racial nation free from the craven fears, suspicions and inequalities of the present! By doing so they would both be true to that blend of imaginative resource and practical common sense which distinguished our people in the past and enabled them, by carrying their libertarian tradition and forms of government across the oceans, "to found", what Tennyson called, "many a mighty State".

*　　*　　*

V

Black Bees in White Bonnets[1]

Every age has its favourite fallacies. Ours is race. More nonsense has been written and talked on this subject in the past half-century than on almost any other, and out of the obsessions and delusions which it has bred an appalling amount of unnecessary unhappiness and destruction has been caused. The second World War was largely motivated by the insane belief of the Germans that they were a superior race whose destiny was to give rule to mankind and subjugate, and even extirpate, inferior races. The world rid itself of this particular piece of pernicious nonsense at the cost of millions of lives, but is now hag-ridden by another, almost equally dangerous. This is that there is an inherent ideological division between the white, black, brown and yellow races which can only be resolved by the subjugation of peoples of one colour to those of another or, alternatively, by a deliberate

---

[1] *I.L.N.* 11 December 1965.

political mingling of men of different colour irrespective of considerations of history, geography and social tastes and aptitudes. The first is the fallacy of the white race-purists or racists and of their opposites, the black and yellow race-chauvinists of Africa, Asia and America. The other is that of unthinking sentimentalists in sheltered nations like Great Britain and the United States, who because, through their forbears' greater skill, enterprise and industry, they enjoy economies and political institutions more advanced than those of peoples of different colour, imagine that they owe the latter some kind of penitentiary amends and should therefore apply to the latter's failings and excesses a tolerance, even an approval, that they would never give to similar malefactors of their own colour.

This view was put to me in an extreme form by a Canadian correspondent writing about the massacre and mutilations perpetrated on the families of European missionaries in the Congo. "What right," he wrote, "has the white race to expect any sympathy at all when our forbears, yours and mine, committed one of the most inhuman acts of all time—the enslavement of the African negro? This act was fully condoned by State, Church and the population at large." What my correspondent implied was that it is wrong to condemn, or even draw attention to, the atrocities committed by black Africans against defenceless and completely guiltless European women and children because the latter, being white, are of the same racial division of mankind as those who two centuries ago made a profit out of the atrocious business of shipping African slaves to America. This, carried to its logical conclusion, is tantamount to contending that all the cruelties and injustices perpetrated by men on one another since the beginning of time should, in retribution, be visited on their descendants.

Yet this plea for racial retributive justice is founded on an assumption without historical justification. African slavery and the slave trade, however unspeakably vile, were not initiated by the British. They were an African institution long before the sails of European traders were seen in the Gulf of Benin. In Africa, as in every other part of the world, slavery and trading in slaves were as old as the history of war and commerce. Here, as elsewhere, it was the custom of primitive tribes to war against one another and, when victorious, to massacre or enslave the conquered. From this arose the practice of trading in and transporting slaves, buying from those who had enslaved them and selling to those who had an economic use for them. When Portuguese, English and other European adventurers—successors of the shipman in Chaucer's *Canterbury Tales*—started to trade with coastal West Africa, they found that the principal commodity the local native chiefs and traders had to offer in return for their proffered wares were slaves. And though by that time, through the cumulative influence of Christianity, slavery was ceasing to exist in Europe—and in England had long ceased to exist—in tribal and pagan Africa it was universally practised. Far more than gold or ivory, its time-honoured and tragic fruits proved the most valuable of Africa's products. When a demand for cheap labour arose in the sparsely inhabited plantations of the new-discovered Americas and the Caribbean, African chieftains and slave dealers and European shipowners and captains avidly pursued the opportunities for profit offered by this vile traffic. The horrors of "the middle-passage" in the crowded Atlantic slave ships are impossible to exaggerate. Yet it is doubtful if its wretched victims suffered more than those who from time immemorial, in every part of Africa and Asia, and, in an earlier age, of Europe, filed in dismal procession across desert and jungle to exile and slavery under the whippings and bludgeonings of merciless captors. Wracked by thirst and hunger, parted from all he loved, scourged, chained and huddled in foetid pit or galley, the lot of the slave has been a pitiful one since the beginning of recorded time. Has my correspondent, and the thousands who like him believe that the trade in African slaves was something unique, never heard of the Moslem galleys of Asia Minor and North Africa which for centuries kept the Mediterranean in terror, each propelled by two or three hundred naked slaves, chained six or seven to a bench, sleeping in their own ordure and scourged at their oars by cruel taskmasters until they died and were replaced by others? And the European nations who contended with the Turks and North African corsairs manned their galleys with prisoners from the jails living under conditions almost as vile and wretched. The diarist Evelyn on his grand tour of Europe saw them at Marseilles and Leghorn, "naked, doubly chained about their middle and legs, in couples, and made fast to their seats . . . and chastised by strokes."

The dreadful crime of the slave-trade —of transporting African slavery to the New World on a vast scale—in which English merchants and seamen engaged in the eighteenth century, was only one of the many ghastly acts of cruelty which man throughout the ages has inflicted on man. Nor is it true, as my correspondent supposes, that in England it was "fully condoned by State, Church and the population at large". On the contrary, it was the conscience of Englishmen, and the principles of English law, expressed first, as always, by a small elite minority and ultimately by a majority in Parliament, that brought about the abolition both of slavery and the slave trade in every land under the British crown. Having outlawed it from British and British colonial soil, British parliaments and the Royal Navy sought to eliminate it everywhere else, willingly paying, as at the Congress of Vienna, a heavy price to do so. Far from having increased the sum total of oppression, suffering and cruelty in Africa, our influence and action immeasurably diminished it.

* * *

VI

Can the Commonwealth Survive?[1]

Can the Commonwealth survive? Is it what it pretends to be? Does it even exist except in the imagination of those who talk and write about it? For a few days, it is true, every few years a number of important-looking gentlemen of almost every variety of creed and colour, attended by deferential lieutenants, aides and officials and wafted about the streets in large, glossy, beflagged, official cars, take up their quarters in the grander and more prestigous West End hotels. From Marlborough House—once the home, in his princely days, of the genial and guttural Edward VII and, more latterly, of Queen Mary—quintessence of all the

[1] *I.L.N.* 25 January 1969.

traditional Britannic virtues of dignity, honour and duty which are now popularly derided but were once the guiding star of a beneficent and immensely formidable global empire—there pours out a flood of part controversial and acrimonious, part nebulous, brotherly and anodyne, ministerial hand-outs which are broadcast to the world by Press and radio. In Palace, embassy, official residence and Government reception-centre there follows a continuous round of stately receptions and banquets of a very exclusive and V.I.P. kind in an atmosphere of beaming cordiality which appears to contradict and make nonsense of all the incompatibilities of belief and viewpoint high-lighted in the Conference chamber. Finally, after being photographed together round a glittering fairy-tale Queen and looking as jolly and relaxed as a collegiate get-together after a bump-supper, the assembled Prime Ministers disperse to the uttermost parts of the earth, having agreed on nothing except the fact that they are as disagreed as they were when they first came together.

Yet sometimes, in this world of compromise, misunderstanding and conflicting self-interest, dreams come true. The Commonwealth may be an illusion; it may, and even simultaneously, be a corridor of aspiration to a human future in which the nations and races of the world will find a common denominator for living together in peace and understanding. Humbug it may be, as Mr. Enoch Powell, in his logical and provocatively uncompromising way, has called it. Yet what is the political history of our country, out of which the Commonwealth sprang, but a wonderful success story of what humbug, if only consistently believed in and long enough maintained, can achieve? All the high-sounding platitudes and phrases which are the stock-in-trade of politicians of all Parties have, for all their contrast with the stark, ugly realities of every day existence, little by little during the ages created in this island what is probably the most humane and tolerable polity for men and women to live in yet seen. There is nothing like saying over and over again, in the face of all evidence to the contrary, that to no men shall we deny or sell justice, that all men are equal, that liberty is the birthright of every subject, to make a society in which these improbables begin to approach reality. And if there is one incomparable benefit which our country has conferred on the world it is that, having, in our favoured island situation, paid lip-service for so long to high-sounding humbug—or, if one likes to put it that way, Christian idealism—it has actually, and to a quite considerable extent, transformed our society for the better. We have become the purveyors-in-chief—far more so even than our American cousins, for we purvey it in a more subtle and, therefore, effective way—of such humbug to others. The Commonwealth is a child—at present perhaps only an embryo—of our, not, as is generally supposed, temporary and now discredited and discarded naval, military and commercial conquests, but of our permanent, consistent and disseminated idealism or humbug. Long may it so continue, thrive and grow!

In his enchanting fairy-tale for adults, *The Happy Hypocrite*, Max Beerbohm relates how a stout and worldly, not to say thoroughly wicked, Regency rip called Lord George Hell became so enamoured of a little dancer that to gain her love he donned the waxen mask of a saint and, courting and winning her under that deceptive guise, put aside his vast possessions and ill-gotten gains and lived in blameless innocence with her until the mask became a part of him and, when torn from his face by a former associate determined to unmask his hypocrisy, revealed beneath it, not the odious visage of his evil past, but, line for line and feature for feature, the saintly lineaments of the deception under which he had hidden. The parable is not without significance; perhaps the relationship between Britain and the astonishing multi-racial Commonwealth she has founded and to which, so improbably and in the face of reason, she clings, will prove something of the same. To resolve so many incompatibles as the divergent national and ideological interests and aims of the Commonwealth present to its statesmen, and particularly to those of our own much-tried and harrassed country—round which at present the Commonwealth conception and corpus, so far as it is a reality, still necessarily revolves—may seem impossible. Yet as all the worth-while things humanity has ever succeeded in achieving, in face of its own imperfections, frailty and impotence, must once have seemed impossible and unattainable, I feel that we of this generation, whether we believe in the Commonwealth's reality or not, should go on trying. "Faith", as St. Paul said, "is the substance of things hoped for; the evidence of things not seen." What happens in the future, as always in this mysterious and baffling world, depends on man's capacity for faith. How many marriages in the light of the obvious imperfections of both partners, would succeed if it were not so? The same is true of political unions.

By far the most important thing a human being—that is, a frail, imperfect and fallible being—can do is to go on trying and, if he doesn't succeed at first, to try, try again. That is what those who wish to preserve the Commonwealth have had to do and will have to go on doing. They will be made to look fools, their idealism will be presented as, at best, lunacy and, at worst, knavery. Yet if, in the fullness of time, the diverse peoples who comprise this curious and tenuous agglomeration of States, nations and tribes learn to trust one another and discover that they have something in common too valuable to discard, it will have justified, and more than justified, its existence. Over the door of the Commonwealth Secretariat office there should be inscribed Shelley's words:

To hope till Hope creates
From its own wreck the thing it contemplates.

CHAPTER 12

Who is for Liberty

... A voice valedictory,
Who is for victory?
Who is for Liberty?
Who goes home?

G. K. CHESTERTON

The Ultimate Evil · Counsel and Consent ·
The Uses of Money · A Flaw in the Financial System ·
The Painful Plough · The Instinct to Create ·
The Need for Education · Student Power ·
Wanted—A Local Democracy · This Sunburnt Face ·
A Choice for Destiny

I

The Ultimate Evil[1]

When I was a boy, slavery was almost unknown. It lingered discredited and seemingly dying, only in a few remote, savage places, and in the political prisons of Czarist Siberia. Great Britain had played the principal part in sweeping it from the world. For nearly a century, wherever the flag of England had flown, the slave's fetters had dropped to his feet and he was free. And happily for mankind, the flag of England flew in more and more places. When A. C. Benson wrote the words of "Land of Hope and Glory," he was expressing his sense of this state of affairs, his pride and faith in it. I grew up in that atmosphere.

I do not live in it any longer. Despite two World Wars, heroically fought to preserve and extend the bounds of freedom, slavery is

[1] *Illustrated London News* 27 March 1948

springing up again on every horizon. I have just heard it announced on the wireless that, following the funeral of Jan Masaryk, action committees in every Czech town and village are to prepare lists of such of their neighbours as are "nationally unreliable", with the object, it is believed, of marching them off to forced labour.[1] In other words, to prepare lists of those they wish to make slaves. We are back where we were before Clarkson and Wilberforce, and long before. For slavery has returned to Europe, the historic stronghold of Christendom for more than a thousand years. We thought we had slain the reviving evil thing when we defied and broke Hitler. But we were wrong. There seem almost as many slaves in the world today, three years after his death, as there were in the heyday of his power.

What are we to do? The answer is: To set our faces against slavery, to lend it no countenance at home or abroad, to refuse to allow it to be extended into any sphere of the earth for which we have responsibility. Slavery is the ultimate and greatest evil. For it is based on a denial of the dignity of the human soul. Under no conceivable circumstances can it be anything but evil. Those who order their fellow-men to be enslaved or kept in slavery are tyrants, whether they enslave them because they are of different race or colour, because they have been defeated in battle or at the polls, because they are poorer or richer, or because they hold different views. To deprive a fellow-creature of personal liberty can only be justified if he has committed a deliberate crime against his fellow-beings, and only when his offence has been proved beyond all possibility of doubt and every safeguard for fair and impartial trial has been scrupulously observed. That is why the multiplication of administrative offences punishable by imprisonment is such a deplorable feature of modern legislation in England. Those who frame such laws forget the supreme importance of liberty and the obligation which free men, who value their own freedom, lie under not to deprive other men of freedom without the clearest necessity. We have become careless of this in recent years and have soiled the statute book with as many offences punishable by loss of human liberty as our eighteenth-

---

[1] Twenty years later history—of the Russian Communist variety—has repeated itself' and in the same place.

century ancestors deemed worthy of death—out of equally well-intentioned motives.

I know there are people who say that there never was any freedom in this country or any other, except for the rich—for landowners, rentiers, and the like. Freedom, of course, like everything else in this world is comparative; some people are freer than others. It is also an attitude of the mind: a man of serene, cheerful and unselfish temper enjoys liberty in a way that others cannot. But slavery—the opposite to freedom—is a thing absolute, definable and degrading. It is that state in which man is left without any freedom of choice. A poor man in this country, in a time of unemployment, might think many times before leaving his job, but he could at least leave it and continue to exist. He was free to express and organise his opposition to government or to his economic lot, free to go where he pleased, free to read whatever others chose to say against his rulers or employers, free to strike against the terms of his employment, free to vote against the plans of his rulers, and, what is more, by his vote, to help dismiss them. These are no small liberties and have been won for free communities by centuries of struggle. They do not exist in Czechoslovakia today, and they do not exist in many other countries. Their restoration is the most important goal before modern man. And the first step in that restoration should be the strengthening of liberty in this country, its traditional cradle in the modern world.

Our problem, as I see it, is to preserve every piece of social legislation which, by strengthening the economic independence of the ordinary man, ensures a wider enjoyment of liberty, yet to do so with a clear realisation that the object of such legislation is not material comfort or benefit for any one class or another, but true liberty for all, and that, wherever such legislation whittles down the liberty of individuals, the gain in liberty sought should carefully be weighed against the individual liberty sacrificed to achieve it. It is the business of a free State, by just laws, to ensure the fullest possible measure of liberty, both political and economic, to all its citizens. But it should not be its business directly to confer material benefits on one class of citizen or another, for to do so is to make a servile state. So far as is compatible with general liberty, material benefits should be apportioned as closely as possible to individual efforts. The strong bent in human nature towards laziness can only be overcome in a free society by the ultimate urges of want and incentive, and to try to remove these urges altogether is not to make society richer but poorer. Direction to labour—a horrible and servile notion of government—is the inevitable corollary to the State's attempts to abolish want altogether by direct action. The State's object should rather be, by ensuring real freedom for all—the freedom which comes from good and stimulating education and environment—to encourage men to abolish want by their own voluntary efforts: the only way it ever can be abolished except by slave labour.

There is one further point—an important one for every lover of liberty. In the last resort, our love of Liberty is founded on our Christian faith. It arises out of respect for the sanctity of the individual soul. The teaching of the Christian Church is clear: that we should love our fellow-men. What we must hate is not the enslaver—the tendency to enslave and constrain others is latent in every man's erring nature—but the fact of enslavement. Our object, as a Christian nation, should be to prevent enslavement and, in the last resort, if need be, to sacrifice ourselves to prevent it. On the clear recognition that we are ready to do so, the liberty and peace of mankind may depend. Yet force, at the best, is a negative and destructive thing. The true means to spread the love and practice of freedom is not by hatred, abuse and self-righteousness, but by precept and genuine human fellowship. There is an iron curtain across the world today, but not all the good is on one side of it nor all the evil. The sword may be drawn rightfully to defend that which is good, but it is not by the sword that Christian men can overcome hatred and oppression. It is by weapons of a different kind.

*   *   *

II

Counsel and Consent[1]

The essence of democracy—if that misused word still has any meaning—is two-way debate. All government, under whatever name, is partly authoritarian; if it is not, it is not government. In any but the smallest and most primitive society, the only alternative to government is anarchy, that is, a continuous conflict of competing and mutually destructive violence and intimidation.

Yet no one likes government when, as inevitably happens, it involves restraints on the individual or acts of authority which the individual feels to be oppressive or unjust. Hence the process which has continued, under various forms, since the earliest recorded times, of those subject to government seeking to compel or persuade those in authority to debate and argue with them their authoritative proposals and acts. To achieve what our Plantagenet sovereigns seven centuries ago called "counsel and consent" in the administration of affairs. To get those in power to recognise—so hard, human nature being what it is, for them to accept—that "that which touches all should be approved by all". If the history of our country has any significance for mankind, it is the patient persistence with which its people over the centuries have contended for this principle and found enduring ways of applying it.

It is often said that there is no such thing as a British Constitution and never has been. This last is nonsense. There never was a continuing society which had so strong and complex a constitution as that which developed in the southern half of this island under the aegis of its Plantagenet, Tudor, Stuart and Hanoverian sovereigns. It is beside the point to say it was not a written constitution, like those which lawyers and philosophers drafted under the eighteenth and nineteenth century liberal revolutions in America, France and other lands. It was not written because there was no need to write it. Having evolved gradually, it was accepted in practice by successive generations of Englishmen,

[1] *I.L.N.* 6 July 1968.

who continuously adapted and applied it to their contemporary needs. What mattered was that it was always concerned with the vital point of how to achieve "counsel and consent" in the ruling of the realm. Sometimes this was sought and achieved by one means, sometimes by another. Written affirmations of constitutional law like Magna Carta or the Bill of Rights were only passing and fragmentary expressions of the enduring national resolve to ensure that those who wielded power should hear and consider what those subject to it felt and had to say about it.

Paradoxically, in what, by our standards, was an anarchical age and land, it was the very resolve of strong sovereigns like Henry II and Edward I to make their rule more effective which gave England the beginnings of its flexible mechanism for ensuring counsel and consent between ruler and ruled. By delegating part of the functions of government to those of their subjects best able to resist and impede their edicts, they made the representatives of the ruled part of the machinery of government. Side by side with the royal instruments of power in the shires— sheriffs, coroners and itinerant judges—they appointed local magnates, "knights of the shire", as they came to be called, and conservators or justices of the peace, to serve on judicial benches and inquisitions and provide the means of a colloquy between the central government and the localities. In the fullness of time they called to their consultations at Westminster and to the meetings of the Great Council of the Realm such knights of the shire and, before long, their humbler trading counterparts, the burgesses of the chartered boroughs. What at first was a temporary and occasional expedient gradually became an accepted and permanent custom. These originally humble representatives of the local communities were able to make their voice felt, and that of those they represented, because they themselves were part of the machinery of royal government and, as such, so necessary to the Crown that the latter could not effectively function without them. The rulers of the realm had to hear what they had to say and pay some heed to it. And the right of these representatives to speak, and the forms of doing so and of voicing the needs and grievances of the subject, grew to be habitual and universally recognised, so much so that when any English sovereign tried to ignore and override them he found his throne in danger.

From Edward II to Richard II, from Richard II to Charles I and James II, the story under varying forms was the same: England could not be ruled without counsel and consent. And when a strong ruler, like Edward I or Henry VIII, wished to do strong and radical things, he was careful to use the mechanism through which his subjects expressed their needs and grievances, to endorse and enforce his will. The greatest, swiftest and most drastic revolution in our history, initiated by the Crown in the sixteenth century, was a parliamentary revolution carried out, at the king's behest, by a consulted and consenting parliament. It was this that made it so difficult to halt and resist. To quote Marvell on a later, but ultimately less successful, revolution, "it cast the kingdoms old into another mould".

Crown, Lords and Commons, the historic components of the High Court of Parliament, have played various roles, but their supreme service has always been that together they provided a two-way debate between rulers and ruled. What is disquieting about our rapidly changing modern polity is that it is becoming felt they no longer do so. In the name of the absolute sanctity of an arithmetical, mechanical and comparatively novel formula of representation, the House of Commons has almost totally monopolised the powers of Parliament at the expense of its other components, while, through the instrumentality of a monolithic party machine and an entrenched and gargantuan Civil Service, the Prime Minister and Cabinet are able to exert a near dictatorship over the House of Commons, whose members too often seem to the man in the street, not so much the representatives of the community, as the instrument and mouthpiece through which the Executive makes its edicts, if not acceptable, compulsorily accepted.

The public is waking up to the discomfort of a situation in which it can no longer effectively argue the toss with those who rule it. It feels that its voice is not sufficiently heard and heeded in the corridors of power. It does not want to see Britain go the way of other so-called democracies where a one-party controlled parliament or national assembly, silent and obedient, is merely the rubber stamp of an all-powerful dictatorial ruler or party caucus.

To restore parliamentary institutions to their former prestige and authority is the greatest of the tasks awaiting statesmen today. As Disraeli put it, "The formation of a free government on an extensive scale, while it is assuredly one of the most interesting problems of humanity, is certainly the greatest achievement of human wit . . . It requires such refined prudence, such comprehensive knowledge and such perspicacious sagacity, united with such almost illimitable powers of combination, that it is nearly in vain to hope for qualities so rare to be congregated in a solitary mind . . . With us it has been the growth of ages, and brooding centuries have watched over and tended its perilous birth and feeble infancy." It resides neither in the procedures of Parliament nor the present-day egalitarianism of the franchise—a mechanical device for ascertaining the popular will which many other countries today share with us and not wholly successfully—but in a far more subtle amalgam of individual rights and corporate powers. The recipe for it, and for what it has made possible in the way of contented and fruitful social living and creative achievement, is to be found in our history.

*   *   *

III

The Uses of Money[1]

How often, in a wealthy and complex society like ours, one encounters perfectly sincere arguments based on the proposition that the making of financial profit is discreditable and that the love of money is the root of evil! Some rest on ideological and political grounds; others on the feeling of kindly and sensitive persons that there is something ignoble in thinking too much about financial matters and that a generous mind should be above mercenary concerns. Yet I have never known anyone who did not have a use for money and a need, great or little, for what it could buy.

[1] *I.L.N.* 3 December 1966; 4 November 1961.

> *Money, I despise it,*
> *Many people prize it,*

sang Archibald Grosvenor in *Patience* to his intended, but was
careful to mention, as the preliminary to his suit, that he was a
"man of property". As for the poor, the thought of money is
always with them; their circumstances scarcely allow them to
think seriously for long of anything else. In the corporate
organisations which artisans and labourers have created over the
years to protect their interests, wage-rates are the very shewbread
on the altar. Even authors, who rate with dairy farmers, house-
physicians and nurses as the lowest-paid of professional workers,
talk with feeling—when they can get anyone to listen to them—
about their royalties; while poets, poor things, whose royalties
are usually of a hypothetical nature, are sometimes, if the correspondence of the late Dylan Thomas is any guide, not above
devoting thought to the gentle fiscal art of "touching" their
friends.

The trouble about money is that everybody wants it. It is
splendid stuff and wonderfully useful, but the competition for it
is terrific and it runs quickly through the fingers. It therefore
causes a great deal of competition, covetousness, jealousy and
heart-burning, though whether more than any other commodity
of exchange—cows or beads or, in the less enlightened parts of
Arabia and Africa, slaves—I doubt. For this reason many worthy
persons contend that mankind would be the better for dispensing
with it altogether. Few of these good men and women, however,
seek to dispense with it themselves.

For though money can act, like every other material object, as
a vehicle for human selfishness, it is selfishness which is the root
of evil, not money. Moreover, the latter tends to operate as a form
of social education. It is a reminder that others have needs and
rights, and that to obtain the satisfaction of one's own, one must
allow for theirs. By its two-way use money forces a man to satisfy
some other person's wishes as the necessary price for satisfying
his own. Except when one party to a monetary bargain is starving
or in desperation, a bargainer cannot dictate his price.

This is where money performs such a valuable social function.
It is a means of satisfying both oneself and some other person

over whose rights and wishes, if one had the power, one might be inclined to ride roughshod. Even if one assumes one is so good and kindly a man that one would never knowingly defraud or oppress another, the capacity inherent in human nature for believing that what one wants is right is so unlimited as to render one curiously blind to any point of view which conflicts with it. Though philanthropically minded persons may seek to benefit their fellow creatures, they often do so in a way which accords with their own beliefs but takes little account of the wishes of their supposed beneficiaries. I read only this morning of a Water Board which, out of the highest public motives, is contemplating compulsorily flooding a valley containing several farms whose owners as a result are prevented either from selling their land or enjoying the benefits they would otherwise derive from it. One of them, seeking to put up a new building to accommodate his cattle, has been refused the Improvement Grant he would otherwise receive towards it, on the ground that it would not be prudent to grant it in view of the possible destruction of his land in eight years' time. Another cannot purchase an expensive piece of machinery essential to his farm's economy because of uncertainty as to its future. If the Water Board and its officials had, like the common ruck of us, to use the ordinary monetary mechanism to bargain for the land it seeks to flood, it would be unable to inflict such gross injustices on those over whose lives and livelihood it has been given despotic authority. It could attain its wishes only to the extent to which the monetary means at its disposal enabled it to satisfy those of others. There would have to be a bargain, and a bargain which left both parties to it feeling they had got something each wanted.

Of course, the officials of the public authority concerned sincerely believe that they are doing right in perpetrating such injustice. They believe that the public is going to be served by their authoritarian dictates, even though innocent persons lose their homes and livelihood as a result. The legislature which authorises such injustice believes the same; it is acting, it is argued, for the general good. I doubt, however, if the subject possesses anything more precious than justice from those who rule him, for, if injustice is to be done to one man or set of men *pro bono publico*, no subject is safe from injustice. It is better for men to enjoy the freedom of choice and bargaining that the mutual use of a money mechanism offers than to have the disposal of their lives at the mercy of all-powerful political and bureaucratic philanthropists freed from the necessity of acting justly. Other things being equal, the more disposal over his own life the State leaves the individual, the more justice, as well as liberty and virtue, there is likely to be.

This is why I do not share the prevailing belief in the validity of what is called socialism. That the State should act as umpire and, when necessary, temper excessive wealth by remedial taxation, that one man should not be fantastically rich and another helplessly poor, I can believe. But to widen the exercise of free choice is one thing; to by-pass it altogether and substitute for it authoritarian dictation is to reverse the entire course of our history and open the flood-gates of tyranny. Money is a passport for free men; compulsory purchase and the whole modern mechanism of statutory confiscation the dungeon key of the servile state. The use of the first produces a community of men capable of realising that others have rights and viewpoints which must be respected. The other breeds men, like the totalitarian dictators, who are incapable of any bargain except one in which they obtain everything they want. It is this that Lord Acton had in mind when he wrote that all power tends to corrupt, but that absolute power corrupts absolutely.

The truth is that without the instrument of money-choice a free society cannot operate or a free man subsist. Money is the means with which, at the expense of conceding to some other a like freedom of choice, we purchase our own. Money gives us the liberty to satisfy our needs and wishes in our own way: to help others, to do what we regard as just or our duty, to do good, or to do evil. It is the only social alternative to a state either of anarchy or despotism, to a world in which the strong exert their will by violence or one in which Government ordains what everyone must do, suffer or enjoy. There is no other mechanism save money by which the individual can enjoy freedom of choice in a law-abiding and peaceful society.

Much, therefore, depends on the proper distribution of money;

that every man who works should have sufficient to exercise a reasonable freedom of choice. And a sufficiency of money, of purchasing-power for all, depends not only on its distribution but on the amount of wealth—of food, clothing, shelter, the material wherewithal for health, transport, recreation and aesthetic enjoyment—which is available for purchase. Such material wealth depends itself on human labour, on the amount of work free men and women, in a free society, are prepared to perform to create it. The most important commodity that money can buy is work: creative, willing and satisfying work to fulfil the needs both of the producer and the purchaser, of the "worker" and the "employer". For everyone when he uses money to satisfy his needs is at that moment an "employer", and everyone when, in return for payment, wages or salary, he labours to satisfy such needs, is a "worker". When the housewife enters a shop and, with the money her husband has earned by his labour, purchases a packet of cereals, she becomes an employer of other people's labour: of the farm and farm-labourer who sow and harvest the grain, of the sailor, railwayman or lorry-driver who transports it, of the manufacturer and factory-worker who process it, of the shopkeeper and his assistants who sell the finished commodity over the counter.

On this interdependence of customer and supplier, of employer and worker, both the justice and wealth of a free society depend. Unless it operates to produce a sufficiency of the material wealth men require and at the same time causes them, customer and supplier alike, to feel they are receiving just treatment, it is not operating efficiently. To make it do so is partly the responsibility of those who rule but it is also the responsibility of us all in our capacities as purchaser and producer, employer and worker.

The efficiency of a free economy thus turns on the wisdom and sense of responsibility with which we exercise our personal freedom of choice in buying, and the energy and skill with which we each do our share of the world's work to satisfy other men's needs and our own. If, whether in our individual or corporate capacity, we misuse our economic freedom of choice by frittering away money on unworthy objects and pleasures, or if we fail to do our share of the world's work efficiently, we endanger the free society the economy serves. The use of money, of its earning and spending is not only an economic question. It is also a moral one—a question of "doing as you would be done by", both as purchaser and supplier or, as we put it, as employer and worker. The health of society depends on a widespread realisation of this. Herein lies the fallacy of the fashionable ideological obsession with compulsorily equalising wealth for its own sake. As the history of Communist Russia shows, the dictatorship of the proletariat, that is, of the rulers of an egalitarian society, is the most absolute of all dictatorships. It involves the abject submission of all to those who, in the name of such a theoretical dictatorship, exercise authority over the egalitarian mass; no one has any freedom of choice except the self-chosen dictators and their secret police. Once the representatives of an elective democracy set out down the slippery slope of equalising all wealth and all incomes, they threaten the very existence of liberty. There is no arrogance, it has been said, like the arrogance of elected persons, or, one might add, of the officials who act in their name. For all the inequalities and injustices which a wise legislature is right to try to modify and temper, the libertarian republic of money is the only answer, save the sword, to the oppression of Big Brother. It is against such oppression that under many names —"the divine right of kings" was one—the British people throughout their history have fought. For though money can be a cause of evil, it is also the root of that without which man is incapable of good: personal liberty. Under an egalitarian dictatorship one does what one is told; one has no alternative. Under a free economy one pays one's money and takes one's choice.

*　　*　　*

IV

A Flaw in the Financial System[1]

Financial systems are complex things—so complex that, like the law, no one can hope to reform and improve them who hasn't spent a lifetime learning to operate them. Yet no one who has is likely to want to alter them or regard it as otherwise than heresy and folly to do so. This is unfortunate because, as nearly all human creations do in the end, financial systems can get out of gear and cease to serve the ends for which their creators designed them. Yet whether they are working efficiently or not, experts always tend to maintain that they are.

There is one way by which even the most ignorant layman can tell that a financial system is not working properly. If a substantial part of the community needs and cannot afford to buy a commodity which other men can make in abundance but are unable to sell for lack of purchasers, the financial system that causes such a frustrating state of affairs is not, whatever experts may say, operating as it should. If, as happened between the two World Wars, millions of men and women are without the very goods and services their own labour, if employed, could have created, because there is no effective financial, as opposed to real, demand for such goods and services to be made, there must be some fatal lack of correlation between the expression of a public need and the financial mechanism for satisfying it.

For money is not wealth itself, or even, as is generally supposed, merely a measure of wealth, but the essential instrument by which under a free system the community's need for goods and services causes those goods and services to be created. Without a sufficiency of purchasing power the goods cannot be made, because the wherewithal is lacking to pay and set to work those capable of making them. Money is like the starting mechanism of a motor; unless applied at the right time and in requisite strength, the motor cannot run. In a free society—one in which men are free to choose their own consumer goods and employ-

[1] *I.L.N.* 5 September 1959.

ment—their possession of purchasing-power is the only motive force which can get the corn growing in the fields and the wheels of production turning. If for any reason there is an insufficiency of purchasing-power in the hands of those whose need for creatable commodities is unsatisfied, there will not and cannot be, without the application of totalitarian methods, a sufficient degree of production. The resources of the earth will not be used to full capacity, nor will those of industry. As a result, there will be unnecessary and frustrating want. All the cleverness, expert knowledge and technical jargon of the priests of high finance or academic economics cannot alter this fact.

Things have changed much since the war. The mass unemployment, which presented, in this and other free communities, the spectacle of simultaneous poverty and enforced idleness for millions, is no longer tolerated, and no political party dares subscribe to any financial principle or expedient that has so feared and detested a result. In many countries freedom itself has perished as a result of the popular hatred which such a consequence of so-called economic freedom aroused in the frustrated masses. Today freedom only survives in Britain because all political parties are at one, and have since the war been successful, in pursuing policies which ensure that the overwhelming majority of the working population is in continuous wage-earning employment.

Yet there are signs that the old malaise of the 'twenties and 'thirties is with us in another form and that full employment is only being obtained at the expense of failing to satisfy some need of the would-be consumer which, under a more efficient financial system, would be automatically satisfied. Miners, for instance, have been told that they are over-producing coal and that mines must be closed because there is an insufficient demand for it. Yet this is not so much because consumers have all the coal they want or could use, but merely because they lack the money to buy it at the price at which the Coal Board offers it. A reduction in the price of coal would almost certainly lead to an increased demand, both at home and abroad. But the rigidity of our present politico-financial regimen of guaranteed and ever-rising wages, prices and taxes prevents it. For financial reasons the full production of wealth is being artificially retarded, and we are the poorer as a result.

Less food, too, is being produced in this country than the soil and the skill of its farming population are capable of providing. As we only produce about half our food and import the other half from abroad it looks as though, here also, our politico-financial system is operating to maintain an artificial brake on the creation of real wealth. It is true there are many plausible reasons for maintaining that it is not to this country's advantage to produce all the food its people want and that the latter are better off manufacturing goods for export in exchange for imported food. Yet with every year of increasing industrialisation in the primary producing countries overseas, this argument is losing force, and it is difficult to believe, as financial pundits argue, that it is really any longer to our advantage to discourage the home producer of, say, butter and cheese in order to reserve the home market for the foreign customers of our manufacturing exporters. Where, of course, domestic agricultural production is dependent on the import of large quantities of foreign-produced feeding-stuffs, there may be no virtue in increased home production of some particular agricultural product, for in that case what would be gained on the roundabouts would be lost, or more than lost, on the swings. But my point is that, wherever there is any slack in the utilisation of the wealth we are capable of creating, and a substantial demand exists for such unmade wealth, there must be a flaw in the nation's financial machinery, since the means is lacking for translating that demand into the purchasing capacity to make it effective and call the desired wealth into existence.

All this is far easier to state than to achieve; for the operation of supply and demand in a nation of free men with a great variety of callings, needs and vested interests, is a matter of infinite complexity. Yet the test of financial and productive efficiency is itself a simple one, and it ought to be continually applied by those responsible for a country's government and economy.

*   *   *

V

The Painful Plough[1]

To farm is to create wealth—the wealth man needs above all other. Sheltered from realities by an elaborate social organisation, urban man is apt to evaluate it lower in terms of money than other forms of wealth, which is why the husbandman is paid less in such societies than any other skilled worker. This is certainly so in Britain, which during the past century has become a predominantly manufacturing and commercial community dedicated to an almost mystical belief that cheap food spells industrial prosperity. While almost every other industry is protected by tariffs, agriculture, still our largest one, is almost completely unprotected against foreign competition. Yet though the price of food is kept at an artificially low level by a system of agricultural price-supports—which is popularly supposed to benefit the farmer but in reality benefits the urban consumer, who, nonetheless, complains of it in his capacity as tax-payer—food remains the most vital wealth known to man. How vital can be realised by imagining a strike of all food-producers throughout the world. Within a few days, even hours, of the exhaustion of mankind's accumulated reserves of foodstuffs, every other form of wealth, from diamonds to uranium, would count for nothing in the market compared with food. A millionaire would be ready to trade a Rolls-Royce for a biscuit, a Rembrandt for a glass of milk.

Yet so long as there is money in the townsman's kitty and food in the shops to suit all tastes and purses, how it gets there and where it comes from seems a matter of indifference to him. All that matters is that it is there and in abundance. Yet a moment's reflection will show that such a state of affairs—one existing mainly in Western Europe and the United States—is an exceptional one. Even today, in our technological and highly industrialised age, the vast majority of mankind is grossly undernourished. Thanks to modern medical and hygienic science, the world's population is increasing at the rate of roughly 100,000 mouths

[1] *I.L.N.* 29 November 1958; 19 August 1961; 5 October 1963.

in every twenty-four hours. Sooner or later, if nothing is done, supplies are going to run so short that the food-surplus-producing parts of the globe will find themselves under dangerous pressure from the leaner and hungrier. Some believe that scientists will be able to grow all the food we want out of trays in their laboratories. Perhaps they are right, but I should not care to rely on it.

What is certain is that without the agriculturalist's skill and labour—the art and toil of the "painful plough"—there would not be enough food in the world to keep alive a fraction of its present population. The scientist, the manufacturer with his gift of mechanised power and quick transport, have great contributions to make to the growing, harvesting and distribution of food, but in the last resort everything depends on the skill of the farmer and farm-worker. The transmitted knowledge and carefully acquired technique of the farmer and husbandman is, in reality, more vital to human life and to the fabric of civilisation than any other single skill. In no country is that knowledge greater or that technique more studied and devotedly pursued than in ours.

The townsman has little idea what it means to ensure that his milk arrives safely on his doorstep punctually every morning. Winter on a farm is a cold, dank business. On the farm in which my own small stake in our agricultural industry is invested, work begins at six o'clock, or earlier, even on the dreariest December or January day. Twice a day without fail, sixty or seventy cows have to be assembled and milked; the elaborate arrangements for ensuring cleanliness of milk and milking-premises have to be carried out, involving formulas of work and habit almost as complex on their small scale as those of getting a battleship to sea or an aircraft off the ground. The production of every cow has to be meticulously recorded, the milk taken by tractor or lorry to the collecting station, the cows driven out to their day's allotted stint in the muddy kale field, and their carefully measured rations of hay, silage and concentrates brought to them. And in the intervals between this twice-daily ritual, begun in the dark and carried out in every kind of weather, the multifarious work of the farm has to be done; the cultivations made, the muck carted, the hedges laid and trimmed, the ditches cleared, the electric fences erected or moved, the machinery repaired and kept in running order, and a hundred matters, both agricultural and administrative, attended to. And if the farm is to remain solvent, once a year every cow has, if possible, to be got in-calf and nine months later delivered of her calf, with all the attendant risks and complications.

The skill, diligence and conscientiousness of those who do the nation's farming never ceases to amaze me. What is so touching about farm-workers is the readiness with which they face conditions of the greatest discomfort and difficulty to ensure that the beasts and the land they serve do not suffer. How many town-dwellers who found the morning milk on the doorstep every day during last winter's arctic weather, and thanked the patient and persistent dairy-roundsman for it, realised what the maintenance of that regular supply involved for the farm-worker in the shires, making his way in the dark across icy fields to start milking at six o'clock, having to unfreeze pipes to be able to milk at all and often having to spend hours in getting the milk-cans by tractor to the nearest collecting-station with every road deep in snow drifts, or having to work all night digging lorries with feeding-stuffs out of snow and ice? Yet the cattle were fed and milked and the milk delivered, and all for wages which many an unskilled worker in the town would regard as derogatory.

At the heart of such a man's work and service to the community is the sense of responsibility which the care of animals evokes: the knowledge that the beasts he tends are dependent on him and, but for him, would starve. The town worker can neglect his task or go on strike without feeling he has done anything shabby or mean: the farm-worker knows that if he did such a thing, the helpless creatures in his charge would perish. Whatever the demands of his own interests, he does not fail them. For all his muddy boots and rough, stained hands, he is a man of honour.

The land disciplines to duty and virtue all her servants. Responsibility to it is the hallmark of any man fit to farm. Most British farmers pass the test with honours. There are many small ones, particularly in the rainy West, who have a hard struggle and lack the capital to take long views. Yet their love for their acres, whether owned or rented, is very real, and they give them a service as devoted as any soldier his regiment or sailor his ship. It is this sense of personal responsibility that the ownership or occupation of land evokes which constitutes its value as an instrument of social machinery. It causes men to identify themselves with the earth and to make its enrichment the means not only of their support, but of their self-respect. Instead of exploiting the land, mankind's chief inheritance, they serve it. They plant and tend trees, they work and manure and re-till the topsoil, they drain and ditch and fence and hedge, build tracks and roads and bridges, barns and granaries, to make the corner of the earth entrusted to them fair and fruitful. To make two blades of grass grow where one grew before is their pride and happiness; for this they are ready for great efforts and sacrifices. There are bad landlords, bad farmers and bad husbandmen; there always have been. Yet in this island they have always been outnumbered by the good, which is why our countryside is so rich and fertile.

It is where, under tyrannical forms of government, private ownership and tenancy of land have been rendered insecure and unprofitable that the earth has become a desert. Men will only serve nature when they have reasonable continuity and security of tenure. For this reason, I doubt if nationalisation of the soil can ever lead to anything but its exploitation and neglect. Slave labour can make a pyramid, but it could never have made a countryside like Kent or the Medoc. The earth responds to love, not rape; the waste and destruction of the African groundnuts scheme was an illustration of how disastrously man's heritage can be impaired when control of the soil is vested in the hands of those divorced from it and who have not endured its salutary discipline. To wed the individual, with his instinctive capacity for creation and self-dedication, to earth, with all its latent potentialities for fruitfulness, is the business of a true statesman. It was this that the early Saxon kings and chieftains did when they made their primitive settlements on the cold clay of this island which their ploughs and ox-dung, sweat, toil and love were presently to transform into the countryside we know. And as one labours in the fields and woods, one feels this sense of the friendly continuity of those who have worked before one in the same spot and the realisation that the landscape whose love inspires one's

work and effort is the creation of predecessors who felt the same
love for it and, because of it, dedicated their lives to its service.
In the words of the Dorset poet, William Barnes,

> *They clear'd the groun' vor grass to teake*
> *The place that bore the bremble breake,*
> *An' drain'd the fen, where water spread,*
> *A-lyen dead, a beane to men;*
> *An' built the mill, where still the wheel*
> *Do grind our meal, below the hill;*
> *An' turn'd the bridge, wi' arch a-spread,*
> *Below a road, vor us to tread.*

*   *   *

VI

The Instinct to Create[1]

Man, it is said, was born to trouble as the sparks fly upwards. He
was also born to work. And there is no recipe in life, I have found,
like work to take the sting out of troubles. By work I do not mean
that activity little deserving of the name, in which someone performs as perfunctorily as he can an unwanted task solely in order
that he may be paid for it; such work, if it brings no other reward,
can never be an anodyne for pain. But when a man, paid or unpaid,
labours, not for remuneration or even prestige, but because he has
discovered satisfaction in doing his work, whatever it may be, as
well as it admits of being done, he has found the recipe for forgetting trouble. He will have learnt the way to lose himself, to
think during the performance of his task of nothing but the all-
absorbing challenge of wrestling with it. It is amazing how
quickly the hours of labour can pass for a man who has this
satisfaction. They will tire him but they will never bore him; he
will know weariness but not tedium. Usually the achievement of
this kind of Nirvana or release from self is attained gradually;
a man comes to realise it only after he has gained the proficiency
from which pride and joy in work spring. But once he has done
so, he is made freeman of the company to which every true

artist and craftsman belongs and has belonged since Adam's breed began. And this applies whatever his labour, though it be only totting up ledgers or emptying municipal dustbins. The test is the resolve to do the job as well as it humanly admits of being done, that is, perfectly. From this everything else follows.

The gravest indictment, as I see it, of modern industrial society is that so few men today find this kind of satisfaction in their work. They are satisfied as consumers to a degree that their fathers and ancestors never knew. It was the kind of satisfaction to which Mr Macmillan referred when he declared that the British electorate had "never had it so good"—a phrase itself wrung from the politically disquieting fact, so palpable to any experienced politician, that, though this was true, the well-paid proletariat of our day appears, from its repeated demands for higher pay, to remain stubbornly discontented with its lot. The reason for this is perfectly clear. Man is, by nature, a producer or creator as well as a consumer, and unless the instinct to create and produce implanted in him by nature is satisfied, he will, to a greater or lesser degree, be an unsatisfactory and discontented being. And our economy, like everything else in our society, depends, in the last resort, on the efficiency of the individual, and if the individual is not satisfied in his inherent nature he will not, and indeed cannot, be efficient. He cannot, of course, be efficient if he lacks the material wherewithal to keep body and soul together —food and clothing and shelter. He cannot, being biologically and sexually incomplete in himself and, therefore, a social creature, operate efficiently in isolation—he needs society and companionship and, to assure the continuance of his kind, the satisfaction of his reproductive needs. Those who control modern society either through the power of the purse or the law are aware of these obvious human necessities, and enjoy status and wealth through their success in satisfying them. They provide, for mass consumption, consumer goods; they also provide—and some of them make large profits by doing so—for the titillation of man's senses. But they fail, and increasingly fail, to provide for that fundamental and deeper need of man's nature: the need through which, by implanting it in him, the Creator fashioned man in his own image: the need, in his own small sphere, to create and produce, to make order and beauty and fertility, to fashion the natural resources of the world to something nearer his heart's desire, above all to forget himself and rejoice in the work of doing so.

It is this failure to see that man is such a creature, with the spark of the divine in him craving to be lit, which bedevils all our hopes of making a peaceful and contented world. For if man is not given the opportunity to create, he will, in his unconscious frustration, destroy. If he cannot love, he will hate; if he cannot lose himself in the selflessness of creation, he will perpetually bicker with his neighbour in an anarchy of competitive selfishness. Being unsatisfied and, therefore, inefficient, he will not build the New Jerusalem of his dreams; he will merely build the Tower of Babel. Ours is a society that, in the words of that great and forgotten prophet, the late H. J. Massingham, persistently puts last things first and first things last, industrialism before agriculture, technology before life, acquisition before function, chemistry before nature and the State before God.

> "Before the war we had become an ersatz people, a seething proletarian or suburban mass controlled by the wage-system and financial dictatorship to produce shoddy or produce nothing, enervated by the clock-work hedonism of mass amusement, living by the senses from the headlines, by the body from the tin-opener, and by culture not at all, existing in warrens of derelict industrial cities or along miles of mean or pretentious boxes strung along highways, like racing tracks, upon the face of a country either desecrated or tumbling into wilderness. Was this living, was this England?"

Those words were written a generation ago. Recalling all that has happened in the past decade and is still happening, they seem, in their essentials, even more true today. What Massingham called "the economic spell of beggaring the whole earth to make profits for gamblers and dealers" still operates, and at an ever-accelerating pace. And as, month after month and year after year, our formerly incomparably beautiful countryside is destroyed and the centre of our cities gutted to serve the ends of a financial accountancy which, however profitable it may prove for some, is based upon a profound social fallacy, men, for all their material prosperity,

grow increasingly discontented, until the only worthwhile recreation of many of the younger generation of factory workers—
enjoying wages beyond the wildest dreams of their hard-used and
industrious grandparents—appears to be wrecking the shops and
amusement-parks of the seaside resorts on which they descend, like
excited and unhappy locusts, for their Bank Holidays. Gambling,
train robberies, hit-and-grab raids, garrotting and the beating-up
of the temporary custodians of other men's wages, are the natural
and, I should have thought inevitable, concomitants of a society
which has adopted as its philosophy the thesis that, provided
someone—whether private individual or statutory corporation—
makes a "profit" out of it, any activity, however destructive of
good, is justifiable and even praiseworthy. That it may uproot
men from their homes, break up families, destroy hereditary and
long-acquired skills, and ravage and waste the accumulated
culture and civilisation of generations is, by this arithmetic of
Mammon run mad, of no account at all. We have made our god of
a false science of figures which ignores nature and, in ignoring
nature, destroys the most valuable of all nature's products, the
virtue and creative capacity of man.

*   *   *

VII

The Need for Education[1]

If I were asked what I considered the country's first priority, I
should reply Education. For education in its broadest sense,
rightly applied, could enable us to overcome all our difficulties
and, in doing so, make the maximum contribution to the peace
and happiness of mankind. It could enable us to produce more
food, manufacture, distribute and export more and better goods,
live more healthily, understand more fully and be on better terms
with our neighbours, be more capable of defending ourselves and
others against aggression and, above all, make a fuller use of our
lives. A Britain in which all her inhabitants, regardless of colour,
creed or origin, were truly educated men and women would have

[1] *I.L.N.* 4 January 1969.

no race problems, housing problem, unemployment, transport or financial problem. Her wise, industrious and self-controlled, above all tolerant, compassionate and patriotic people, and those they elected to represent them in Parliament, would be capable of solving all these problems in a spirit of mutual amity, understanding and good sense.

All this is obvious. Yet it is well to have a measure between what is and what should be. If it is obvious what such an ideal education could do for this country, it is equally obvious what our present system of education—that vast administrative and teaching machine to which we devote so large a part of the national income—is failing to do. For we are far from being a fully educated people. We are not producing anything like as much food as our soil is capable of raising and are forced, unnecessarily and at great expense and labour, to import vast quantities of food from other countries, many of whose own people are grossly undernourished. Too often the goods we manufacture and export to pay for these are of poor and shoddy workmanship with delivery dates which, owing to suicidal labour disputes, are notoriously unsatisfactory. The majority of our people have pasty complexions, bad teeth and impaired digestive and nervous systems, and spend, through our vaunted but wasteful National Health system, almost as much on drugs and other remedies as they spend on food, much of which they impair by careless and inefficient cooking. Despite modern means of communication and of transmitting knowledge, we are still fantastically insular and persist in behaving, often to our own hurt, as though all other nations and peoples had exactly the same standards, aptitudes and interests as ourselves, while we are so incapable electorally of elementary reasoning that we allow our politicians to reduce to a point criminally below the margin of safety the armed forces capable of ensuring, in time of war, the passage to our shores of the food and raw materials on which our continued existence depends. In short, for all our expenditure on education, we are fools. Properly educated men and women need not, and should not, be fools.

Everything in this world is a matter of comparison; other people are foolish too, and many, no doubt, even more foolish. Yet this is no reason why we should be complacent about ourselves. How many of us, on any subject not intimately and immediately connected with our own personal affairs—and even then only in the narrowest sense—think for ourselves or do anything but take our opinions at second-hand from others? We are brain-washed most of us, from morning till night, because we lack the thinking and reasoning capacity to sift the evidence on which those second-handed notions are based. It isn't that we lack brains; we all have them. It is merely that we have never been taught, or have taught ourselves, to use them properly. During most of our time we go about in a kind of trance with our minds only half functioning. The *reductio ad absurdam* of our mental state of vacuity is to be found in the words—I say nothing of the music—of our so-called "pop" songs. A baby drooling in its pram is no more mindless. Yet our young people of both sexes, who in their leisure hours, and frequently in their working ones too, listen to and intone these fearful lubrifactions of lugubrious idiocy and regard the sentiments they express—so far as they express anything at all— as the fine flower of their cultural heritage, have been educated for years, and at vast expense, in a wide variety of branches of knowledge.

Is there, therefore, something wrong with our educational system? Is there anything we can do about it? The fault, of course, does not lie wholly in our schools. Our children are subjected to a range of influences which have little or nothing to do with the class room; to those of their homes, the streets, the cinema, the wireless and "telly", the books, papers and strip cartoons they read and pore over. And many of these influences are very far from good, educationally, culturally or morally. Yet the greatest of all educational influences in the lives of our children, except those who come from very good homes—homes where thought, knowledge and the love of beautiful and worthwhile things is part of the air they breathe—lies in the kind of teaching they receive at school. And this depends on the teacher and curriculum.

Of the teacher I would say that nothing is so important as the quality of those who teach. On them the whole future of our civilisation and nation now depends. The most valuable service to his country a young man or woman can perform today is to dedicate his or her life to teaching the next generation of Britons and giving them the very best of all he or she has to give. It is more important than going into business or finance, than being a civil servant or sailor or soldier, than being a scientist or inventor, a doctor or farmer, a politician or diplomat. For all the work that these do depends on the quality and capacity of the ordinary Briton, and that depends on those who teach in our schools. If we are to become a great nation again, to make the most of our inherited capacity, it is essential to raise the whole status of the teaching profession, to recruit to it the best of our people and to make the conditions of those who serve in it second to none.

As for what the teacher teaches—the subject and curriculum—here, too, I believe a radical reassessment is called for. Today the emphasis is on the acquisition of as much dessicated knowledge as possible; on quantity rather than quality; on stocking, usually only temporarily, the memory instead of training and exercising the powers of thought, reasoning and self-discipline. The two most important lessons one can teach a child are to control himself for the benefit of himself and those about him, and to concentrate on whatever he is learning or doing so that he becomes master of his subject. The hallmark of an educated man, whether he is a university don or a farm labourer, is that he has learnt to do at least one thing thoroughly, that is, as well as it admits of being done. Of how many today, in any walk of life, can one say that? And the hallmark of a good man is that he is what, for want of a better word, we used to call a gentleman: a man, that is, who is gentle in his relations with his fellow-beings, who is true to his word, honourable in dealing, faithful to his trust, if necessary at the expense of himself and even his life. When we have a nation of men like that we shall be able to call ourselves educated.

*　　*　　*

VIII

Student Power[1]

A conflict between the generations—between youth and age—seems the most stupid of all conflicts, for it is one between oneself as one is and oneself as one will be. Or between oneself as one was and oneself as one is. Everyone in the course of life is young, and everyone who survives long enough becomes old. And it is the same person who is both—the same soul, the same mind and, unless Dr. Barnard and his disciples have got at one, the same heart. So if any kind of conflict can properly be described as suicidal, it is this. Persisted in, it would make the continuance of human society impossible.

Indeed, when one thinks of it, all society is fundamentally based on a compact or understanding between age and youth. The mother and father sacrifice themselves to rear, feed and educate their offspring, who in their turn, rear, feed and educate their own. Society, as Burke said, is a partnership between generation and generation, "a partnership in all science ... in all art, in every virtue and in all perfection, not only between those who are living, but between those who are dead, and those who are to be born." Youth and age are alike parties to it.

Part of this generation-partnership or compact is expressed in the Mosaic commandment: "Honour thy father and thy mother that thy days may be long in the land which the Lord thy God giveth thee." It is only among the beasts and the most primitive savage communities that this commandment is unknown. It is because it is, that which we call "progress"—the cumulative steps by which a civilisation is made—is virtually non-existent in animal and savage communities. With them each generation devours or destroys its predecessor, and the act of procreation is unaccompanied by any creative act or achievement. With experience ending only in puberty, for such a society there is no future, for nothing is ever added to it. For, though it does not follow that men and women grow wiser with age and experience, there

[1] *I.L.N.* 29 June 1968.

cannot without them be what we call wisdom. There can only be instinct, emotion and need, and not the means of co-ordinating and satisfying these on which both civilised society and any full and completed individual life depend. To allow the mind to mature and deepen, to feed and enrich it on the transmitted thoughts, wisdom and garnered intellectual and artistic achievements of the past, trust and partnership between the generations are as necessary as the action of sun, air and rain on the growth of plants.

For the old must place their wisdom and experience at the service of the young yet allow the vitality, energy and enthusiasm of youth freedom of scope, while the young must respect and honour the achievements and practical sense of their elders and place their physical strength and vigour, while they still possess them, at the service of the continuing community. Both, for their mutual benefit, must be tolerant of one another and of the frailties that are common to all. Human nature being what it is, it is not easy to achieve this tolerance and understanding between crabbed age and impatient youth, yet nothing enduring or worthwhile can be effected without it. It is the parent of all political and material progress.

It is this that makes most of the current fuss and frenzy generated by the phrase "student power" not a little absurd. In any just and wise world, power must be based on knowledge, not on its absence, and the business of a student is not to exercise power, least of all by force and violence, but to study so that he or she may possess knowledge and so become worthy of the power which in the fullness of time it will automatically be his or her turn to exercise. The purpose of education is to enable men and women to be better workers, craftsmen, parents, electors, administrators, statesmen, than they could hope to be without it. There is a time in the life of man for all things, and the age that immediately follows puberty is the time for intensive learning, for apprenticeship to the business of adult existence. Schools, colleges and universities exist and are supported by the community to provide the training on which its future well-being depends. A university which degenerates into a youthful pressure-group or a cell for mob demonstrations is failing to fulfil the purpose for which it exists and becomes a handicap, not an asset, to society. When it does so the implication is that those who administer and teach in it do not know their business. It is not the fault of its students if they abandon study for agitation, but of those who direct and teach them. No great teacher, with wide and generous sympathies, ever failed to win a response from his pupils. When a regiment fails in morale and discipline, the failure is the fault of its officers.

If, therefore, there is a breakdown in the work of our universities, there must be something wrong with our conception and technique of education. The young who spend the hours, when they should be learning, in such activities as making barricades, carrying revolutionary banners in procession and shouting down any expression of opinion contrary to the accepted ideology of the hour, are wasting, and therefore losing, the opportunity of learning while they have the chance to learn. And the blame must lie with what they are being taught and how they are being taught. If the result of their teaching is to turn them from study and rational discussion into violence, intolerance and the dialectics of the closed mind, there must be a flaw in it. Instructors who produce such results merit Milton's classic indictment of—

> *Blind mouths! that scarce themselves know how to hold*
> *A sheep-hook or have learned ought else the least*
> *That to the faithful herdsman's art belongs!*
> *What recks it them? What need they? They are sped;*
> *And when they list, their lean and flashy songs*
> *Grate on their scrannel pipes of wretched straw.*
> *The hungry sheep look up and are not fed,*
> *But swoln with wind and the rank mist they draw,*
> *Rot inwardly and foul contagion spead;*
> *Beside what the grim Wolf with privy paw*
> *Daily devours apace, and nothing said,*
> *But that two-handed engine at the door*
> *Stands ready to smite once and smite no more.*

As a commentary on the politically disturbed state of Western university life today, the poet's lines could scarcely be bettered.

Even the grim wolf with privy paw, waiting for its prey behind the iron curtain, was foreseen.

Yet though few in this country feel much sympathy for unkempt adolescents using mob violence to enforce their shallow and aggressive views while neglecting the studies for which they are financed by the working taxpayer, there is one aspect of "student protest" which deserves consideration. It is the claim that modern industrial society and government are ignoring and repressing the creative and libertarian impulses of man. Those, who make it, see and resent—I believe rightly—a society in which the validity of every major activity that affects men's lives is being increasingly decided by purely materialistic and mechanical standards. Thus, if it is considered to be the financial interest of some large-scale bureaucratic, industrial or commercial institution to transform and destroy a local community and its people's traditional homes, amenities, customs or livelihood, or to outrage their ideals and beliefs, no peaceful and constitutional expression of opinion and protest has much chance of prevailing. Nothing is allowed to weigh against the overriding authority of incorporated tycoon or administrative mandarin. It is the kind of automatic steam-rollering in the name of mass numbers and accountancy, disguised usually under some sham democratic façade, which is making anarchy a popular cause for the young. They fail to see, having so pathetically little knowledge or experience of how the world runs, that anarchy invariably becomes the parent of even more rigid and far more ruthless and cruel tyrannies than those they fear and resent. Yet their instinct that something is "rotten in the state of Denmark" and needs amending is not at fault. Vietnam, Porton, Aldermaston are the symbols to them of nightmare fears that encompass humanity's pilgrimage towards the light, with Giant Despair in his castle and Apollyon straddling the way.

* * *

IX

Wanted—A Local Democracy[1]

Someone described democracy as the divine right of kings standing on its head. This is a paradox more startling than accurate. What is true is that the edifice of bureaucratic government which today operates in the name of democracy can become, and often is, democracy standing on its head. In so many of the matters where government impinges on the life of the ordinary man, the latter has no effective control over his life at all. He has to do what Government tells him and, if he objects, however sound his reasons, is without appeal or redress. He is steamrollered by the immense, irresistible forces of our centralised Treasury-controlled, police-enforced bureaucracy into passive obedience.

The essence of democracy is that the citizen—or, as we say in England, the subject—should have some real say in the political and social regulation of his life. Now there are many things which concern ordinary men and women today about which they are not consulted and which would not be approved by them if they were. Public opinion-polls show, for instance, that the majority of men and women in modern Britain—and especially, and not unnaturally, women—do not share the enlightened faith of their parliamentary rulers in physically painless and reformative, as opposed to the traditionally more drastic, punishment of perpetrators of violence, particularly of violence towards women and children. But as our three parliamentary Parties, and presumably the Civil Service which frames such legislative enactments and administrative rules, are all united in disapproving of capital punishment and the use of the birch, the subject and his wife and daughter are compelled, contrary to their wishes, to live in greater danger of violence than they need or, at any rate, believe they need do. In what to them is a major matter, they have to accept the fact that the man in Westminster and Whitehall

[1] *I.L.N.* 5 August 1961.

knows best. The enlightened conscience of the constitutionally entrenched minority overrides the will of the constitutionally impotent majority.

In theory, of course, the subject—the numerical majority of electors, that is—is the ultimate arbiter of all legal and statutory action. Unless Parliament should use its constitutional power to deprive him of his vote by prolonging its own existence or in some other way disfranchise him, he can exercise his aggregate right of decision at the next General Election. Yet unless one or other of the principal and highly organised political Parties, who alone can create a Government, chooses to sponsor the particular measure vital to him he has no real means of securing its adoption as law. Owing to the vast size of our national community today and the high and exceedingly costly degree of organisation required to win an election, the issues offered to the decision of the electorate every four or five years are of a very general and nebulous character. The electoral mandate given to a victorious political Party, or rather to its leaders who then form a Government, is rather like that given to Sir Christopher Wren when the committee responsible for rebuilding St. Paul's Cathedral approved the design he had submitted to them. He was instructed to follow the design in broad outline, but was to be allowed to modify it from time to time as he thought fit. As a result, the finished St. Paul's bore little resemblance to the design which the committee had approved and adopted. It was His Majesty's Surveyor-General, not the committee, which—fortunately, in this case—built the cathedral.

This practice, applied to democratic government, is in some ways a sound one: the only one in certain matters compatible with a large-scale national democracy. The man in the street cannot direct a great nation's foreign policy or control the intricacies of, say, the bank rate or overseas exchange. He has neither the time nor the knowledge to do so either wisely or effectively, and any nation whose ruling system, or rather lack of system, left it to him would soon find itself in trouble. There has to be delegacy to the trained expert in such matters, and this means that the expert, whatever his nominal limitations of power, has, in effect, the controlling voice. Yet there are other matters on which the man in the street's views are as valid, and should be as capable of being made effective, as those of any official or professional politician: in which, as the man on the spot directly concerned with the minutiae of his own life, he has far more first-hand and expert knowledge than the remote bureaucrat behind the plate-glass windows of Whitehall or the busy committee-man in the Palace of Westminster. He is concerned closely and intimately with the question of whether or not an arterial road should be driven through the village in which he lives, whether there should be a speed-limit on the stretch of highway which he and his wife and children have to cross daily, whether a factory or chalk-pit or nuclear power station or open prison should be established there, or an airfield or helicopter landing-place within ear-drum distance of his home.

If democracy is not to be regarded merely as a façade or form of words, in such matters the decisive voice should be that of the man and woman on the spot and not that of the expert in Whitehall, however wise and far-sighted. For it is those most directly affected who, by the true principles of democracy, should have the right not only to be heard but ultimately to decide. The power given in the name of democracy to remote, and usually concealed, functionaries to impose their will on local communities is despotic power and should have no place in peacetime in a free and self-governing polity.

Unless democracy is to perish—as it has perished so often before in human annals—and is not to be supplanted by Communism or some new species of Fascism, we have got to find a way to give more adequate expression to the wishes of ordinary men and women in matters that most directly concern their lives. We need to give the local community far greater powers to express itself and to make its wishes felt, both through local assemblies and by representation at Westminster. We shall have to seek a way to return to the realities, as distinct from the conventions, of democratic government. Our polity needs refashioning so that the people's representatives once more become the effective mouthpiece of those who elect them instead of professional members of an assembly, the sympathies and interests of whose

ruling majority tend to be primarily with the Executive whose
power they were originally intended to control but of which,
in the course of ages, they have, without realising it, become a
part.

* * *

X

This Sunburnt Face[1]

There seem two things common to the new nations in Africa,
and Asia which formerly suffered, or enjoyed—whichever way
one looks at it—British rule and have now been granted independence and, either as a compensation or an uncovenanted benefit,
financial aid by this country. One is the vehemence with which
so many of their elected, or self-elected, rulers denounce Great
Britain and all she does today or has stood for in the past. The
other is the passionate desire of scores of thousands of humble
Asians and Africans to leave their own countries and, by hook or
crook, enter this one with their wives, children and dependants
and, thereafter, settle here for ever.

To borrow the adjective coined by the advertisement department of *The Times*, "top" Asians and Africans distrust and
condemn Britain, ordinary or penny plain ones apparently love it.
Judging by their actions there seems nothing the latter want so
much as to mingle with and become part of us, their former—so
their statesmen and intellectuals tell them—oppressors. This
cannot be due entirely to the free benefits offered by our public
health service. It certainly cannot be our climate! Nor, I think,
is it ourselves, with our pale faces, stand-offish manners and
insular notions and customs. One is forced, therefore, to the
conclusion that one of the things these newcomers find so
attractive about this overcrowded, overclouded, over-taxed island
is that it has a constitution under which the individual can live
more happily and do better for himself than under any other.

What really appeals to them, I suspect, is our libertarian form
of life and rule: the old-fashioned British political and legal

[1] *I.L.N.* 9 March 1968; 28 June 1969.

spécialité de la maison, expressed in the words of our eighteenth
century ancestors' favourite song, 'Rule Britania:'

> *The nations not so blest as thee*
> *Must in their turn to tyrants fall;*
> *But thou shalt flourish great and free,*
> *The dread and envy of them all.*

Or, as A. C. Benson put it, "Wider still and wider shall thy bounds
be set!" Only nowadays the bounds, instead of being widened
geographically, are, while contracted in terms of geography,
expanded in those of domestic population. Pakistanis, West
Indians, Ghanaians, Cypriots, Indians, Maltese and Kenyans, like
the Irish, Poles and Jews in the nineteenth century, all want to
come here and share our libertarian heritage and our now
rather straitened means.

It is strange that this unlooked-for triumph of the Whig
tradition—of the principles of the "glorious Revolution of 1688"
—in what used to be called by our pious and insular ancestors
"heathen lands afar", should have occurred at the moment when
the Whig tradition has become so apparently discredited in the
country of its origin. While our university-trained intellectuals
contemptuously explain away, on Marxist or Freudian lines, every
act in our past of what used to be regarded as libertarian virtue,
the simple peoples of African townships and Indian villages see
in this island the one place in the world where true liberalism
flourishes—the kind of liberalism that allows a man of whatever
creed, race or colour to do what he would with himself and his
own. With a touching and pathetic enthusiasm they clamour to
be let in and to count themselves and their progeny among the
heirs of Hampden, Russell and Sidney.

It is also a historical irony that this demand should have come
when the cumulative effects of Britain's political withdrawal
from the Orient and Africa, and of the long-drawn-out erosion
of her share of world trade, are confronting her with a seemingly
intractable economic dilemma. An open door policy to all comers
is no longer practicable for a small island state whose population
has almost doubled in the past half century, and which has now
been further swollen by the influx in little more than a decade of
over a million coloured immigrants.

Twenty years ago there was no colour problem in Britain and no seeming likelihood of there ever being one. As a global trading nation our great international ports like London and Liverpool had long had coloured communities of settlers, temporary or permanent, from the Orient, Africa and the Caribbean, but no one resented them or regarded them as any more of a problem than the masts in the river or the welcome oranges and bananas on the fruit-barrows and the tea-chests in Twining's warehouse. They were part of the British heritage and one in which a trading and imperial-minded people took pride and pleasure. In the eighteenth century Dr. Johnson, the very embodiment of the traditional Englishman, had his faithful black servant, whose dignity he scrupulously honoured and respected. Queen Victoria had her Munshi, and there were valiant black as well as white bodies stripped to the waist among the gun-crews who won Britain a century of peaceful and beneficial command of the world's sea-lanes in the days of Nelson and the great admirals. It was among the proudest of our boasts that, when a slave's feet touched British soil, his fetters fell from him. Lord Chief Justice Manfield's famous judgment was as much an English political legend as Magna Carta, to which, indeed, it formed an appendix.

Today we have a permanent coloured population of at least a million adults with a coloured child population increasing, it is believed, at a far faster rate than that of our native stock. Some of these newcomers, those from the Caribbean and, in particular, those from that tough and tenacious offspring of seventeenth century England, Barbados, share many English beliefs and habits, even though they are mostly descendants of African slaves, just indeed as we ourselves—though at a greater remove in time—are partly the descendants of Celtic and Saxon slaves. Others from the villages of Southern Asia, though formerly British subjects, share neither our language, beliefs or habits but are as different, many of them, from us as any of Adam's offspring can well be from one another. The gulf, therefore, to be bridged is enormous, and is taxing, and is long going to tax, all the resources, mental and physical, of our administrators and teachers. The responsibility for this titanic and, for anyone with a grain of imagination or historical foresight, frightening problem lies with the creators of

our open-ended Welfare State—an obvious magnet for the under-
privileged in a grossly unequal world; with the legislators and
officials in Westminster and Whitehall who allowed the greatest
migration in modern history to take place without the slightest
attempt, until it was too late, to plan or control it; and with the
demand of British employers and employees for high profits and
high wages, which resulted in a demand for cheap labour from
underprivileged lands to perform for us the more menial and less
rewarding tasks we had become too avaricious or lazy to do for
ourselves. Part of the responsibility also rests on the shoulders of
those who in the past—statesmen, financiers, publicists and, in
the last resort, electors—who so repeatedly failed to heed the
warnings of prophets, like Ruskin, Froude and Joseph Chamberlain, who had seen that the necessary concomitant of global
empire was a sustained policy to make every part of it economically viable for all its many peoples. Those who believe that the
natural and best place for Pakistanis is Pakistan, and for West
Indians the Caribbean, ought first to ask themselves what has been
done in the past and, what could be done now and in the future,
to make Pakistan and the West Indies, and all those other places
from which immigrants have come and are still coming to our
small overcrowded island, better able to support and afford a full
and happy life for those born in them. The story of the Sibylline
books is not without relevance here.

All this is past history. The immediate problem created by mass
immigration is the strain placed on the country's housing accom-
modation and schools. This is one which, provided the flow of
immigration dwindles or ceases, could be solved in time; it is
one, too, which is confined mainly to certain urban areas, though
in some of these it is distressingly acute. The other two problems
likely to stem from this astonishing migration—one which
future historians may see as one of the most extraordinary events
in our history—belong to the future. At present, despite all the
talk of dedicated or professional racists—and these are to be found
on both sides of the controversial fence—there is surprisingly
little racial prejudice in this country; the ordinary Englishman,
once he has got used to the presence of neighbours and working
mates of different colour or nationality, good-humouredly

accepts them as fellow-creatures with as much right to consideration and fair treatment as himself. And seeing how naturally
white and coloured children accept one another in our schools
and playgrounds, racial prejudice, in this sense, would seem likely
to decrease rather than increase but for one circumstance. This is
the precariousness of our economic position. For if our foreign
creditors were to reach the conclusion that we were no longer
credit-worthy, or if for some other reason we became unable
either to sell our goods abroad or to get sufficient raw materials
from overseas for our dependent industries, there could be a
massive increase in unemployment. And were a situation to arise
similar to that which existed before the War when there were
two or more men seeking every vacant job, those whose colour
proclaimed them to be immigrants or the descendants of immigrants would almost certainly be resented as interlopers and get
the raw end of the deal in the labour market; and no amount of
anti-discriminatory legislation could prevent this happening with
all its tragic consequences. The other danger is that the distinguishing colour of the newcomers and their descendants is going
to make it much more difficult for them to think of themselves
and be thought of as "mere English" than has been the case with
the descendants of, say, the Eastern European Jews who settled in
England in such large numbers in the last century and most of
whose descendants today yield to none in their love of their
adopted country and acceptance of its ways. This could result in
something very dangerous in our polity, a large racially minded
electoral pressure-group whose sympathies lay primarily with the
peoples and nations to which they were racially akin, instead of
with the country which had become their new home.

For these reasons both integration and a limitation of and, if
possible, with justice and humanity, some modest diminution of
the size of the immigrant population to be integrated, seem
advisable. For the larger the immigrant population, the more
difficult integration must be to achieve and the more essential
and urgent it must become. In this sense both Mr. Enoch Powell
and the Chairman of the Race Relations Board, however little
they may realise it, may be seeking the same end. What both
presumably want to ensure is that every naturalised coloured

immigrant or descendant of coloured immigrants will in the future feel himself to be, and be seen to be, as good an Englishman as, say, Mr. Emanuel Shinwell, and no one could be a better Englishman than that. For all the abuse showered on that stormy political petrel, Mr. Powell, his latest proposal of a settlement grant of £2,000 for every immigrant who voluntarily elects to return to his own country seems on the face of it both sensible and humane, whatever may be thought of his earlier speeches on the racial problem. Where he differs from his critics is that he recognises what so many of them, in their very proper zeal for integration and racial equality, fail to recognise, that the problem of integrating so many immigrants differentiated by nature from the indigenous population by their colour, is made so much more difficult by the magnitude of the numbers to be integrated. It is a problem which cannot be solved by ignoring it or pretending that it doesn't exist, but only by bringing ourselves, white and coloured alike, to accept a self-evident truth, and then, without rancour, exaggeration or mutual reproaches, setting ourselves to find just and humane ways both of reducing the dimensions of and solving a political, social and economic problem which should never have been allowed to arise on such an enormous scale but which, having arisen, must be faced with realism, tenderness and imaginative sympathy, and with due regard both to our own national and future cohesion as a people and the human rights and needs of the newcomers who have joined us.

Perhaps the wisest thing ever said on the subject were the words which the poet Blake put into the mouth of the little Black Boy's mother in 'Songs of Innocence':

> *Look at the rising sun: there God does live,*
> *And gives His light, and gives His heat away;*
> *And flowers and trees and beasts and men receive*
> *Comfort in morning, joy in the noonday.*
>
> *And we are put on earth a little space*
> *That we may learn to bear the beams of love;*
> *And these black bodies and this sunburnt face*
> *Is but a cloud, and like a shady grove.*

For when our souls have learn'd the heat to bear,
The cloud will vanish; we shall hear His voice,
Saying: 'Come out from the grove, my love and care,
And round My golden tent like lambs rejoice.'

*   *   *

XI

A Choice for Destiny[1]

There are many arguments against Britain joining the Common
Market. Some are political, some economic. But there is one overriding one, which springs from the very meaning and purpose
of democracy.

For democracy means that men and women should have some
say in controlling those who rule them, and so ensure that the
latter govern them in accordance with their particular needs and
desires. Because human needs and desires vary from region to
region and country to country, the larger the community that
has to be governed, the more difficult it is to ensure this. As
pointed out by Coleridge—a political philosopher as well as a
poet—a constitution equally well suited to England, France,
Prussia, Spain and Russia must be equally unsuited to them all.
A peasant living in the Sicilian sunshine has needs and dispositions
different to those of a coalminer in County Durham. His government, if it is to be the kind of government he wants, must reflect
those differences.

Of course, there are respects in which all men are the same.
There are attributes which a poor tribesman in a savage and
primitive land shares with the most sophisticated aristocrat or
cultured intellectual in an advanced civilisation. It is true, too,
that, with increasingly rapid communications, the world is
growing smaller. Yet the variations which shape the feelings and
dispositions, as well as needs, of its inhabitants are still immense.

Those who overlook this, as many progressive-minded persons
do, are in the position of the eloquent feminist who, while
assuring her audience that there was only a little difference

[1] *I.L.N.* 13 July 1968; *Sunday Express* 23 February 1969.

between man and woman, was interrupted from the back of the hall by a cry of, "Three cheers for the little difference!" When, with emotions which we find it difficult to define, we sing the National Anthem, or, if we are French, the Marseillaise, we are in reality saying this. We are expressing our thankfulness for a distinguishing attribute which is precious to us. We do not, if we are true patriots and respect the patriotism of others, imply by it that we regard ourselves as superior to men of other nationalities. We merely mean that we are different, have a valued separateness of our own, and feel drawn to our fellow countrymen because of that separateness.

The more intensely men feel this love of their country, the stronger their sense of common belonging with those who, regardless of class, calling or material circumstances, feel about it in the same way. The more strongly they share this feeling, the easier that community is to govern and the more effectively can its Government give effect to their desires and wants. In such a community there is a readiness in its members to give and take, to subordinate the more separatist needs of the individual to the wider and common needs of the whole. It is a readiness which animated the men and women of Britain during the war, when our feelings of oneness with one another were sharpened by common perils and awareness of the greatness of the human cause for which we were fighting.

In the face of nuclear weapons and the capacity for mutual destruction with which science has endowed quarrelsome mankind, the need for some system of international co-operation is obvious. But it is not going to be achieved by eliminating the ties which, by binding men to one another in their national communities, render them more public spirited and less individually selfish. On the contrary, the closer knit and, therefore, the more satisfied the human components of existing communities are, the better the chances of their co-operating in a global system in which justice is done and violence avoided.

This is why national sovereignty should be cherished and respected and why any international or supranational system which aims at its destruction is bound to break down on the divisive elements, so dangerous and destructive, in human nature.

Without sovereignty there can be no democracy, for it is through sovereignty that democracy makes its will felt. And it must be a sovereignty that expresses and enforces the will of those who basically share a common idealism and interest.

If we were to join the Common Market and accept—as we should have to—its bureaucratic and rigidly legalistic constitution, we should lose the ultimate control over our rulers which Englishmen have enjoyed for centuries, and still enjoy, through the libertarian formula of the sovereignty of the Crown in Parliament. Though it has operated during our history through many changing forms, that sovereignty ensures that, while there is no limit to what the elected Parliament of the hour can do in giving effect to the popular will, it cannot bind any succeeding Parliament. In other words, while the existing generation of British electors and their representatives can bind themselves as they please, they cannot bind those who come after them and who, through the same magic and simple formula—the supreme and absolute sovereignty of the Crown in Parliament—will, when their time comes, be ensured the same control of their destiny.

It is this democratic freedom and right of our successors and heirs which we should destroy if we were to subscribe to the terms of the Treaty of Rome. That Britain should belong to, and join some wider economic grouping of nations for the purposes of trade, finance and credit, is clearly desirable. But it should not, and need not, involve the sacrifice of our own and our children's democratic birthright, the freest and most elastic, and, by virtue of that very elasticity, most stable system of self-government on earth. If, for the sake of international co-operation and freer trade, we are to join such an economic grouping of nations, it seems most likely to be successful between nations whose peoples speak the same language, share a common history and literature, and inherit similar legal systems and political institutions.

In the British nations overseas, in the United States and in some, at least, of the new Commonwealth nations, these common conditions already exist. It would seem wiser, therefore, to build on them, instead of seeking to merge our identity with countries however friendly, whose development and history and, as a result, character and institutions, while tending to unite them to their mutual benefit in a continental grouping, are fundamentally different from ours and those of the ocean nations who share our libertarian heritage.

For though Britain is an off-shore island of the European mainland, by history and temperament she is something far more. She is a port of departure, a base from which adventurous men have gone out to trade across every sea. The essence of that global trade was freedom; the freer it was, the more Britons flourished. In pursuit of trade and freedom for the individual they founded, on the far shores of ocean, great nations whose peoples still share the same freedoms, speak the same language and live under the same libertarian systems of law.

For Britain to turn her back on those nations and her Commonwealth and withdraw inside a restrictive and inward-looking European autarchy would be to betray her nature and history. The Treaty of Rome has helped to reduce tariff and political divisions between one part of western Europe and another. But in its relationship to the outer world it reeks of commercial restriction. Politically, it suffers from the fatal flaw in all authoritarian schemes of government; that it seeks to bind the future. The virtue of the British Constitution is that it leaves future parliaments—and generations—free. It is this which has enabled us to secure change without bloodshed, and, unlike the great continental nations, to avoid revolution.

For though we have much in common with our fellow-Europeans—Germans, Italians and French—we have far more in common with the Americans and Canadians whose shores border the North Atlantic, an ocean now bridged in less time than it formerly took to cross the Channel. Since we can only join with our Teuton and Latin neighbours at the expense of sacrificing our political freedom, why should we not seek a wider economic union with our oceanic neighbours who would require no such sacrifice? Already, through the European Free Trade Association, we have such a union with the North Atlantic nations of Scandinavia and Portugal, as well as with Switzerland and Austria. It could serve as a model for a free-trade area for industrial products under which all the Atlantic nations, including the United States, Canada, Great Britain and the E.F.T.A. countries, agreed, within the provisions of G.A.A.T., to abolish for a term of years all tariffs on one another's industrial goods.

Such an Atlantic Free Trade Area, open to any like-minded nation to join, including our fellow-English-speaking nations in the Pacific—Australia and New Zealand—would free us from the fatal disability of having to accept the costly agricultural provisions and dear-food policy of the Common Market, which, by sending up our cost of living, wage-bills and export prices, could have a grave effect on our balance of payments. For industrial products it would offer a wider market even than the E.E.C. And it would leave our traders free to expand in traditional and existing markets. For less than a fifth of our exports go to Common Market countries, more than four-fifths to the rest of the world. The countries which buy most of our products are the United States, South Africa, Australia and Canada, in that order. Why should we join with France, Germany, Italy and the Benelux countries in putting up tariff barriers against our best and oldest customers? Nor would our joining a North Atlantic Free Trade Area necessarily preclude closer commercial relations with the Common Market countries. If the latter wished to enter into free trade in industrial products with N.A.F.T.A., there would be nothing to prevent their doing so.

Here is the real alternative to pleading for admission to the E.E.C., or waiting supinely for it while the world moves on without us. By pursuing it we should be following the true course of our history instead of contending against it. Churchill pointed the way in 1940 when he predicted that the great English-speaking democracies would have increasingly to merge certain of their affairs for their mutual and general advantage. "I do not view the process," he said, "with any misgivings. I could not stop it if I wished; no one can stop it. Like the Mississippi it just keeps rolling along. Let it roll. Let it roll on full flood, inexorable, irresistible, benignant, to broader lands and better days."

CHAPTER 13

To Thee My Country

"I vow to thee, my country—all earthly things above—
Entire and whole and perfect, the service of my love."

CECIL SPRING RICE

Witnesses from our Past · All Things by a Law Divine ·
A Heritage Worth Preserving · The Case for Patriotism ·
Naval Tradition · The Passing of the Regiments ·
An Unassuming Service · Imperilled Shrines

I

Witnesses from our Past[1]

As one travels through England by car, dodging, overtaking or
fretting behind the continuous stream of traffic which pours
along its narrow, congested highways, one glimpses behind the
petrol stations, the new council houses, the ugly Victorian and
Edwardian suburbs of the towns and larger villages, the remnants
of an older England. Here is the Georgian coaching inn; the
Hanoverian lawyer's handsome red-brick house with carved
portico behind its stately garden wall, topped by mulberry trees
or a pair of cedars; a row, fallen on evil days, of decaying but
neatly-built cottages once inhabited by unlettered but immensely
skilful craftsmen in stone, wood or metal—the men who made
the furniture, silver, glass and china which sell at such fabulous
prices at Christie's and Sotheby's today. Side by side with them
are vestiges of a still older England, Stuart and Tudor—a fine
almshouse with beautifully lettered inscription over the door,

[1] *Illustrated London News* 23 May 1959.

a cloth or market hall, a great mansion like Burghley, Hatfield or Levens, hidden or half-hidden from the highway, with stone terraces and topiary paths,

> where stately ladies once did use
> To walk wi' hoops an' high-heel shoes.

Beyond them again in time, though still sharing the same space, are the church-towers and naves, the last barns and granaries of the old open-field agricultural system, like Coxwell and Tisbury, the collegiate buildings, gateways, bridges and ruined castles, and, towering over all, even over the huge, clumsy factories, gasometers and silos of our own unseeing, imperceptive age, the cathedrals of the later Middle Ages—Lincoln and Salisbury, York and Exeter, Ely, Norwich and Canterbury, still to this day the crowning glories of our land. These in many cases incorporate buildings of still greater antiquity, like the Norman arches of Peterborough and Durham and the humble choirs of little parish churches which once rose, spireless and towerless, above the minute wattled and thatched huts of our peasant ancestors in the days of the Normans and Saxons. Their survival into the era of the internal combustion engine and jet plane seems almost a miracle. How much longer, one wonders, will they evade destruction at the hands of the vandal and the nuclear bomb, or perhaps more imminent, of the Borough Engineer and Council Surveyor?

Yet there is something more surprising than their survival. How was it that our forbears, with nothing but their skilful, industrious hands and a few simple manual tools, raised these magnificent edifices, of which, incidentally, those that survive into our own age are only a fraction of what they originally created? What inner driving force could have inspired them to be so determined, industrious and heroically ambitious to build, as they did, not for their own age alone, but for a seemingly eternal, though, as it has turned out, largely unheeding, posterity? And the answer, however inexplicable to our generation, is a simple one: the explanation of the history of England from the days of St. Augustine and St. Cuthbert to those of Milton and Bunyan, and even, in a diminishing degree, to those of Wesley and Wilberforce. They were animated by a passionate desire to understand the meaning of life and by an intense belief in God as the creator and ruler of the Universe. We no longer possess that desire or belief; are content with what the *Daily This*, or, if we are aspiring "top people", *The Times*, tells us, and all we want is to make as much money for the satisfaction of our bodily comforts—or, if we are socially-minded, those of the aggregate community—as seems, without over-tiring ourselves, reasonable. We want a rising wage or salary, a forty-hour or less week, holidays with pay, refrigerators, washing-machines and telly-sets, a garage beside every house and a car in every garage. And soon, no doubt, we shall want other things—helicopters and free daily injections of happiness-drugs and State-provided monkey-glands to make us live longer! But, as a people, we feel no desire to raise great monuments to the glory of God—"*ad majorem Dei gloriam*", as our ancestors put it—or to go out into the waste and pagan places of the earth to found Christian colonies and convert and save the souls of the heathen. As a result, with a few isolated exceptions to prove the rule like Liverpool Cathedral, no architectural monuments of enduring beauty and faith are being raised amid all the vast conglomeration of modern utilitarian and transient architecture, while the heathen, beyond the Iron Curtain and the China Sea, remain stubbornly unconverted and are growing more heathen every day. Whether this is a good thing or not remains to be seen. Personally, I believe we are likely to be the losers by it, both in this world and, if—contrary to general modern belief— there be another world, in the next. For, unlike those who look back in anger, I look back in regret. This is because I look back, not to the immediate past, but to a more distant one—not to the golf links, Edwardian Ascot and Clapham Junction—but to the age of Fountains, Bell Harry tower and Salisbury spire; to the Age of Faith.

I know very well, of course, that the Age of Faith was no utopia on earth; that there was disease, war, poverty, squalor, malice, jealousy and all unkindness then as now. One has only to read Chaucer—that wonderful English mirror of a vanished age— to realise it and how unchanging the manifestations of human nature are. But unlike the men of the era in which I grew up and which preceded ours, I doubt if human nature is perfectible or whether the world can ever be made a utopia. It is right, of course, to try to make it so, but, knowing myself and a little of my fellow men, I find it hard to suppose that it is an end achievable merely by human effort. Original sin, and even more strongly original folly, seem to be part of the soil in which we grow. Though it cannot banish these from the earth in which our transient lot is cast, faith is essential to enable human beings to do the work and achieve the stature of which they are capable. Their lives are as poor and stunted without it as plants without rain. It was because in the past the people of England and their rulers were touched by faith that they achieved so much, and their achievements in grace and comeliness still stand, unmatched, today. The more I think of it, the more I am convinced that everything of value in our history between the Dark Ages and our own time grew out of the Christian faith and the attempts, however imperfect, of our ancestors to apply its principles. It is true of what happened before the Reformation, it is true of the Reformation itself and the great Puritan movement which sprang from it, and it is true of what happened after the Reformation until comparatively recent times, even when, as often in the age of declining faith after the seventeenth century, it was no longer done in Christ's name. No one can understand English history and the testimony of its ancient buildings and monuments who fails to enter into the feelings that caused our ancestors to believe what they did and, believing, do what they did. The ruined arch at Croyland and the soaring vault of King's College Chapel tell the secret of their power.

*   *   *

II

All Things by a Law Divine[1]

There is a village station within a few miles of my home. It stands, like all the pleasantest stations, some way from the place it serves and has grown, as it were, into the fields. No doubt when it first came into the broad vale, the iron railway and its brand-

[1] *I.L.N.* 5 April 1941.

new brick buildings and appurtenances were an eyesore and a great offence to the humans and cows thereabouts. They are so no longer. For time has had a hand in their shaping, has toned down the colours of the bricks so that they blend with the soft browns and greens of the vale, and has weathered their hard lines and edges. What hasty man performed imperfectly, Nature, that leisurely worker, has gone over again with her cool contemplative chisel until almost all traces of that first raw job have been removed. The little station of today has something of the organic simplicity of a tree or stream. It serves its purpose without self-consciousness or friction. And as one awaits the train there—or the next train, for there is no better place in England to miss a train—one can look across three or four great meadows, full of cows and, at the right season, of buttercups, and fill one's eyes with the sight of the little village under the hill, with its wind-mill, grey church tower and clustering, mellowed red-brick houses. Beyond rises the soft, rounded hill on which I love to walk, with its occasional groups of Grecian trees, its fugitive ghosts of Arcadian nymphs and shepherds. For in this place, with its still unbroken peace of centuries, the past is very near the present. All English history—its strength, its sleeping fires, its patient consistency—are contained in its speaking silence.

The men and women who, like their forbears, inhabit this village share many of its attributes. They are slow of speech and thought, kindly and unshakable. They are the best sort of citizens, for their virtues preserve and nourish the State. They are the kind of people without whom no democracy could long exist: they preserve a leaven in the body politic. They have little in the way of the showier graces, yet are essentially healthy. They put first things first, not by any process of reasoning, but by instinct. A few weeks before the war I spent an hour wandering round the village church, examining its lovely seventeenth-century monuments and resting in one of its cool, stillness-washed pews, while the sound of birds and insects, making the best of that sun-drenched August afternoon, drifted in through the open, curtained door. On one wall was a list of the young men of the village who gave their lives in what was then called the Great War that the village and the England of which it was part might live. More than half the village manhood, born between 1875 and 1900, was comprised in that proud but mournful record.

Remembering the many small kindnesses and courtesies I have received from its friendly people, I could not help contemplating, as I stood once more on that familiar platform, the association between natural beauty and human goodness. Is ugliness a cause of hate and greed, and beauty of kindliness? Anyone could think of examples to the contrary. Yet my own experience suggests they are. Other things being equal, I have usually found that the inhabitants of a place with a long heritage of beauty share some of that beauty in their character, and of an ugly place the reverse. The process of cause and effect may be, and is, slow: it takes more than one generation of sordid surroundings to destroy the natural virtue and tenderness of those who dwell among them, just as it took more than one generation of living in a Tudor manor-house and deer park to make gentle—I use the word in its literal term—the blood of a greedy and harsh-tempered profiteer. But the connection between aesthetics and conduct exists even though our knowledge of its working is still far too inadequate to reach any practical conclusion. If we only knew it, it is probably as close as that between digestion and temper. The impressions of the eye may be more delicate and indeterminate than those of the tactile senses, but their effect on the human brain, and through the brain on the whole system, is a scientific phenomenon which scientists will have to tackle if the way to Utopia is going to be found by the exercise of human reason.

For here we are face to face with a fundamental rule of existence: one which the ancients recognised even though they could not comprehend and apply it and which our nineteenth century men of science forgot or ignored in their painstaking study of natural phenomena. That everything in the universe is in some way connected with everything else: that nothing in God's creation can stir without everything else, vast or minute, feeling to a greater or lesser degree its effect. That in such movement there is almost infinite elasticity and room for recompense and adjustment is clear: what we have got to recognise is the fact of movement. It is something which scientists, after a century of denial, are beginning to be aware: that there is interlinked purpose and order in the universe, as in the human body and as in every machine—man's clumsy imitation of God's larger creation—that works. Life is a pattern, moving in an ordained rhythm: the stars in their courses and the tides of the sea and those subtler tides in the souls and bodies of men and women, beasts and birds all form part of the pattern. Mar it at any point, and you mar it at some other: when you dislocate the thigh, you warp the neck as well. This is the secret which those who regulate society and the body politic have to master as well as the scientists: there will be no peace in Israel until they do.

Today everything that is happening in the world bears out this truth. The wolf dog, starved by the stringency of the times of the proper food ordained for its body by providence, develops hysteria and becomes a raging maniac, flying with blazing eyes and bared fangs at the master to whom it had given its heart. The child deprived of protective vitamins by the usages of modern hygiene or commerce, falls a prey to the germs of wasting diseases from which it would otherwise have been immune. The great wars of our century which have devastated the world can be traced to natural causes, intricate and manifold. No one who makes a study of the effects of ill-nourishment on German and Austrian childhood in 1918-19 can escape the connection between the same rickety and nerve-diseased youth and the hysterical manhood with which a diabolical Vienna house-painter of genius was to scourge the world twenty years later. So between ugly and unrhythmical surroundings and sour and acrid tempers there may well be a vital connection of which we have still to find the secret. The great poets and artists—men gifted by God with instinctive apprehension of His universe—have always felt there is.

*   *   *

III

A Heritage Worth Preserving[1]

England is a small country and though more damaged aesthetically, in relation to its former beauty, than any other in the world, still a very beautiful one. It owes its beauty partly to its climate, but chiefly to what successive generations of Englishmen have done to make it beautiful. Even the Victorians, while recklessly despoiling certain areas in their exploitation of the country's mineral and industrial resources, made a contribution to its heritage of visual beauty, for they were great gardeners and landscape planners. Whatever their architectural infelicities—at their worst, less vulgar and obtrusive than ours—they passed to their heirs what was probably an even more beautiful landscape than they inherited from their Georgian forerunners.

For it is difficult to believe there can ever have existed on earth a lovelier countryside than that of this island seventy years ago, before the coming of the motor and the break-up of the hereditary landed estates which preserved and enriched the national heritage of woodland, meadow, park and village. For all the horrors of the grim utilitarian drabness of South Lancashire and the smoking Staffordshire and Warwickshire heaths, the Durham minefields and South Welsh valleys, and the nightmare East End of London, the England on which I opened my eyes as a boy at the turn of the century was transcendently beautiful. To watch it being increasingly ravaged and destroyed, piecemeal, beyond recall, has been by far the worst penalty that those who knew it undefiled have had to pay in their middle and old age for the benefits of the social and technological revolution through which this country is passing. The saddest thing about it has been that, unlike high taxation, restriction of individual liberty, and loss of national power, prestige and moral influence, most of this destruction has been unnecessary. It could have been avoided, and could still be stopped, if our rulers had the will and capacity to do so.

Every great achievement—and there could be none greater than

[1] *I.L.N.* 27 May 1967.

to preserve, at the eleventh hour, the visual heritage of our country—requires a decisive act of will. Nearly always, such an act has to be that of a small number of resolute and dedicated men, like those who at the end of the eighteenth century made up their minds to destroy the immensely powerful vested evil of the Slave Trade and, within a generation, in the face of overwhelming opposition, succeeded. Such, too, was the act of those who, in the heyday of *laissez-faire*, resolved that the social evils which flourished and multiplied under that economic theory of political and moral abdication were too vile to condone any longer, and who made it their life-work to combat the horrors of child labour, slum housing and factory exploitation. Of the greatest and most persistent of them all, Antony Ashley Cooper, 7th Lord Shaftesbury, his biographers wrote: "The devil, with sad and sober sense on his grey face, tells the rulers of the world that the misery which disfigures the life of great societies is beyond the reach of human remedy. A voice is raised from time to time in answer: a challenge in the name of the mercy of God, or the justice of nature, or the dignity of man. Shaftesbury was such a voice. To the law of indifference and drift, taught by philosophers and accepted by politicians, he opposed the simple revelation of his Christian conscience. This was his service to England; not the service of a statesman with wide plan and commanding will, but the service of a prophet speaking truth to power in its selfishness and sloth. When silence falls on such a voice, some everlasting echo still haunts the world, to break its sleep of habit or despair."[1]

It is such a voice—and such a will—that are needed today to save the living body of our country. Every week that passes, in the name of technological progress, financial profit or bureaucratic uniformity, some part of England's dwindling heritage of beauty is being transformed into a noisy and dreary wilderness of concrete, biscuit-box or bungaloid architecture, racing-track motorway or airfield whose hideous uproar is apparently to continue, day and night, for all eternity. As frequent as the daily news items about sex-murders and wage-grab coshings and break-ins, are the reports, affecting far larger numbers and

[1] J. L. and B. Hammond, *Lord Shaftesbury*, p. 276. Constable.

depriving unborn generations of their birthright, of schemes for spanning the landscape with giant pylons, bull-dozing farms, woods and villages out of existence to make airfields, factories and roads, or for erecting gasometers or forbidding towers of concrete and glass in the heart of ancient towns. Opposition by those whose homes are uprooted and whose familiar and loved neighbourhood is forcibly changed against their will, cannot prevail against the financial interests of promoters and contractors supported in the name of the public weal by the dialectic and compulsory powers of State and Local Authority. The ultimate word—against which there is no real appeal—is spoken by a tiny minority of faceless bureaucrats and "planners" into whose hands Crown and Parliament, by a thousand acts of complex delegation, have committed the custodianship of the country's soil.

What is needed is a master Ministry with the duty and power to impose order and the rule of sanity and proportion on the hundred-and-one-authorities, public and private, who with the licence of the State but without the State's overall control or, indeed, any control at all, are tearing the body of England to pieces. Anyone— Minister, private person or corporate body—seeking to alter the face of the country should have to submit his plan to and receive the licence of such supreme Authority whose function it would be to consider, not merely the sectional requirements of administrative convenience or departmental pride, fast transport, cheap power or financial and commercial advantage, but the common interest of the continuing nation and the health, beauty and productivity of its most enduring asset, its living space and soil. If the scope and duty of the Treasury, with its supra-departmental powers, could be enlarged to protect not only, as at present, the country's financial and fiscal economy but its supreme treasure, its land, the hand of the destroyers could be stayed and controlled. A far-sighted Prime Minister by a single and simple act could bring this about. Liberty in a framework of law has always been the English answer to anarchy; never has that framework been more needed than in this matter going, as it does, to the very root of our existence as a nation.

*   *   *

IV

The Case for Patriotism[1]

Much is said today about the evils of patriotism. It is supposed to lead to wars and every kind of irrational and reactionary prejudice and to be an influence for bad from which the young should be guarded at all costs. At best, it is seen as a species of old-fashioned nonsense, deserving the ridicule of every well-educated and progressive person.

Yet before discarding it altogether one should first ask what it is. In its original sense, patriotism means love of the land on which one lives. It arises out of the look and feel of the familiar soil and landscape of home, of its tilth, contours and colours, its plants and vegetation, its woods and rivers, its horizons and minutest blade of grass. This is one of the strongest and most elementary feelings of man, though one of which modern town-dwellers have been partly deprived by the artificial character of urban life. Even here, it is remarkable how much affection men can feel for the urban and industrial entity in which they have grown up, however hideous to the eyes of strangers. Glasgow, for instance, is scarcely an Athens or Florence, yet Glaswegians sometimes sing with emotion, and even tears, a not particularly inspiring ballad, of which the refrain runs—

> *I belong to Glasgow,*
> *Dear old Glasgow town.*

Even the most enthusiastic internationalist could hardly regard such a sentiment as anti-social or would object to a similar song about Leopoldville or the capital of Ghana, by one of those cities' grateful sons or daughters.

For those who live by the soil and grow the world's food, love of country is not merely a sentiment but a force of great economic and practical importance. It is love of the soil, of the dear familiar fields he has wrestled with and tended and expended his sweat and treasure on, month after month and year after year, that makes your dedicated countryman, the man who is always trying

[1] *I.L.N.* 3 February 1962; 4 November 1967.

to give more to the land than he takes. The English rural landscape, as we know it, has been made by such men over the patient
centuries:

> *These homes, this valley spread below me here,*
> *The rooks, the tilted stacks, the beasts in pen,*
> *Have been the heartfelt things, past-speaking dear,*
> *To unknown generations of dead men.*[1]

Out of this natural love, this feeling

> *deeper than our speech and thought,*
> *Beyond our reason's sway*

arises, in the course of civilisation, another love—the love for the
ideals which have become associated with the national community
serving the land. So the Scottish peasant in the harsh wars of rival
lordships in the fourteenth century developed an intense feeling
for liberty, the feeling expressed by the poet Barbour when, in his
epic, "The Brus", he apostrophised the ideal his hero embodied
for his countrymen:

> *Ah! freedom is a noble thing.*

So, a Frenchman, when he thinks of *la patrie*, thinks not only of
"the fair and pleasant land of France", with its beautiful capital
and noble provinces, but of that fierce intellectual spirit and sense
of common humanity and human dignity which is France's
supreme gift to mankind. And we in England developed over the
centuries a deeply-felt patriotism, based on the belief in certain
common ideals, for whose continuance men were ready to die
and any violation of which by those who governed or spoke for
her could fill them with shame and dishonour. Such ideals may
have been obscured and lost sight of today, yet they can still be a
potent force in crisis to rouse the emotions and inspire the services
of Englishmen. Among them are justice or what we call "fair
play", tenderness towards the weak and courage in protecting
and championing the oppressed, fidelity to pledged word, endurance in adversity, loyalty to cause and comrade, that playing
for one's side and not letting it down which is such a strong, even
if, at times, dangerous force. These ideals, which used to be
traditionally associated with the name of England's patron saint,
St. George, grew out of our Christian faith and the virtues which

[1] John Masefield, *1914*. Heinemann.

the Christian Churches taught to successive generations of Englishmen. So Charles Lister, before he fell in action, wrote of his friend, Julian Grenfell, that "he stood for something very precious—of an England of my dreams, made of honest, brave and tender men, and his life and death must have done something towards the realisation of that England".

Twice in our generation this binding force proved of immense value in preserving the decencies and liberties of Christian civilisation. Without it the ugly ideals of totalitarian despotism could not have been withstood. Those patriotic virtues inherent in Englishmen and in their Scottish, Welsh and Northern Irish compatriots—and which have nothing to do, as is commonly supposed, with race but everything with creed—were epitomised in the wartime speeches of Winston Churchill. Even if Britain plays no further part in shaping the affairs of mankind, these will always be remembered for the love of country they expressed and the effect on the world's history of the response they evoked.

It seems strange that, at a time when in so many places— where hitherto the binding force of nationality has meant little —an almost hysterical consciousness of it prevails, in Great Britain, whose people have long been famed for their national pride and cohesion, patriotism has become almost an ugly word. Even to praise the corporate virtues which only a quarter of a century ago turned the triumphant tide of totalitarian tyranny, is to label oneself a reactionary. Sacrifice for one's country, courage, discipline, devotion to duty, are denigrated by those who mould the nation's beliefs and teach its young. Yet in Russia and China, Yugoslavia and Poland, Egypt, Indonesia, Tanzania and Somaliland, indeed in almost every country except this, patriotism is regarded as the first of the social virtues, and treason against one's country and its corporate ideals, even the mildest criticism of them, as a crime. The very organs of international co-operation, which to us appear as a sacred altar on which to sacrifice national self-interest and pride, are used by other countries as a mechanism for furthering their national policies and exalting their patriotic ego.

What explanation is there for a phenomenon so contradictory? Why is it right for anyone living in, say, Zambia who is suspected of criticising the Zambian State and its rulers to be imprisoned without trial and threatened with confiscation, expulsion or death, while here anyone who advocates the protection of British rights or British nationals is denounced as a "gunboat imperialist"? Is the explanation that given by the present Prime Minister for the Rhodesian deadlock, that we here and those of our now despised "kith and kin" in Rhodesia are living in two different centuries; that we have passed out of the age of the topee, the sundowner and the Union Jack, while they, Edwardian-minded "hearties", colonialists and "racists", are still, deplorably by our standards, living in it? Yet the weakness of this explanation is that, if it be true, the Zambians and Indonesians, Egyptians and Chinese, and, indeed, the peoples of almost all countries but ours, with the possible exception of the United States, are doing the same. Can it be true that the rest of the world in pursuing the nationalistic delusions of the past is half a century or more behind us? That we alone are marching along the highway to universal understanding and global peace and unity?

An alternative explanation, however, is that we are wrong in supposing national pride to be a conception mankind can afford to discard. For patriotism, which means so much to others, is still one of the only ways in which human beings can be induced voluntarily to act selflessly, instead of selfishly, for a common purpose. A nation is an instrument—and probably, in mankind's present state of development, an indispensable instrument—for social well-being and progress. To evoke their full potentialities and harness them to a common creative end, men need some corporate ideal to which they can dedicate and, when necessary, sacrifice themselves. It must not be too universal, or the sense of personal identification and stimulus becomes lost; yet it must be large and comprehensive enough to unite all sorts and conditions of men and talents in a great communal pursuit. In no country has this stimulus been stronger than in ours. Think of the achievements, in almost every field, of early nineteenth century Britain— of Nelson and Keats, Wilberforce, Constable and Faraday, Livingstone, Wordsworth and Florence Nightingale—and one can see what patriotism has done for us—and the world—in the past. Much of the inertia and drift from which all classes in the community, especially the young, are suffering today arise from the vacuum caused by the rejection of patriotism. It was the reaction brought about by the terrible casualties of the First World War—during which love and pride of country spurred men to endure sufferings almost too great to be borne—which still causes so many of our intellectuals, publicists and teachers to inveigh against patriotism and bring up the young to despise it. Yet when in 1939 a second assault was made on the liberties, lives and decencies of free men, a temporary revival of patriotism in the young alone enabled us to stem the tide of despotism.

Can all the king's horses and all the king's men put Humpty-Dumpty together again? It is anybody's guess. But, short of a world-wide religious revival to evoke the selfless and co-operative qualities inherent in men, I can see no other way in which the disruptive and destructive forces threatening to tear modern materialistic society apart can be withstood. I believe we have got to teach the young—the not so young can only learn from bitter experience and disaster—the ancient lesson that men owe to their country and her traditions almost everything which makes civilised life worth living and that, having received so much from her and those who served her in the past, it is incumbent on them to repay that debt by giving themselves to her service. It is not necessary to be a soldier and face death in battle to be a patriot. The husbandman, the craftsman, the professional man, the poet and artist, and all who devote their gifts and skills to enriching their native land, are serving her no less. Therein, for those who realise it, lies happiness and fulfilment.

> *O pray for the peace of Jerusalem: they shall*
> *prosper that love thee. Peace be within thy*
> *walls and plenteousness within thy palaces.*
> *For my brethren and companions' sakes I*
> *will wish thee prosperity.*

The psalmist understood what he was talking about.

* * *

V

Naval Tradition[1]

During the War I put to a naval officer a question to which I had often tried to define an answer. In what, I asked, consisted the genius of the Royal Navy for evoking virtue from men and winning their affection and loyalty—a genius which has been evolved through the centuries. He answered, "a system of manners". Based on long experience, it has been directed to solving the practical problems of enabling men to live together in the confined and crowded conditions of life afloat. Without it a sailor's life would be intolerable and discipline impossible. Remembering the many occasions in history in which the sea service of great nations with a less clearly defined naval tradition has broken down, one can see what he meant.

What is this system of manners? It can be summarised, I think, in four words: consideration for other seamen. By this is not meant a weak or sentimental consideration; life at sea, and most of all in wartime, is hard, and anything but a stern and realist consideration for the other man's lot would be a mistaken and cruel kindness. The most useful gifts one sailor can give another are courage, capacity for endurance and self-respect, for without these he must face ultimate disaster and shame. To enable a man to be a man, in the Navy's view, is the highest service one seaman can do another. And the great admirals who built up the unwritten code of naval behaviour and tradition have always borne this fundamental truth in mind. Yet the basis of British naval discipline, stern and spartan though it is, is never obedience for its own sake, but obedience for the sake of ship and crew and the common well-being of all. Whenever that ideal has been departed from— and sometimes, in the easy times of peace and in the hands of lesser men, it has been—the glory of the Navy has suffered an eclipse. Yet such eclipses have never been for long; always some master educator, steeped in the highest traditions of the Service, has appeared to remind it of the truths by which it lives.

[1] *I.L.N.* 22 September 1945.

Nelson was such an educator; so, in more recent times, was Jellicoe. The supreme service of the latter was not so much that he defeated the threat of the Kaiser's High Seas Fleet to Britain's existence and the world's liberty—there are two opinions as to his strategic and tactical ability—but that he retouched the entire Service with something of the magic of Nelson's selfless spirit. Years later, when, after two decades of neglect of its maritime traditions, a seafaring people was grappling with the greatest peril in its history and facing almost insuperable odds, it was saved by the courage, faith and leadership of admirals and captains who had served as young lieutenant-commanders, lieutenants and midshipmen under John Jellicoe. Nelson once said that he had the happiness to command a band of brothers. It was Jellicoe's lifelong study to do the same.

The source of both these men's power, and that of the many officers who modelled themselves on the same great tradition, was studied and habitual selflessness. "It was no wonder," wrote Mahan, "that the common sailors idolised Nelson, since he was always thinking about them, and won their hearts by showing his own." "Officers," Jellicoe laid it down, "must be taught that their first duty is the well-being of those under them." In that phrase he summed up the whole British naval tradition. Though at times it may have seemed otherwise to superficial observers, it is the very antithesis of Prussianism, for it is based, not on administrative machinery, but on humanity. And humanity not at its lowest level but at its highest, it being the constant reminder of all naval precept that man is not only a body but a spirit. It is not automatic obedience to orders that the Navy seeks to instil, but the active habit and spirit of discipline: not the mechanical performance of duty but the instinctive resolution to do one's duty on all occasions. "Pride of service," Jellicoe wrote, "is essential to the true spirit of discipline."

It is this insistence on the spirit, this practical and transmitted belief in its all-importance, which has made the Royal Navy what it is, a Service of gentlemen. "Recollect," Nelson declared, "that you cannot be a good officer without being a gentleman." The same proud motto may be said to govern, however unconsciously, the rough and homely mind of the Lower Deck. The author of the beautiful ballad, Tom Bowling—and there are few more beautiful in our language—knew what he was writing about. It is the unspoken pride of the humblest British seaman to honour his word, to be gentle to the weak, to be loyal to his comrades, to do his duty. It was this which made our undisputed command of the seas not a curse to mankind but a blessing.

It is time to realise that we can learn other lessons from our great fighting Services than those of valour and technical skill. For they are repositories of certain human truths which have been forgotten almost everywhere else. "Manners," runs the old saying, "makyth Man." But in our eager, clever, greedy machine age, man is the one thing we have forgotten how to make. The Services, almost alone among our adult institutions and establishments, have remembered. Once, flying over Scapa Flow in the critical middle years of the War, I remarked to the naval officer who was accompanying me that it was strange to think that on these few great ships lying below at anchor the fate of the world depended. "No," he replied, "not on the ships, on the men."

* * *

VI

The Passing of the Regiments[1]

When I was a boy, learning to be a social instead of a solitary creature at a preparatory school on the Kentish coast, one of my great treats was to be marched on Sunday afternoon in crocodile—then the universal scholastic formation—to Shorncliffe a mile or so away, there to file through the lines of the soldiery and see the British Army taking its Sabbath rest in the famous camp where a century before John Moore had trained the Light Brigade to be the finest fighting corps in Europe. It was still an army recruited mainly from the plough and the gutter—the army which Kipling had sung and Florence Nightingale sought to humanise and which cloaked the hardships and rigours of its existence beneath uniforms of scarlet, gold and gleaming pipe-clay. To see it was an

[1] *I.L.N.* 27 November 1965; 10 August 1957; 28 March 1959; 20 August 1968; 25 November 1944; 22 July 1950.

aesthetic as well as a martial experience. I think it was the former, even more than the imagined glamour of war, which made me— an untidy, ill-co-ordinated lad, always with his head in the clouds—passionately resolved to be a soldier. At that time it scarcely seemed conceivable that my life could take any other course but the conventional military one of crammer, Sandhurst, a Regiment of the Line, India and, if I was fortunate—for wars were then supposed to be on their way-out—participation in some glorious charge or forlorn hope in which, contrary to all probability, I should distinguish myself and win the notice of my Sovereign, promotion and one day, for I spent much time studying the campaigns of Napoleon, a major-general's plumed hat or even a field-marshal's baton! None of this came to pass— though in the fullness of time, like all my generation, I became involved in a war, though not at all the kind of war I had en- visaged—and my life took a prosaic civilian course very different from that of the coloured dreams of my youth. I saw that fairy- tale Victorian Army for the last time at King Edward VII's funeral procession and on the coronation day of his son, when it pitched its tents and pavilions in the London parks, lined the streets and marched with its glittering jangling accoutrements in seemingly unending columns of scarlet, crimson and gold, blue, green and silver, behind bands of sounding brass, drums and bugle and fife, and beneath the sheen of bayonets and lances. A few years later, in sober khaki, it held the breach on the dusty roads of northern France and the mud of Flanders while England girded on her neglected armour, and, in doing so, almost ceased to be, surviving only in the spirit it handed on to the mechanised, motorised British armies of the twentieth century:

> *These in the day when heaven was falling,*
> *The hour when earth's foundations fled,*
> *Followed their mercenary calling*
> *And took their wages and are dead.*

Pride in corps and the perennial education in virtue and valour it fostered have always been the cement of the Army's greatness. It would be a mistake to attribute any virtue in the British soldier to the innate courage of his race. Britons, untrained for it, are as capable of behaving badly in the face of danger as anyone else.

It has been discipline, training, above all, *esprit de corps*, which, superimposed on certain basic hereditary dispositions, have enabled their troops to achieve the impossible when all the odds were against them. In them pride of corps has always attached to the small unit, to what Sir Thomas Browne called "the little platoon". Round the organisation and transmitted traditions of the Regiment has grown up a wonderful continuing pride and loyalty which again and again has caused men to transcend their natures and attain to the highest peaks of nobility and sacrifice. In how many hopeless fights against odds has defeat been averted or victory won because the officers and men of some particular regiment have refused to yield ground when, by doing so, they would have fallen short of the highest traditions of their corps or shamed it in the eyes of other regiments! "There we unflinchingly stood," wrote Captain Leslie of the Worcesters on the field of Albuera, "and there we unflinchingly fell."

It has been the British soldier's belief that his regiment is the best in the world, and the efforts of its officers and N.C.Os. from generation to generation to prove it so, that, despite the almost impossible conditions under which he has been expected to fight at the outset of our wars, has usually enabled him to cover himself with glory and to emerge at the end victorious. This love of regiment and desire for corporate emulation has been a constant source of efficiency. It has made men do their duty when without some such stimulus they could not have done so. For in the last resort the end of all military training—and the deciding factor in battle—is that, sooner or later, as Lord Wavell put it, Private So-and-So will have to advance straight to his front in the face of the enemy. All the immense preparation, expenditure, training and equipment of war are designed for, and dependent on, what happens at that moment. If the soldier fails the test, all is in vain.

Bureaucrats and politicians never seem to understand this. Because an Army composed of small units which have grown accidentally out of its long history presents administrators with what would seem to be unnecessary and irrational complications, reformers are for ever trying to change the regimental pattern of the British Army. Yet though, with their amalgamations and disbandments and, thanks to the vagaries of our foreign policy, subsequent re-incorporations, they have repeatedly altered the Army's pattern, they have never succeeded in destroying, or for long damping, the regimental spirit which makes it what it is. Again and again, when old units have been "reformed" almost out of recognition, the spirit and *esprit de corps* of the old has reappeared in the new. The sacred flame that burns so brightly in battle has merely been borne from one hearth to another. The "legend" of the regiment lives on, and old prides and traditions are grafted on to new. The Oxfordshire and Buckinghamshire Light Infantry may have seemed to some at the time of the Victorian Cardwell reforms to be a new regiment. But as we now can see it was nothing of the kind. It was two great and ancient regiments made one—the 43rd and the 52nd Foot, both of them preserving everything which had made them distinctive and glorious in the past, while becoming a single whole. Today it is part of an equally great regiment, the Royal Greenjackets, which also embodies the two historic Rifle regiments, the 60th or King's Royal Rifles, and the 95th or Rifle Brigade—that shining examplar of all the fighting soldier's virtues.

The greatest miracle I have ever witnessed was the transformation of the Army between 1940 and 1945; between the collapse of France and the return to Europe of British arms when, with our American allies—still the junior partner in fighting skill and experience—we fought our way back from the south into the continental fortress from which we had been driven at Dunkirk. In 1940 the Army, which between 1916 and 1918 had broken the back of the Kaiser's invincible host, was the Cinderella of the Services. When, after a generation's neglect, rearmament began in the late 1930's, the Army had of necessity to yield precedence in every requirement of equipment to the Royal Navy and Air Force. Its tanks—the decisive new weapon Britain had evolved in the First World War—were few and fragile, its battalions under strength, its stores depleted. Only its higher command, with its staff-trained and dedicated professional veterans of the Somme and Arras—men like Wavell, Alan Brooke, Alexander, Montgomery and Bernard Paget—was outstanding. And the new civilian entry with which its depleted ranks were filled in the melancholy months before, and the desperate months after, Dunkirk, was drawn from a generation which had been taught to regard war with horror and soldiering as a stupid activity unworthy the consideration of civilised beings. In the summer of 1939, when war broke out, Blimp was almost the dirtiest word in the language.

Yet, paradoxically, Colonel Blimp was to save us. Under the regimental officers who had won their Military Crosses on the forgotten battlefields of Flanders and Picardy, and who returned to their regiments at the call of duty from long years of retirement, the young men of the generation whose intellectual elite had voted that it was wrong to fight for King and country, were transformed into soldiers who could have held up their heads with the men who stormed Badajoz or fought their way to Lucknow. Before most of them had had a chance to fire a shot in anger they had become imbued with a fighting spirit and soldierly pride equal to those of the finest armies Britain had raised in the past.

This astonishing change was brought about by a resort to the Army's living history. It was an educational *tour de force* accomplished by middle-aged officers from the sporting shires and tough hard-baked non-commissioned paragons of the barrack-square who could never have conceived of themselves as teachers. They were men of upright bearing, good manners, incisive but unassuming ways, a gay liking for the pleasures and pastimes of earth, tempered by a lifelong mastery over self, men who neither cut nor attempted to cut much figure in the piping times of peace but who, in the hour of danger, became the personification of constancy, calm in storm, serenity and heroism in disaster. Well-groomed colonels and general officers with grizzled hair and red tabs, watching the guns among bursting shells with the same quiet assurance as they took their turn at the tape in the Senior or Rag, regimental sergeant-majors with neatly creased trousers and waxed moustaches, "old sweats" with the stamp of their profession as unmistakable upon them as the king's head on a golden sovereign, such were the men who re-made Britain's Army.

Yet educationists they were, and of an astonishingly effective kind, exhorting by word, deed and example those temporarily committed to their charge to emulate the men of old who, by their valour and fortitude, had created and handed down the legends by which their regiments lived. The surprising thing was how quickly the magic of that teaching worked. It would never have been possible to get the great mass of civilian and, at first, reluctant soldiers to absorb the history—and, with it, by implication, the tradition—of the British Army as a whole. But the history and tradition of the individual regiment did what such wider study could never have done. Building on the ordinary Briton's love of playing for his side, every regiment transmitted its legends to its new members. And because every regiment was different, the response was as personal and enthusiastic as that of the peacetime supporters of Tottenham Hotspur or Glasgow Celtic. Young men, who a year or two before had never dreamed there was any difference between one type of soldier and another, almost burst with sinful pride to think of themselves as Durham Light Infantry or Seaforth Highlanders, and privately, and sometimes not so privately, turned up their martial noses at other and, as they were convinced, inferior units. 'Lucasta,' sang Robert Graves of the Royal Welsh in the First World War,

> *he's a Fusileer,*
> *And his pride keeps him there.*

What a strange and unique tradition that of the British Army is! Most of the usual military attributes, of course, are there: courage, constancy, discipline; where indeed have they been surpassed? But others are almost wholly lacking: the consciousness of might, for instance, is one which the Army, unlike the Royal Navy, has scarcely ever enjoyed. It had it for a few months in 1918, only to vanish like snow in 1919. Even in 1944 it was small compared with the armies of Russia and the U.S.A. Its greatest field strength under Marlborough and Wellington was never more than 50,000 men; its most famous victories were won when it was outnumbered. The episodes in its past on which English historians linger most fondly—like the legends over our wayside inns—are those when it was most lacking in might and, therefore, by its reckoning, most glorious and true to itself— Inkerman, Rorke's Drift, Mons, Dunkirk, the Rifles dying at Calais. For the English have never claimed that their St. George was bigger than the Dragon. Their pride has been that he was so much smaller!

As for ruthlessness and fanaticism—martial qualities which

the comparatively youthful German Army was always claiming for itself and repeatedly proving by its acts—what attributes could less suggest the British Army? What could be less fanatic than a British cavalry subaltern on his way to Ascot? Or less ruthless than the Tommy of 1919 in the streets of conquered Cologne? "The British Army," wrote its historian, John Fortescue, at the conclusion of his noble work, "will be remembered best not for its countless deeds of daring and invincible stubbornness in battle but for its lenience in conquest and its gentleness in domination."

The very nicknames of our regiments reveal their character. The Dorsets—the regiment which carried on its Colours the proud text, *Primus in Indis*—were known, not as the Conquerors of the East, but the "Green Linnets". The Wiltshires were the "Moonrakers" because some of their countrymen were once found on a dark night dragging a pond with hay-rakes, looking, as wits said, for the moon, but, as they themselves confessed, for smuggled brandy kegs. The Norfolks—that grand corps whose representatives still wear mourning for the great soldier they buried "darkly at dead of night" on the ramparts of Corunna—were the "Holy Boys" because a century and a half ago the pious folk of Portugal, seeing the Britannia on their cap-badges, prostrated themselves at what they took to be an image of the Virgin. The first Regiment of the Line, with its long—to its brother regiments almost over-long—history, was kept in its place with the sobriquet of "Pontius Pilot's Bodyguard". And one regiment of Hussars, which lacked the patronage of the various royalties which adorned the titles of its companions, christened itself cheerfully "Nobody's Own" and took pride and courage from the fact in battle.

It is curious how almost unknown this regimental history of the British Army is to the ordinary Englishman. Our highbrows have never heard of it; our learned historians ignore it. With a few exceptions the annals of the Regiment have been compiled at the end of each campaign by some pious but unlettered veteran whose sense of reverence for his dead comrades and pride in his corps has done gallant but halting duty for experience in research and skill in writing. Yet the theme of any one of these regiments is worthy of the muse of a Trevelyan or Macaulay. Where in so little is so much of human achievement and virtue as in the annals of a British Regiment of the Line? Here is triumph over toil, monotony, discomfort, hardship and adversity; here is constancy and loyalty, true to the sun of its faith in the darkest hour; here is love and companionship without reward; here is heroism and self-sacrifice and devotion. And when a great Regiment salutes its Colours, it is expressing this truth. Its members are commemorating their predecessors who suffered, endured and died in its service, and are dedicating themselves to do likewise.

* * *

VII

An Unassuming Service[1]

Lecturing at the R.A.F. Apprentices' School at Halton shortly before the War, I used a phrase that was truer than I knew. I had been speaking of the close relationship between the historic British command of the sea and the development, preservation and expansion of our liberties. After outlining the naval occasions by virtue of which it had been won and maintained, I looked up from my notes and, on the spur of the moment, added, "Gentlemen, it now depends on you!"

"For what we have received," I was taught to say as a child after meals, "the Lord make us truly thankful!" Every year, when the anniversary of the R.A.F.'s victory in the Battle of Britain comes round, we of our generation recall with thankfulness the men, living and dead, who by their courage and devotion won that salvationary victory. There never was another quite like it in the whole of our history since Alfred won his victory over the Danes at Etheldun more than a thousand years ago. Even in the defeat of the Armada wind, tide and weather played a part. No such climatic aid was afforded in the defeat of the Luftwaffe, for throughout that summer the weather was Hitler's ally. If divine aid was given to British arms during that providential year—and many believed it was—it took the form of the moral inspira-

[1] *I.L.N.* 13 September 1952.

tion of those fighting in the air for Britain and the world's victory.

For they fought like men inspired. And the ground crews who serviced their aircraft, and the workers in the aircraft factories who made their machines and components, worked like men inspired too. So did the personnel of the Radar stations, the crews of the anti-aircraft and searchlight sites, the men of the Observer Corps, and all those engaged, in one form or another, in the Battle of Britain. Nor should it be forgotten that the battle was fought principally to prevent a Channel crossing. It was, in part, a sea battle, fought not only by the R.A.F. in the air above the Channel and southern England, but by the Royal Navy on the waters of the Channel itself and on the High Seas.

In that epic autumn, the R.A.F. saved this country, and, with it, the world's freedom. It did so again in those laborious years of preparation and endurance before the assault on Hitler's western wall, when night after night the crews of Bomber Command went out on their perilous missions, suffering losses in proportion to their strength unparalleled in any sustained and successful operation in the history of war. But they won by them a stranglehold on the aggressor's production-centres and communications without which D-Day would have been a shambles and disaster, following which the flying bombs could have destroyed London, leaving the Nazis in permanent control of Western Europe.

We can never be sufficiently grateful. The Royal Air Force in its thirty years of existence has won its place in the British heart beside the Royal Navy for its service in preserving all we love and value. Today the strains of Walford Davies' R.A.F. March arouse the same associations and emotions as the sound of "Sunset" played at a naval ceremony. They remind us, with a sense of pride, pity and tenderness too deep for words, of the valour, sacrifice and unselfishness of those who, transcending their own needs, laid down their all for their country and gave her existence continuance. They commemorate all that was beautiful in those freely-given and dedicated lives, the love of their comrades and dear ones, the hours of life and happiness and preparation that had gone to make them what they were and, in doing so, to serve Britain. They remind those who hear them that in her service

there is no finality or discharge, that life for every one has a
purpose and that its highest achievement is sacrifice—the key
which alone opens the door to the enduring aspirations of men.
For, if their sacrifice has meaning, it is that the end of life is not
material satisfaction but mastery over self in the cause of something more satisfying and lasting than self.

*   *   *

VIII

Imperilled Shrines[1]

Returning the other evening to Wiltshire after absence, I had to
break my journey at Salisbury, and made my way, as most
travellers halted in Salisbury do, to the Cathedral. It was almost
dark and the beauty of the Close—perhaps the loveliest in England
—was shrouded, but the silhouette of the spire and the great
building out of which it rises was glorious against the darkening
sky. It was too early for Evening Service, but, as I entered, the
lights on the High Altar were already lit and the interior had
ceased to be a processional ground for tourists and become wholly
devoted once more to the purpose for which it has existed for
seven centuries—the contemplation and worship of God, so that
casual entrants like myself and a few remaining sightseers were
awed into stillness and participation in the mystery within. I took
my seat near the west end of the central aisle, looking up through
the darkness at the distant altar, and above at those wonderful
arches, the hard, brassy, nineteenth-century renovation of the
stonework and marble no longer visible and only the miraculous
achievement of the thirteenth-century builders shining through
space and time. Then, as I waited, a single bell began to sound,
filling the whole cathedral with the sense of serene imminence—of
waiting in peace for an answer to all the confused questionings
of the illusion called life outside. I was on my way to my own
place—the place to which I ultimately belong so far as man
belongs to any place on earth, because there, and in my birthplace,
Norfolk, my life had its beginnings, and to our beginnings we

[1] *I.L.N.* 27 October 1956.

inevitably return. It made me feel very grateful and strangely at peace to be allowed to stand and kneel in this great Wiltshire shrine, the heart of the land of chalk and greensand downs and valleys to which I owe so much and whose lifelong inspiration I am trying, in some small measure, to repay by planting trees in a little corner of its soil. For part of the miracle and meaning of a cathedral is its link with the countryside it serves, whose sons made it, and the fruits of whose husbandry paid for its making. How right John Betjeman was when, in his poem on King's College Chapel, Cambridge, he stressed its territorial associations.

In far East Anglian churches the clasped hands lying long
Recumbent on sepulchral slabs or effigied in brass
Buttress with prayer this vaulted roof so white and light and strong,
And countless congregations as the generations pass
Join choir and great crowned organ case, in centuries of song
To praise Eternity contained in Time and coloured glass.

For in a cathedral or minster or great collegiate church more than in any other place, space and time are narrowed and brought together. As I sat under that noble, arched roof in the darkness waiting for the bell-broken silence to merge into music and the Service to begin, I could almost, by putting out my hand, feel the cool spring water of the Wiltshire river which rises in my ground and touch the familiar stone of the little church where I worshipped as a boy and in the shadow of whose walls my father's ashes lie.

Out of the clay the Saints were moulded,
Out of the clay the Wine and Bread.

For England is a Christian land, and only by contemplation of her long Christian history can one comprehend her. Her cathedrals and parish churches mark the milestones of her passage through time. Stand at dusk in any English cathedral or parish church and remain there in the silence and gathering darkness, and our history as a people becomes plain.

If you came this way,
Taking any route, starting from anywhere,
At any time or at any season,
It would always be the same: you would have to put off

Sense and notion. You are not here to verify,
Instruct yourself, or inform curiosity
Or carry report. You are here to kneel
Where prayer has been valid. And prayer is more
Than an order of words, the conscious occupation
Of the praying mind, or the sound of the voice praying.
And what the dead had no speech for, when living,
They can tell you, being dead: the communication
Of the dead is tongued with fire beyond the language of the living.
Here, the intersection of the timeless moment
Is England and nowhere . . . A people without history
Is not redeemed from time, for history is a pattern
Of timeless moments. So, while the light fails
On a winter's afternoon, in a secluded chapel
History is now and England.[1]

This is why, to any lover of England and her history, the
preservation of her cathedrals and parish churches matters so
much. Despite our immense technological and mechanical resources—resources beyond the wildest dreams of the craftsmen
who first made them—in no period of our history have our
churches been so neglected as in the half-century since the out-
break of the first of the two German wars. Probably it is no
exaggeration to say that something like half of them are in need
of urgent repair despite the efforts of their dwindling congregations and the work of the Council for the Preservation of
Historic Churches. Yet our civilisation was made by these
churches, grew out of the arts, learning and creed which those
who raised and tended them taught, and, when they crumble or
are destroyed, will perish with them. Their aisles and towers
have witnessed our whole history as a nation; were there when
the news of Crecy and Agincourt, the defeat of the Armada, and
the deliverance of the Nile and Trafalgar set their bells ringing;
and through all the peaceful years of springtide, summer's suns,
harvest and winter's snows have been the centre and inspiration
of all the great moments of ordinary men's and women's lives.
They knit us together as a people, like the Abbey at Westminster
"make us we"; without them ours would be a raw materialistic

[1] T. S. Eliot, *Little Gidding*, pp. 8, 15. Faber.

polity of concrete factories and offices and purposeless urban populations fast receding into barbarism. Lincoln towering in shafts of light above the city, Canterbury's "Bell Harry" and glorious nave enshrining the earliest home of English Christianity and the grave of the "holy blissful martyr" who died to ensure that the Church should never be the mouthpiece of a soulless State; York, Gloucester and Winchester, where Jane Austen's ashes rest under the feet of passing worshippers and sightseers; it is these and all the thousands of churches like them in every corner of the land which link us to those who have gone before and give meaning and purpose to our lives as members of a continuing nation.

> *By altars old their banners fade*
> *Beneath dear spires; their names are set*
> *In minster aisle, in yew tree shade;*
> *Their memories fight for England yet.*

The Faith Within Us

The Creed of Creative Love ·
Answer to a Dilemma · A Recipe for Happiness ·
The Christian Message · It Came upon the Midnight Clear

I

The Creed of Creative Love[1]

In a recent televised protest demonstration a young lady was seen carrying a placard labelled, "I hate everyone!" Whether this *reductio ad absurdum* was a serious gesture of student unrest or the work of some humourist masquerading among the humourless I have no idea. But it is immaterial, for the words epitomised the suicidal illusion of our age. It is one that, if persisted in by the peoples of Western and, formerly, Christian Europe and America, must ultimately result in the end of our civilisation and the beginning of a new Dark Age. It is an illusion deliberately supported and fostered by those who direct the oriental despotism —new in its ideology, but old as time in its methods—which today dominates the great land-bloc of Northern Asia and Eastern Europe, and whose policy is to undermine and destroy by every means in its power the national forces of the formerly Christian and, as they believe, decaying States which alone stand between them and the dominion of the world. Among those States is Britain which, until a generation ago, was the centre of a commercial and increasingly libertarian empire comprising nearly a quarter of the earth's population.

Now when this empire has disintegrated, and the Christian

[1] *Illustrated London News* 24 August 1968.

civilisation of which it was for so long a principal pillar and support, is everywhere in question, it is worth considering how that civilisation came into existence. It arose out of the Christian religion. And the essence of the Christian religion was a belief in the creative importance of love. The central tenet of Christ's teaching was that through the exercise of love men could create a heaven, not only on earth, but in another world beyond the grave, though so far as the latter was concerned, the existence of that heaven was unprovable in terrestrial terms and depended on faith. Yet what was clearly provable, and was the rock on which the Christian Church rested, was that the exercise of love in this life was capable of creating—and alone was capable of creating wherever it flourished, even in the most unlikely places and circumstances—a little world of mutual happiness which, so Christ taught and Christians believed, was in itself the mirror of that greater timeless and unbounded happiness in the heaven to come. The Kingdom of Heaven, he said, was within you.

On the basis of this belief western civilisation was built. It was the gradual production of centuries of cumulative works of love which created expanding islands of light in the great ocean of barbaric hatred, cruelty and darkness that swept over western Europe after the disintegration and collapse of imperial Rome. History and observation alike show that the natural state of human society, unless redeemed and ennobled by this principle of creative love, is one either of anarchy or despotism, either of that kind of existence described by the philosopher, Hobbes, in which there is "no arts, no letters, no society, and which is worst of all, continual fear and danger of violent death and the life of man solitary, poor, nasty brutish and short", or, as the only alternative, a rule of law brutally enforced by the physically strong on the weak for the former's exclusive benefit.

Such alterations between anarchy and despotism would seem to have been the human norm, the successive despotisms of ancient Asia or the savagery of the African jungle. Yet out of Christ's teaching arose a higher option for mankind: the creation of law and order through the exercise of love. It was an option only very gradually, and never anything like wholly or perfectly, realised. Yet the transformation which in the course of time

it wrought on human existence can be seen by comparing the
life of, say, Hampstead Garden City at the beginning of the
twentieth century with that of the fetish-worshipping tribes of
the Gold Coast in the days of King Kofi Kari-Kari and the
Kumasi ritual massacres of a century ago, and beside which
even what is now happening in Biafra or the Congo pales into
insignificance.

It was the philosophy of love as a creative force that established
over a large part of the earth's surface the kind of life which we
in this fortunate island know today and have long taken for
granted. Yet in the centuries that followed the withdrawal of the
last Roman legions, life in Britain was as uncertain, wretched
and bloodstained as it used to be, and is again threatening to
become, in large tracts of tribal Africa. If one wants to understand
how Christian civilisation grew out of anarchy and barbaric
tyranny one cannot do better than study the story of how in this
country Roman monks and Celtic missionaries preached Christ's
gospel of love to the heathen, that is, to ordinary primitive non-
Christian men, and established germinative centres of example
where that gospel could be put into practice.

It was because, where the monks and missionaries made their
settlements men lived together in amity, that they and their
disciples were able to achieve advances in agriculture, the arts
and ways of living that were impossible for societies torn by
perpetual strife, fear and mutual destruction. Everything that
was educative, creative and enduring in European society in the
Middle Ages was the legacy of the Christian Church and its creed
of creative love. And in the fullness of time the lessons taught by
the Church were carried by European colonisers and traders into
other continents beyond the oceans—the Americas, Southern
Asia, Australasia and Africa.

That they also carried with them, and displayed, the faults and
weaknesses inherent in all human nature does not alter the fact
that the civilisation they planted beyond the oceans was of
immense benefit to mankind. To destroy it, whether there or at
home or in both, would be a suicidal act of folly. And destroy it
we are in danger of doing. The more vocal part of the younger
generation, both in Europe and America, has been, and is being

taught by those who should know better, to denigrate and revile the virtues—truthfulness, honesty, courage, tolerance, industry—which have built the house in which civilised man lives and has his being. Above all, they have been taught, and are being taught, often in the name of high-sounding abstractions like pacifism, equality and anti-racism, to hate and, the inevitable fruit of hatred, to destroy.

What is wanted, in a world still riven by two great global wars, is not anger, violence and destruction, but tolerance, understanding, love and peaceful creation. If those responsible for our schools, universities, books, television, broadcasting and newspapers could only realise this and apply their realisation of it to their work, they could do more to remove the causes of war, racial intolerance and class conflict than all the protest marches, demonstrations and sit-downs that have ever taken place.

*　　*　　*

II

Answer to a Dilemma[1]

G. K. Chesterton once observed that modern man had not only lost the way but lost the map. Today, only one thing about the future of humanity seems clear: that man has no idea where he is going. He wants to travel faster and further, but beyond a vague aspiration to colonise the moon—for what precise purpose no one seems to know—he does not appear to have any ultimate objective at all. He would like, of course, to increase his material comforts and diminish the amount of pain attendant on his brief physical existence and to postpone, as long as possible, the hour of his personal demise. He would also like to do less work for more material reward. But there his aspirations end; the meaning of his destiny, as seen by himself, is as confused and indeterminate as that of a Picasso picture. Indeed, that great but perverse artist affords, like so much contemporary music, a perfect reflection of the thoughts and mood of the age—an age of Uncertainty and Bewilderment.

[1] *I.L.N.* 6 December 1958; 31 December 1966.

Of course, those who don't know where they are going sometimes reach their destination quickly; the Gadarene swine did.
Robert Louis Stevenson wrote that it is better to travel hopefully
than to arrive. Yet his accent was on the word hopefully, and part
of modern man's trouble is that he hasn't much hope. Despite
pipe-dream platitudes about future peace and prosperity, the man
in the street, so far as he thinks about the future, is more afraid
than hopeful. He expects nuclear wars and slumps, dole-queues
and strikes, civil strife and authoritarian regimentation. And he
does so with a fatalistic indifference which, in this country at
least, is quite alien to the spirit of her past. The pessimism and
defeatism of his attitude would have amazed and horrified his
cheerful, vigorous great-grandfather of a century ago.

If I had to find in a word an explanation for the contrast between
the philosophy of the mid-nineteenth century and that of the third
quarter of the twentieth century I would seek it in the word God.
By God man implies an intellectual idea or abstraction which he
cannot define in concrete terms. He has often tried to do so, but
always in vain, for it involves a contradiction in terms. Even
those who fashioned graven images to represent their gods and
worshipped and offered sacrifices at their feet never really believed
that the God they feared or sought to propitiate was contained
in the inanimate stocks or stones before which they knelt. What
they were concerned with was an intangible, invisible and
mysteriously indefinable Power behind the outward form of their
man-fashioned idols. That Power was the explanation of life and
all its mysteries and perils, the key to their future, the arbiter and
guide to their conduct—a spiritual king and lord by serving
whom they hoped of find a way through the storms and perils
which encompassed them. And history suggests that great
human achievement, both individual and corporate, has always
been preceded and accompanied by religious or spiritual faith.
The religions have varied, but faith and the hope and energy
begotten by faith have been the common denominator of every
major outburst of human vitality. "They that wait upon the Lord
shall renew their strength; they shall mount up with wings as
eagles: they shall run and not be weary." It was not only the
prophet Isaiah who noted this phenomenon. Nor has it only been

the God of Israel who inspired and heartened man to do great things. The cold God in the Kremlin and the bloodthirsty racial Gods of Valhalla and Berchtesgaden have set men marching too.

But we in the West now apparently have no god. Formal obligation to the Christian God is still paid by the official leaders of the Western nations on ceremonial occasions, but in the pursuit of national policy the conception of God and God's will plays little or no part. Some modern historians, who not unnaturally are swayed by the philosophy of their age, maintain that it never did. In this, I am convinced, they are wrong. Belief in God and God's will played an enormous part in the policy of this country, not only in the Middle Ages and in the religious ferments of the sixteenth and seventeenth centuries, but also in the Victorian, and even in the Edwardian, era. Great Britain did not go to war in 1914, as is often argued today, because of some abtruse diplomatic accident in one or more of the European capitals and chancelleries, but because the people of Britain and their pacifically-minded representatives believed that it was contrary to Christian conscience and morality that an aggressor should be allowed to violate with impunity the frontiers of a small nation whose territorial integrity and neutrality both we and that aggressor had sworn to maintain. Even as late as 1939, though religious faith in Britain was rapidly declining, we went to war for similar reasons. As a people we were prepared to lay down our lives and material possessions sooner than see what we believed to be a moral principle flouted and trampled under. That principle derived from the Christian religion and belief in God.

I am far from supposing that this country is incapable of the same conviction and unanimity of sacrifice. Nor do I believe that the Christian faith in Great Britain and Western Europe and America is dead; in many places and among large and powerful minorities it is still very much alive. Yet running through so much of what is now taken for granted is the idea that God— and, as an implied consequence, God's will—are outmoded notions that no longer have any validity. In an interview which that brilliant astronomer, Mr. Fred Hoyle, gave to a popular newspaper on the creation of the universe, he was reported as saying that there was no room for a super being in a universe where there is continuous creation. Since the latest scientific observations and conclusions suggest that creation itself is a ceaseless and continuous process, Mr. Hoyle contended that, if a super being exists at all, he must stand outside space, time and the universe itself. I am not quite clear what Mr. Hoyle's own view of the matter is, but, according to his interviewer, "In Hoyle's universe there is no beginning and no end; there is no limit to space and time; and there is no God."

Now if the third of these propositions is supposed to follow from the first and second, I cannot see it as anything but a colossal non sequitur. It is, of course, perfectly true that in the past a large number of unthinking persons supposed God—the old-fashioned name for Mr. Hoyle's hypothetical "super being"—to be Himself confined within the bounds of time and space, a part, as it were, of His own Creation. In its crudest manifestation this supposition took the form of picturing God as a kind of extra large and venerable, though all-powerful, male being with a long white beard floating over the cosmos like a figure in a Blake engraving. But no one who has thought deeply about religious experience or probability has ever supposed that God was confined to His own visible Universe or was incapable of standing outside it. It seems, therefore, puerile to suggest that because modern science proves—so far as it is capable of proving such a thing—that God cannot be confined within existing Creation, no God can exist. The first condition of an all-powerful God is that He is outside the bounds of His own Creation, outside time and space—for in Eternity time must be non-existent—outside, except so far as He chooses to manifest Himself to man's limited perception and intelligence, human comprehension. It is because we know ourselves to be creatures of finite mind and capacity and helpless in a universe of infinite possibility that we crave for, and seek to believe in, an infinite and eternal God. Everything science reveals only heightens the sense of the necessity of God and man's dependence on Him.

*   *   *

In a consortium published in the *Weekend Telegraph*[1] called "God in the Scientific Age", my friend Ludovic Kennedy, has given his views, with other contemporary thinkers—including a cardinal, a bishop, a dean and a scientist—on how religion has been affected by recent discoveries. He begins by stating that he is a humanist and that the humanist does not believe that God created man in His own image but that men, at all times, have created gods for their own needs. "Because," he goes on, "the humanist's deepest beliefs are concerned with man's relationships to men, not gods, they are not initially affected by the prospect of widened horizons. He asks himself the same questions as the Christian. When and where did it all begin? Why are we here? What lies beyond the furthest star? But unlike the Christian he does not know, or expect to know, or feel a need to know, the answer."

In this frank avowal of his belief, or rather disbelief, Ludovic Kennedy is at one with a large proportion, probably a majority, of the younger generation in this country. It is not merely that they do not believe in a future life—an attitude which explains their intense concern, even obsession, over the horror of premature death, as shown by the popular campaigns against the nuclear bomb, the Vietnam war and capital punishment—but they cannot see the need to concern themselves with an event so seemingly remote to them as death in the course of nature. In this island, at least since 1945, much of the harshness and discomfort of life that men have had to face in earlier ages has been eliminated by the Welfare State and a host of scientific and mechanical devices for easing existence. It has become for most people what Ludovic Kennedy describes as a "cosy" world. Yet, with his habitual honesty, he makes a reservation which, though it does not in itself invalidate the case for "humanism", may well weaken its appeal. "In this cosy world in which we live and whose workings we think we know," he writes, "humanism is easy enough. But when at last man is launched into space, groping his way through the dark pit of the universe, he may feel the need of a loving hand to guide him. He may turn, as his ancestors turned at the dawn of their history, to a god or gods to succour him." And this bears out something which I observed lecturing to

[1] 16 December 1966. 'God in the Scientific Age.'

Servicemen during the war; that those who, in Wordsworth's words, are

> *. . . doomed to go in company with Pain,*
> *And Fear and Bloodshed, miserable train,*

seldom evince much enthusiasm for a philosophy that dispenses with God and the hope of a future life. Soldiers, sailors and airmen, whose lot and duty it is to stake their lives for others, usually feel the need for some spiritual force outside of, and stronger than themselves, to sustain them in the hour of danger.

Yet the question whether scientific knowledge has made religion superfluous goes deeper than this. One of the contributors to the symposium—Sir Bernard Lovell, director of the Jodrell Bank Observatory, put it in this way: "There is no possible scientific answer in the strictest sense to the vital question of the condition of the universe at time zero, at what, that is, the Bible describes as 'In the Beginning'. In any discussion of the beginning the theological and metaphysical approach has equal validity with the scientific. Neither does it seem that the scientists can ever answer the question as to whether the universe we observe is the totality of the cosmos." As another contributor, the Bishop of Southwark, writes, "God can neither be proved nor disproved." For the validity of belief in God and our own immortality turns on a single question. It concerns the human capacity for understanding. If we claim that with our terrestrial intelligence we are capable of comprehending all things, including the mystery of our own existence, the case for both God and our personal immortality goes by default.

For centuries great Christian philosophers, like Thomas of Aquinas, have tried to prove the truth of the Christian credo by rationalising it, by irrefutable intellectual and logical arguments in its support. They have always failed, and always must. For this reason it is untrue to say that science and human understanding of the material world have knocked the bottom out of the Christian Faith. They may have done so to many of the legends that have attached themselves to Christianity, but they have neither destroyed nor weakened the central tenet of Christian belief—that, through faith in Christ and observance of the truths he taught, men can transcend death and find immortal life.

The first principle of Christianity, as of all religion, is wonder—wonder at the inexplicable miracle of God's creation, the miracle of life itself. The second is humility—the overriding sense of one's own mental limitations and powerlessness in the presence of the great mysteries of birth and death, the mysteries which no scientist has ever been able to solve or throw the slightest real light on. He can show, as men have been able to show for countless centuries, how the physical body is born from the womb, and how disease, injury and decay deprive it of life. But how that life comes to be and whence it comes, and where, if anywhere, it takes its way when, in the instant of physical death, it deserts the body, we are no nearer discovering than our remote and primitive forbears.

> *A thousand times I have heard men tell*
> *That there is joy in Heaven and pain in Hell,*
> *And I accord right well that it is so;*
> *And yet indeed full well myself I know*
> *That there is not a man in this countrie*
> *That either has in Heaven or Hell y' be.*

So wrote Chaucer in the heyday of conventional Christian belief and orthodoxy, and his lines are still true as on the day they were written. We are forced back onto our own manifest incapacity to solve the mystery of existence, not only the existence of the universe, but what concerns us as conscious and sentient individuals, the explanation of our personal being. The wider the range of terrestrial knowledge and science, the greater our command over matter, the more humiliating becomes our inability, and that of all the impressive philosophies, machines and appliances we have created, to answer that, to us, insoluble conundrum. We can only shut our eyes to it and, if we wish to claim omniscience, conceal our powerlessness to understand, let alone master our destiny, behind an unreal barrage of brave words, or alternatively fall back, as Christ bade his disciples fall back, on faith—the faith that can enable a man to face all dangers, bear all suffering and overcome seemingly omnipotent might.

"And Jesus answering saith unto them, 'Have faith in God. For verily I say unto you that whosoever shall say unto this mountain, be thou removed and cast into the sea, and shall not doubt in his heart but shall believe that those things which he saith shall come to pass, he shall have whatsoever he saith.' " That mountain is the inexorable inexplicability and seeming purposelessness of life; inexorable and unanswerable, that is, without this act of faith in the divine spirit which we cannot prove by our intellect yet feel the need of in our hearts, and which we call God and which Christ by His life on earth made manifest. And so at the end of it all, in this age of computers, astronauts and omniscient commentators on every subject under the sun except the one that most concerns us all—the meaning and purpose of our personal existence—the only answer which satisfies is the one we learnt in childhood: the answer of that unique life: "Never man spake like this man"—that began two thousand years ago when the wise men from the East asked their question: "Where is he that is born King of the Jews? for we have seen his star in the east and are come to worship him."

*   *   *

III

A Recipe for Happiness[1]

According to an article in a popular monthly entitled 'The Young Agnostic', "We are witnessing the death of the old morality. We are sensing a complete breakdown in our sense of duty, our sense of obligation. Duty to whom? Obligation to what? Am I anything more than a happy or unhappy accident. These are the questions that are being asked today, in quite genuine incomprehension." From this beginning, expressing a dilemma which many people, particularly the young, feel, the writer goes on to draw the conclusion that Christianity is becoming a mere moral code to which most people pay only lip-service. "The god of society is money . . . Which should we be—successful, rich and immoral, or poor, inefficient and Christian?"[2] This dilemma, he asserts, is insoluble if one accepts what the New Testament says.

[1] *I.L.N.* 25 January; 1 February 1964.

[2] John Meredith, 'The Young Agnostic', *Harpers Bazaar*, January 1964.

Yet does the New Testament say anything of the sort? If by the New Testament one means Christ, the creator of the Christian religion, one should look to what Christ himself said and taught. Fortunately this is not difficult, for, by what to a student of history must seem a miracle of survival, Christ's words, notwithstanding centuries of intervening barbarism and ignorance, have been handed down in a language which has the clear and unmistakable hall-mark of a unique and immediately recognisable mind and personality. In each of the four Gospels, different though the characters of their writers were and the circumstances of their writing, Christ's words stand out from the text in language which to anyone used to judging words are as palpably that of one and the same man as are, say, certain passages of Shakespeare or Churchill's wartime speeches. Whether one attributes to Christ supernatural and divine qualities or not, his sayings reveal him as a unique and most original genius.

Now Christ laid down certain principles for living whose observance, he declared, would enable a man—any man—to enter into what he called the Kingdom of Heaven. The Kingdom of Heaven, he said, is within you. He didn't say it was in the sky or beyond the grave; it lay in a man's attitude to his own life and that of his fellow-creatures, and on the conduct that expressed that attitude. It was within the reach of poor and rich, Jew and Gentile, Pharisee and sinner. According to the author of 'The Young Agnostic', "the Church has a reputation for being clearly against certain things, yet it rarely stands clearly for others; its official statements, presumably following the example of the Ten Commandments, are precise about what one should *not* do without being intelligible about what one *should*". Yet, if Christ's words are the test, this is completely untrue. Christ stood most clearly *for* certain, and at the time he advocated them, startlingly original things, and was particularly emphatic about what one *should* do rather than what one should not do. What is more, when it comes to practice and not mere lip-service, these positive recipes for living are just as revolutionary and original as they were on the day when they were first enunciated. They are as difficult as then to put into practice, for they run diametrically counter to the line of least resistance which men, following their selfish instincts, usually pursue. Yet they are also just as attainable, now as then, by any man or woman who deliberately bases his or her life on them and to the precise extent that he does so. They constitute a recipe for living happily which works, unlike selfishness and self-indulgence which, however much they appear to be the way to happiness, almost always in the end lead to unhappiness and frustration.

For the pursuit of what the self at the moment desires is, paradoxically, an unsatisfying pursuit; when it has been achieved, the self usually ceases to desire it. The appetite for self-indulgence grows on what it is fed, and the goal of selfish satisfaction, when attained, as constantly recedes, leaving the pursuer still unsatisfied. Sooner or later the man who always insists on getting his own way encounters, too, a resistance from others which engenders the self-consuming evils of anger, jealousy and resentment. The "rat-race" of every man for himself is as old as human existence. So is its failure as the key to contentment.

In his revolutionary Sermon on the Mount, Christ denied that the pursuit of self-interest and pleasure led to worldly happiness. He claimed precisely the opposite: that the only enduring happiness was to be found in serving others—a happiness, therefore, within the reach of everyone, rich and poor, old and young, hale and halt. It could be had at any time by anyone, however hitherto self-centred and selfish, and therefore, sinful, who applied Christ's recipe which, unlike the exclusive regimen for Heaven prescribed by scribes and Pharisees—the intellectuals of religion— was available to all, workaday men and women as well as recluses and scholars, publicans and sinners as well as priests and saints. It was this that, in a little book published shortly before his death, caused Lord Beaverbrook—a man who had had ample opportunity to learn from experience the vanity of worldly power and its pursuit—to describe the Sermon on the Mount as the most cheerful sermon ever preached. "It points directly," he wrote, "to an ideal of life which can be lived here and now, and the living of which will in itself bring happiness and contentment."[1] This layman's attempt "to understand Jesus in the flickering light of a limited intelligence", as he called it—a reasoned declaration of faith coming

[1] Lord Beaverbrook, *The Divine Propagandist*, Heinemann.

at the end of a long, famous and often stormy public career—
is illuminating not only because it is expressed with great simplicity and in language the ordinary man can understand, but because, being concerned solely with Christ's actual words as transmitted by the Gospels, it sees in the latter only what Christ himself
put there and nothing else. "The mission of Christ, as revealed
in them", he writes, "was to tell mankind how to achieve happiness in this world and, as the direct consequence of that achievement, the gift of eternal life ... The Sermon on the Mount was
His first and greatest sermon. It contains the essence of His
message on how to attain happiness by thought and conduct."

"The Kingdom is a state of mind into which a man enters in
this life . . . This internal state of grace has little to do with
external conditions. It does not concern itself with systems of
government: it does not really matter in the least whether the
man who possesses it is rich or poor. Of course, it is true that if
the doctrine of the Sermon on the Mount were universally
accepted by mankind great changes might take place in the
internal and external structure of society. But this would be a
mere consequence, a by-product of the acceptance of the
Kingdom, making it easier for others to follow. Such changes
were not the immediate aim of Christ who spoke directly to
the individual soul, offering that peace and happiness which
the material world alone cannot bring.

"In reading the Sermon distortion soon creeps in if this
fundamental idea is not borne in mind. 'Blessed are they that
mourn for they shall be comforted' does not mean that a
follower of Jesus should desire a series of terrible family
bereavements. It means that when he has to face sorrow his
spiritual state will find him consolation. . . . Jesus does not mean
that in order to attain salvation it is necessary to be persecuted—
but that, if you have the Kingdom of God, persecution does not
matter. If you prefer personal safety to your faith you will lose
the Kingdom of real happiness . . . Selfishness, graspingness,
narrowness, self-righteousness, hypocrisy, self-seeking are
shown to be sure precursors of misery, and their antithesis the
road to joy."

What struck me most about this unassuming little book was the similarity of its interpretation of Christ's teaching to that of my mother, whose life, background and temper of mind were, on the face of it, about as far removed from those of its author as it would be possible to conceive. She was a mystic and a poet, a dreamer who as a young girl from an exceptionally sheltered home married, out of some instinctive sympathy, a man much older than herself with an iron discipline of life, a dedicated sense of duty and little of this world's goods. For the sake of his work and their children she turned herself into a practical and frugal housewife, mistress of every domestic resource and expedient. Yet, under a self-made cloak of common sense so closely woven as to become second nature and which she used to shelter and help all in need of it, she retained her poet's capacity for dreaming, and a wisdom, born of it, which every now and then filled me with wonder—for, as we do with those we have long known, I took her too much for granted. Looking back on her life and re-reading her letters, I think she was one of the wisest people I have ever known. Devoted and, to outward appearance, completely orthodox churchwoman though she was, her view of Christianity reflected both the independence of her mind and the mysticism that underlay it.

To her, Christ's words were not so much a sacred text remote from life as an obvious explanation of how everyday existence should be lived. Hatred, envy, greed, jealousy, malice and their consequences of cruelty and violence were the certain precursors of unhappiness, bringing to those who harboured them a retribution which, deserved and inevitable though it was, made them objects of her pity and compassion. There was nothing weak or sentimental in my mother's tenderness of heart towards the erring. She saw clearly that punishment for evil was part of the law of creation and as necessary for its doer as rain for the earth after drought, for her instinct told her that the hardness of heart which was its cause—a thing alien to her own tender and generous nature—could only be softened by affliction and suffering. Yet, though, unlike the modern world with its unrealistic aspirations, she accepted this, she also perceived and felt, with an intense conviction I have never seen equalled in any other being, that love was the governing and redeeming principle of the universe capable of transforming all its creatures, even the most depraved and abandoned. To her this, and this alone, was the meaning of Christ's teaching and life and the explanation of what he meant by the Kingdom of Heaven. It was a Kingdom that could be entered by any man at any moment; all he had to do was to escape from the prison of his own selfishness by turning the key of love.

Because of this, notwithstanding her indifference to wealth and its comforts and trappings, my mother would never accept the contention of many ardent Christians that it is necessary to salvation to forgo all worldly success, to give everything to the poor and, turning the other cheek to the unjust and aggressor, to submit to wrongful violence: in other words, to act diametrically contrary to healthy instinct and prudent reason. Such assumptions, she held, arose from taking Christ's words out of their context and failing to perceive the far deeper, poetic truth they illumined. For our Lord was not speaking literally as materialists supposed, or seeking to reform the body politic, but was addressing himself solely to the individual soul which alone held the key to the Kingdom of Heaven on earth. Lord Beaverbrook in his book expresses the same view. "Jesus," he writes, "was neither a theologian nor a Communist. He was the Son of God who came to give comfort to our souls; to teach us how we could live in this world with the most supreme happiness by fulfilling all the charitable laws of God . . . Many teachers tell us that we should try to accept the doctrine of the Sermon on the Mount and apply it in our daily lives. They say that society would be reconstructed and that international relations would undergo vast changes. Christ never sought such universal acceptance. He spoke to the man in the field, to the wayfarer, to the powerful and mighty, to the lowly and the humble, offering them the many benefits which cannot be gained by material success. Over everything, He offered the gifts of peace and tranquillity . . . The Sermon on the Mount . . . points to an ideal of life, the living of which will in itself bring happiness and contentment." My mother not only believed this; she practised it and, by doing so, proved it to be true, retaining, through all the tribulations and trials of her life, which were many, a wonderful serenity. And her life perfectly illustrated the truth of another passage in *The Divine Propagandist* which refers to the Christian precept that one should love one's enemies.

"This has always been taken as a hard saying—a commandment transcending the capacity of ordinary life. But is it really so? Does not Jesus give us a piece of very sound practical advice ... Hatred rarely does any harm to its object. It is the hater who suffers. His soul is warped and his life is poisoned by dwelling on past injuries or projecting schemes of revenge. Rancour in the bosom is the foe of personal happiness."

In his book Lord Beaverbrook gives two very interesting reasons for a rational belief in immortality. "The desire for eternity is one which nature has implanted in the human race. Now nature, working under the Providence of God, does not bestow instincts on her creatures and at the same time refuse to satisfy them. Looked at from one point of view, nature is the fulfilment of instinct. When, therefore, the sceptic suggests that we cheat ourselves in this matter, consciously or unconsciously, and believe in immortality because we wish to have it so, he is really putting forward one of the strongest arguments in favour of future existence." The other ground is the doctrine of the conservation of energy. For if a man does not try to create in himself an immortal soul—if "he prefers pride, selfishness, materialism and lust to the ideals and life of the Kingdom of God and does so deliberately and persistently"—in other words, if he stifles his emergent soul with sin—he cannot enter God's kingdom in this world and cannot, therefore, transcend the death of the body and inherit eternal life.

As the title of his book suggests, the author—much of whose life was spent in propagating a deeply felt political belief which, for all his genius as a journalist, never won acceptance—was profoundly impressed by the means Christ used to bring home to men the original and revolutionary truths He came into the world to reveal. As His message was directed solely to man as an individual, that is, to every separate individual, living and unborn, it could only be disseminated gradually and in the course of centuries. "Any overwhelming manifestation would, like the proclamation of Christ's kingdom on earth, have defeated its own object ... Jesus had convinced a limited number of men that He was the Son of God. He had taught those followers what the relation between man and man ought to be. Finally He had by one supreme act shown the observers who were to carry on the work that submission and sacrifice, meekness and charity, even to the torturers, are the supreme end of life upon earth . . . The Message of Calvary . . . is a cry directed to the heart . . . The Cross was a beginning, not an end."

" The Crucifixion was a deliberate and necessary act intended to fix indelibly in the mind of man, so that never throughout history could he forget it, that supreme goodness made the supreme sacrifice. The figure on the Cross is lifted up in order that it may call to what is best in us across the ages. The response will vary, and so will the demand. Sometimes much will be demanded of a man, sometimes little; some men will give generously, others hardly at all. The difference between the age before Jesus and the age after Him is that the greater part of the world accepts the moral obligation that the death on the Cross entails. By slow degrees, by imperceptible gradations the Kingdom of God, which is humanity, tenderness, love of others, has been conquering the world ever since Calvary."

The history of the last fifty years, since the lights of a great civilisation made by Christianity began to darken in the summer of 1914, may seem to give the lie to this thesis. But fifty years is a very brief time in the history of mankind. If one looks at humanity today and contrasts it with what it was two thousand years ago, a historian can hardly avoid the conclusion that, this in fact, is what has been happening.

*   *   *

IV

The Christian Message[1]

At the heart of the Christian tradition lies one word—Love. It was Christ's unique achievement that, alone of the great teachers known to history, he taught that the Kingdom of God resides within every human heart and that God is love. Others, the

[1] *I.L.N.* 23 December 1950; 21 December 1957.

founders of the Buddhist faith in particular, have emphasised the essential oneness of created nature, and have seen that the secret of life must lie in its pursuit. But only Christ of Nazareth has shown how every man, even the saddest and most defeated, has the key to Heaven within his own heart. This is the truth that all his disciples have laboured, first to learn themselves and then to teach by precept and word, and this is the truth—the rock—on which the Christian Creed and Churches are founded:

> *But, when so sad thou canst not sadder,*
> *Cry; and upon thy so sore loss*
> *Shall shine the traffic of Jacob's ladder*
> *Pitched betwixt Heaven and Charing Cross.*

That creed—the creed of the all-importance of individual human love—was first proclaimed at a moment when the civilised world appeared to be on the threshold of a new and eternal era of material power, progress and dominion. It emanated from a member of a small and divided people who, unknown to themselves, were on the threshold of a dreadful disaster. Its full and universal significance only became apparent some centuries later when the great Mediterranean civilisation of Imperial Rome was dissolving under the hammer-blows of armed barbarians. In the fullness of time, as Western man emerged from the long, dark ages of violence and destruction, it became the inspiration of a new and greater civilisation—that on which our modern world, also now threatened with disintegration, has been founded.

Everything that is worthwhile in the European tradition, which today also comprises the American tradition, sprang originally from that respect for the individual to which the new Gospel of Love gave rise. For as it was a Christian's duty to love his neighbour and even his enemy as himself, how could he deny that neighbour the right to live his own life in the fullest freedom? From that inescapable logic the intolerant and selfish mind of man has sought, age after age, to escape, only to find its inexorable, inevitable conclusion gaining on him. This, not the Marxist thesis of the inevitability of the triumph of the majority's materialistic self-interest over that of the minority—a thesis which history has disproved again and again—is the real explanation of the advance, first political and then economic, of democracy in this and other Christian countries: an advance still continued, though dreadfully endangered, since the decline of conscious Christianity during the last half-century among the peoples of the West. The widespread belief in the democratic countries that every man should have a fair chance in life, so contrary to the promptings of the selfish, competitive instinct inherent in untutored human nature, could have originated only from this revolutionary precept of Christ that a man should love his neighbour, every neighbour, as himself.

This is not a belief which receives any acceptance in the great Communist communities of the East. No good Marxist supposes it to be his duty to love, or even to give a fair chance to, a reactionary or a diversionist or any other species of human being who disagrees with or is under the displeasure of the edicts and rulers of his iron State. Yet the Liturgy of the Christian Church of England, itself the historic conscience and moral mentor of the English State, expressly enjoins on men and women the obligation of prayer for "all prisoners and captives"; for all, that is, who have offended against the laws of the community. No wonder that Christ, the architect of so strange a creed and practice, seems, even apart from the testimony of the Gospel story, to have had in his nature something superhuman, something which, in our search for words to express the inexpressible, we call divine. He taught men to act outside and beyond the scope of their apparent natures.

Yet—and here lies the explanation of the success of Christianity —Christ, himself transcending human reasoning and vision, founded his Creed on the innate capacity of every living creature both to love and to learn from love. In the confusing and desperate dilemma which terrestrial existence poses to every living, and ultimately suffering and dying, being, love affords the sole explanation of, and the sole justification for, the individual's lot. Everything else on which the individual sets his heart—wealth, happiness, power, success, progress—is seen in the end to be vanity and a delusion. In the hour of death, the one certain earthly consummation to which all our actions and all our minutes tend, man can derive no comfort from any of these conceptions. Only the affection of the heart remains. If only it be true and absolute affection—such affection as causes a man to lay down his life for that which he loves—even death can become a personal achievement and triumph. "Herein is my Father glorified; ... these things have I spoken unto you that my joy might remain in you and that your joy might be full. This is my commandment, That ye love one another as I have loved you. Greater love hath no man than this, that a man lay down his life for his friends." Though it required a mind of more than human clarity and perception to grasp and enunciate such a paradoxical truth—one that after nineteen centuries of Christian teaching we are now able to take for granted, but which at the time of its first utterance must have seemed so revolutionary and paradoxical as to appear insane—it needed only the inner experience open to every man and woman, even the humblest and most degraded, to prove its truth. A poor, starving, outlawed waif of a dog that gives its heart, absolutely and unreservedly, to a tramp who, in a spasm of pity, feeds it a bone, proves the truth of Christ's saying and lives, dies and glories in the overriding, all-powerful validity of love. Stalin, in all his splendour and power and with all the obedient millions and machines at his command, could not touch the glory and power of the meanest creature that loves wholly and purely. It was this which caused the mediaeval Christians, in their images of the humble nativity of the Founder of their Faith, to find room in that inner sanctuary of Love for the poor beasts of the field, the Ass and the Ox, who in dumb, loving adoration and service, took their places beside the Virgin and the Holy Babe. It is not only in the heart of humankind that the mystery resides which Christ showed to be the key of our existence, but in that of all created and sentient beings.

* * *

V

It Came upon the Midnight Clear

Within a few days it will be Christmas. The banks, shops, offices and factories will be closed, and except for the main public utility services and on the farms, where work never ceases, men will have ceased to labour. The streets will be quiet, with little traffic, the roadways strangely empty, and in the afternoon, after the royal broadcast, the London parks will fill with strolling citizenry. And in a million homes, all over the country, families and kinsmen will sit down together, eat possibly a little more than is good for them, be a little happier than usual and make merry. If there are children present, they will make very merry indeed.[1]

What does it all mean? For a minority in Christian Britain, as elsewhere, Christmas is a religious commemoration, the highlight of the Christian year. For the majority, probably the vast majority, it has little more religious significance than New Year's Day. For them it is merely a feast and holiday, and is kept by them because it has been so kept from time immemorial, because their fathers kept it, and because their earliest memories of celebration and family reunion go back to Christmas Day. The giving of presents, the decorations on the walls, the songs and tunes of the familiar carols, the particular kind of fare prepared and eaten on this great day are all sanctified by memory and repeated usage. There is nothing more to it, or seems to be nothing more, except, perhaps, a slight temporary, yet perceptible, all-round rise in the temperature of human kindliness. If the emotion of love and loving could be measured by statistics and represented by graphs, the 25th day of December would almost certainly be marked by a sharp rise and peak.

The "Christian myth": that is how clever men who wish to be thought in tune with the prevailing ideology of our time, refer to the body of Christian belief out of which the Christmas feast arises. Perhaps they are right in doing so; perhaps there was a Christian myth which is now no more—a man-made, temporary, evanescent idea that is now dying as other man-made ideas die. Yet there are certain historical facts which, before we dismiss the "myth", we should do well to remember; but for these facts Christmas would not be kept at all. The first is that on a specific day—a day in history on which the sun rose and fell, both in distant Palestine and on this dark, misty Atlantic island—there was born in the manger of a poor inn in Judea a child called Jesus who, without any of the material advantages and without doing

[1] *I.L.N.* 22 December 1951; 24 December 1960; 24 December 1955.

any of the things that ordinarily give men fame and power, succeeded in influencing profoundly the minds and actions of countless millions still unborn. He was not a prince or statesman or warrior. He was not a member of a conquering race. He wrote no book and raised no artistic monument. His years on earth were few and lived out in a poor, obscure, conquered province where he was regarded by most of his more cultivated and educated contemporaries as a person of no consequence whatever. His only crown was one of thorns placed on his head in the hour of his final torture and death by the mocking, merciless men into whose hands he had fallen. As a matter of strict prosaic history, it is to celebrate this man's birth some 2000 years ago that we shall all sit down on Christmas Day, Christians and unbelievers alike, to eat roast fowl and plum pudding and put paper caps on our heads and read, amid laughter, little rhyming texts taken out of crackers. It therefore takes, one might think, a good deal of explanation.

It is not wholly answering the historical conundrum set by this apparently baffling non sequitur to reply that countless people for a great number of generations have affirmed, as millions still affirm today, that Jesus was the Son of God. The theological interpretation put by churches and scholars on Christ's reported words has varied in all ages and varies to this day; where men have only their reasoning to guide them, there can never be any ultimate certainty in theological meanings. What there is, and never has been, any doubt about is that those who knew Christ best during his life, and particularly after his terrible and agonising death, became convinced that he both was and knew himself to be more than man, and that they succeeded, in the teeth of every opposition, ridicule and persecution, in communicating the conviction to others. Yet it is not the belief of those others that constitutes the heart of the matter; it is what Jesus himself did during his lifetime to create that belief. What Jesus did caused men to worship what he was. For what he did, created, both in those who were witnesses of it and in those who came to learn of it only by hearsay, a conviction of what he was so intense that they regarded his existence on earth as infinitely the most important thing which had ever happened; so important that not only did they try to alter their own lives, to live, however unsuccessfully, as he had lived, but even, in many cases, deliberately—in order to testify to his existence—elected to die as he had died. This is not a myth; it is documented and ascertainable history.

For this wonderful man, whom those who call themselves Christians believe to have been more than man, and the Son of God—though the meaning of that phrase is manifestly far beyond our limited human comprehension—possessed an attribute which far exceeded the capacity of normal human nature as we know it from our own personal experience. He possessed, and was possessed of, an infinite capacity for love which enabled him to regard—and treat—every other being's personality, need and suffering as though they were his own. He did not love only individually and spasmodically, as all human beings, even the worst and most selfish, at some time or another do. He loved so much that all human suffering and need mattered to him as though they were his own. Anyone who has ever considered at all deeply the nature of human perfection—the quality which we are always ludicrously expecting in others and always, even more ludicrously, expecting others to see in ourselves, and never finding in either—must realise the incompatability of moral perfection with human nature. For if a perfect man existed in a world such as ours he would die of horror and compassion at all the terrible things which happen in it every day and every second. However tender and loving, however shaken and moved by the sufferings and tragedies that affect them personally, men and women instinctively close their hearts to other tragedies every whit as great as their own and those immediately around them. But a perfect being would not in self-protection shut his heart to the grief and misery of others; he would suffer with them and give himself utterly and unceasingly to endure, relieve and succour them.

The whole meaning of Christmas, the miracle of Christ's birth —and death—is that once, and once only, in human history there was such a being. He loved his fellow men so much that his whole life, and his terrible, tragic death, were dedicated, without the least alloy of self or selfish indifference, to the relief and service of all who stood in need of them and, being so, was lived as no man's has ever been before or since. He left us two command_ ments: that we should love God, whose nature he revealed by his own, with our whole being, and that we should love our neighbour as ourselves. However far we are from fulfilling either, we all of us—as a result of Christ's life—come at Christmas for a moment a little nearer to doing the second and, for those who acknowledge our debt to him, a little nearer the first.

*   *   *

"The child Christ enters in"—in this season it is not the end of Christ's life that we recall, but the beginning. We think of the manger, the babe in the straw, the mother looking down on her treasure with eyes full of love and wonder, the Wise Men kneeling before them in awe and thankfulness, and the simple shepherds receiving the tidings in the starlit fields. It is the story of a nativity —one that happens in the life of every man and woman and of every mother, and out of which all the things of life which we take for granted, good and ill, noble and ignoble, arise: a story which, with that of death, is the supreme miracle, when a living spirit, made we know not how, and coming from we know not where, clad in corporeal flesh, enters the world through the suffering body of a woman whose heart, for all her suffering, sings for joy that a babe is born. But in the case of this particular miracle there was something added, something which infinitely heightened the mystery of even that great moment, and made it, in time, a meeting point for earth and heaven, past and future, life and death. Around that birth, and out of the life, teaching and sacrificial death of the great soul who entered the world in human flesh at that moment, grew the conception, strengthening with the years and spreading from land to land until, 1,500 years later, it encircled the earth, that an eternal, all-loving, all-creating God cared for suffering, erring man so much that His own spiritual offspring crossed the mysterious threshold of human birth and, sharing man's full lot—so painful, so inexplicable and often so shaming and humiliating—suffered the utmost agony and in-dignity man can suffer in order that the Divine in life should be revealed and its purpose made manifest and the way of fulfilment through love and sacrifice, in the shadow of Golgotha and the

Cross, made radiant. And on that far Christmas night, when shepherds watched their flocks on the tawny hills of Judea and the three Kings of Orient travelled along the desert track towards their beckoning star, the recurring miracle of it began: the miracle which recurs in every Christian heart, even in the hardest, when the Christian message is remembered and the meaning of that small helpless babe, born to poverty and persecution, in the manger of the crowded wayside inn. "I am sure I have always thought of Christmas," said Scrooge's nephew, "when it has come round—apart from the veneration due to its sacred name and origin, if anything belonging to it can be apart from that— as a good time; a kind, forgiving, charitable, pleasant time; the only time I know of, in the long calendar of the year, when men and women seem by one consent to open their shut-up hearts freely and to think of people below them as if they really were fellow-passengers to the grave, and not another race of creatures bound on other journeys." For a few hours a whole community starts to act on the selfless, instead of the selfish, principle and finds itself merry and glad. Even if the attempt lasts only till the first pang of indigestion after the second mince-pie, in commemoration of Christ's birth we make the selfless choice and put others before ourselves and are surprised to find how happy it makes us.

> *And girls in slacks remember Dad,*
> *And oafish louts remember Mum,*
> *And sleepless children's hearts are glad,*
> *And Christmas-morning bells say, "Come!"*
> *Even to shining ones who dwell*
> *Safe in the Dorchester Hotel.*[1]

Today Christmas has become a very secular affair. Even our Christmas cards seem to have strayed a long way from the first Christmas and the meaning of it all, depicting stage-coaches and soldiers in Georgian or Victorian regimentals, landscapes and London streets, yachts racing and geese by Peter Scott, and the faces of one's friends, their houses, dogs and even, sometimes, if one has such elevated friends, their crests and coronets. It is all very friendly and harmless, and as such in the spirit of Dickens's Christmas, and yet there seems to be something missing—the

[1] John Betjeman, *A Few Late Chrysanthemums*, p.11. John Murray.

inner flame and intensity of belief from which the whole occasion
derives and without which it can be little more than make-
believe and mummery. For those who are not churchgoers there
are only the carols to remind us—that exquisite echo of the faith
of our fifteenth century ancestors which are heard in their supreme
setting in the service relayed from King's College Chapel on the
afternoon of Christmas Eve.

Yet to a historian, however worldly and secular-minded he may
be, the mysterious significance of the thing, the inexplicable
mystery of it all, keeps plucking at his shoulder. A historian's
business is the contemplation and, so far as he can compass it, the
explanation of what happened; and here is something that indubitably happened at a particular moment in history—the birth
of Jesus of Nazareth, and the astonishing chain of circumstances
that followed from it. Disbelieve all the miraculous phenomena
that are said to have accompanied it and the obscure, brilliant,
heroic life and death which followed, and the miracle of it, the
immense canalisation of human purpose and energy which sprang
from it remains, I am convinced, man's greatest achievement on
earth. Even in our age of vast machines and scientific wonders the
Gothic cathedrals still stand as the greatest works we men have
ever made. We can destroy them but we cannot replace them. We
have not the faith, and, because we have not the faith, we have not
the power. For human creation comes from faith. Without it
creative power withers and dies; one must believe in the purpose
of what one does, or the force of inertia, like that of gravity, will
flatten out oneself and one's work. And the Christian Faith has
been the greatest continuing germinator of human energy at all
levels of which there is any record in the annals and achievements
of man.

That is why of all the Christian virtues, faith is fundamental.
It is not the greatest of the Christian virtues—love and courage,
forgiveness and mercy, truthfulness, honesty and purity are all
much greater, viewed from the individual angle of human effort,
because they are so much harder to achieve. But it is the greatest
of the Christian necessities. For faith is not something one makes
oneself, even though, having been given it, one can do something
to keep it. It is a treasure handed down from generation to

generation and should be treasured and defended, in the last resort with life itself, and never wantonly destroyed. "And certes," wrote Chaucer, "faith is the key of Christendom." In the last resort Christianity and the Christian virtues depend on faith—on the belief that Christ was born on that far day in Bethlehem, that He lived his life and preached his Credo—our Credo, as the Gospels and Christian tradition and learning teach us—and that He died on the Cross and rose from the dead. If one doesn't believe that, the Christian conception falls to the ground and becomes nothing more than an interesting and dying myth, and the morality and humanitarianism which derive from it an automatic reflex from the past, like a chicken going on walking after its head has been cut off. One can be unselfish, charitable, a good husband, a good father and citizen, one can be filled with the spirit of love, can be a great scholar or a marvellous orator or artist, but if one lacks faith all will ultimately avail nothing and be swallowed up in death. And the corollary is also true: a man may be a very great sinner and weak and selfish and yet, if he has faith, possess the key by which, in the end, he may still, by an exercise of inspired will and effort, redeem his own frailty and imperfection and turn a life of failure for himself and others into something which, however imperfectly, testifies to the enduring power of the great life given for man under the skies of Palestine two thousand years ago.

> *And all the bells on earth shall ring,*
> *On Christmas day, on Christmas day,*
> *And all the bells on earth shall ring,*
> *On Christmas day in the morning!*

Acknowledgements

The author is indebted to Lord Thomson and the Proprietors of Thomson Newspapers for permission to reprint 'The Summer of Dunkirk' which appeared in the *Daily Sketch* in May 1943, and to the Editor of the *Sunday Express* for permission to embody part of an article published in that newspaper on February 23rd 1969. Grateful acknowledgement is also made to the Hon. Sir Max Aitken and Messrs. Heinemann for permission to quote passages from Lord Beaverbrook's *The Divine Propagandist*, to Messrs. Constable & Co. for Walter de la Mare's poem 'England' on the dedicatory page; for a passage from George Santayana's *Soliloquies in England*; to Faber & Faber for a passage from T. S. Eliot's 'Little Gidding'; to Sir John Betjeman and Messrs. John Murray for passages from two of his poems; to the literary executor of T. H. White for a passage from T. H. White's *England have my Bones*; to Faber & Faber for a quotation from Edward Thomas's 'Collected Poems'; to Macmillan & Co. for a passage from Sir Osbert Sitwell's *Sing High, Sing Low*; to Messrs. William Collins Sons & Co. for a quotation from Edmund Blunden's *Undertones of War*.

The original of the George III Coat of Arms used on the dust wrapper hangs in the beautiful Grinling Gibbons room at Compton Chamberlayne and has been reproduced by kind permission of its owners, Mr. and Mrs. Derbe Berry.